The Seven Deadly Sins

Jewish, Christian, and Classical
Reflections on Human Nature

SOLOMON SCHIMMEL

THE FREE PRESS
A Division of Macmillan, Inc.
New York

Maxwell Macmillan Canada
Toronto

Maxwell Macmillan International
New York   Oxford   Singapore   Sydney

The Free Press
A Division of Macmillan, Inc.
866 Third Avenue, New York, N.Y. 10022

Maxwell Macmillan Canada, Inc.
1200 Eglinton Avenue East
Suite 200
Don Mills, Ontario M3C 3N1

Macmillan, Inc. is part of the Maxwell Communication
Group of Companies.

Printed in the United States of America

printing number
1 2 3 4 5 6 7 8 9 10

Library of Congress Cataloging-in-Publication Data

Schimmel, Solomon.
    The seven deadly sins : Jewish, Christian, and classical
reflections on human nature / Solomon Schimmel.
        p. cm.
    Includes bibliographical references (p.   ) and index.
    ISBN 0-02-927901-1
    1. Sin (Judaism) 2. Deadly sins. I. Title. II. Title: 7 deadly
sins.
BM630.S35   1992
296.3'85—dc20   92-4059
                                                              CIP

Grateful acknowledgment is given to the publishers for permission to reprint excerpts from the following:

Donald Campbell, "On the Conflicts Between Biological and Social Evolution and Between Psychology and Moral Tradition." *American Psychologist*, 30 (1975)

Geoffrey Chaucer, "The Pardoner's Tale," from *The Canterbury Tales*, translated by Nevill Coghill (Penguin Classics, Revised edition 1958). Copyright © 1951 by Nevill Coghill, copyright © Nevill Coghill, 1958

St. Basil, Ascetical Works, volume 9 of *The Fathers of the Church*. Catholic University of America Press, 1962

Richard Fitzgibbons, "The Cognitive and Emotive Uses of Forgiveness in the Treatment of Anger." *Psychotherapy*, 23 (4) (1988). Reprinted with permission of the editor, *Psychotherapy*

From *The New English Bible*. © The Delegates of Oxford University Press and the Syndics of the Cambridge University Press 1961, 1970. Reprinted by permission

The New Oxford Annotated Bible: Revised Standard Version. National Council of Churches

New York Times, April 5, 1989, and May 27, 1991. Copyright © 1989/91 by The New York Times Company. Reprinted by permission

Solomon Schimmel, "Education of the Emotions in Jewish Devotional Literature," *Journal of Religious Ethics*, 8 (2) (1980); "Anger and Its Control in Graeco-Roman and Modern Psychology," *Psychiatry: Journal for the Study of Interpersonal Processes*, 42 (4) (1979); "The Book of Job and the Psychology of Suffering and Doubt," *Journal of Psychology and Judaism*, 11 (4) (1987); "Free-will, Guilt, and Self-control in Rabbinic Judaism and Contemporary Psychology," *Judaism*, 26 (4) (1977); "Joseph and His Brothers: A Paradigm for Repentance," *Judaism*, 37 (1) (1988)

Seneca, "On Anger," "On the Happy Life," in *Moral Essays*. Harvard University Press

The Tanakh: A New Translation of the Holy Scriptures. Jewish Publication Society of America

George Will in *Newsweek*, February 25, 1991. By permission of *Newsweek*

Janet P. Wollersheim in *Behavioral Approaches to Weight Control*, E. E. Abramson (Ed.). Copyright © 1977 Springer Publishing Company, Inc., New York 10012. Used by permission

To Yehudit, David, Atara, and Noam
with love

Contents

The Persistence of Sin

The hell to be endured hereafter, of which theology tells,
is no worse than the hell we make for ourselves in this
world by habitually fashioning our characters in the
wrong way.

—WILLIAM JAMES, *Principles of Psychology*

The seven deadly sins—pride, anger, envy, greed, gluttony, lust, and sloth—are with us every day. Consider these events, typical of many regularly reported in the press:

- Arrogant and self-centered yuppies suffer depression and other psychological problems during the recession of 1990–91 when they find themselves out of jobs and suddenly realize that they are much less important than they had assumed themselves to be. " 'My patients are very bitter,' said . . . a psychoanalyst to whom patients are referred from employee assistance programs in troubled Wall Street organizations. 'Many of them came from upper-middle-income families and went to all the correct schools and felt they had a passport to success.' " (*New York Times*, November 7, 1990).
- Millions of men and women are so distraught about their body image that they subject themselves to plastic surgery, breast and hair implants, and seek psychological counseling for low self-esteem. " 'Negative body images carried into adulthood are a major component of eating disorders,' said . . . a psychology

1

THE SEVEN DEADLY SINS

professor. . . . 'While most American women confess to being unhappy with their weight, . . . for some it becomes a consuming preoccupation that leads to bulimia and anorexia.' . . . Another psychologist reports that hair loss is especially devastating to a man in his twenties. 'He thinks no one will love him and the door to his future is blocked' " (*New York Times*, February 7, 1991).

- A man, upset at complaints and legal threats made by neighbors about the unruliness of his children, "stormed upstairs to confront . . . the board member he thought was behind the letter. He took a 9-millimeter pistol with him . . . pulled the gun from his waistband, . . . and, in a fury, shot the . . . man eight times, killing him right in front of his wife. An acquaintance says that the murderer "had a hot temper" and "was very nervous from working too much" and at the time was also angry at his employer (*New York Times*, May 16, 1991).
- Premed students, envious of the academic success of a classmate, maliciously destroy her laboratory experiments in which she had invested long hours of painstaking work. They hope thereby to ruin her chances of being accepted to a prestigious medical school.
- A distinguished senator with a reputation for the highest integrity is investigated by a Federal grand jury for possible illegal acceptance of gifts, and suspected of many other financial improprieties. A former senatorial colleague of his comments: "I don't know anybody that would have taken all those gifts. I still don't think he's a bad person. But he got greedy somehow. [He] brought it all on himself. He shouldn't have let this happen" (*New York Times*, June 6, 1991).
- A major pharmaceutical company is working to develop a new "miracle" drug that will wean smokers from tobacco, curb the appetite of the obese, and keep alcoholics away from liquor. It has the potential to earn billions of dollars. In the meantime millions of Americans smoke, eat, and drink themselves into a plethora of illnesses because they fail to control their cravings for food, drink, and drugs.
- A prominent female neurosurgeon at Stanford University resigns from her position because she can no longer tolerate the

sexual harassment she has been subjected to by some of her
male surgeon colleagues. The harassment included unsolicited
physical caresses in the midst of performing surgery.
· Several members of a street gang set out to look for a party on
Halloween night but instead end up beating, raping, and stab-
bing a woman 132 times before leaving her in a field to die.
The motive, one alleged assailant told the police, was boredom.
"There was nothing to do and so I guess we had the impression
of going out to the field and kill somebody." (*New York Times*,
May 27, 1991).
· Lee Atwater, known for his vicious election campaigning, reflected on his life as he faced death from a brain tumor at the
age of 41, not long after attaining the pinnacle of political
influence. "The eighties were about acquiring—acquiring
wealth, power, prestige. I know. I acquired more wealth,
power, and prestige than most. But you can acquire all you
want and still feel empty. What power I wouldn't trade for a
little more time with my family!"[1]

For the most part these vices are manifestations of our refusal to
master our physical and psychological impulses. To eat as much as we
like, to sleep with whoever is willing, to garner wealth illicitly when
there is little chance of detection, and to lash out at those who frustrate
or hurt us is easier than exercising restraint in the face of these temptations. In the case of sloth, we choose to turn our eyes and hearts away
from the sufferings of others so that we can avoid involvement. This
failure to develop and use self-control reflects modern American culture's reduced interest in moral values and the cultivation of good
character.

కు

All of us are engaged to one degree or another in a personal, ongoing
battle with sin and vice, although we may not think of our conflicts
with our natures in those terms. Although our anger doesn't make
most of us murderers, our lust doesn't make most of us rapists, and our
greed and envy don't make most of us outright criminals, they, to-

gether with gluttony, arrogance, and sloth, often make us and those who have to live with us miserable. Moreover, when we give in to our low passions we debase our humanity. Our failure to live up to the best we can morally be is as tragic as the unhappiness our evil causes.

The vices also operate at the social level. They permeate politics and commerce, and saturate popular culture and entertainment. Some, such as pride, greed, and anger, profoundly influence domestic and foreign policy. If we were more aware of and troubled by our personal vices, and learned how to control them, the positive impact would carry over into our social and political institutions. Generous, compassionate economic leaders, imbued with the value of social stewardship rather than greed and ambition, would not have tolerated the neglect and even corruption that have been exposed in the banking, securities, and insurance industries. Every deadly sin fuels harmful social phenomena: lust—pornography; gluttony—substance abuse; envy—terrorism; anger—violence; sloth—indifference to the pain and suffering of others; greed—abuse of public trust; and pride—discrimination.[2]

Because sin is associated with religion, secularists think that it is irrelevant to them. But many of the sins of tradition, and particularly the seven deadly ones, are primarily concerned with what it means to be human and humane and the responsibilities that we have to fulfill if we want to be considered as such. The theologians and moralists who wrote so perceptively about our inclination to hurt others in order to satisfy ourselves and what we must do to change ourselves for the better were profound psychologists. Not only did they excel in analyzing human personality, but because they wanted to guide us to self-improvement they were very action oriented. They never lost sight of the practical implications of their psychological theories. Their primary concern was to teach us how to help the good in us dominate the evil. They also were concerned with our happiness. They believed, rightly, that in the long run those who are moral and ethical are also happier. Conversely, by succumbing to immediate gratification of our impulses, usually injuring others in the process, we may experience pleasure. But in due time the pleasure will give way to unhappiness because it alone cannot sustain us spiritually.

The relaxed moral and ethical standards of our society, its unbridled egotism and exaggerated claims to individual freedom, are reinforced by many proponents of modern secular psychology. But since psychology professes to make us happier, and our sins and vices do not, psychology should be teaching us how to regulate rather than indulge our desires. Why doesn't it emphasize what was commonly accepted by our ancestors, that we must recognize and overcome our vices? For one thing it considers the notions of sin, vice, and virtue to be relics of antiquated theological and philosophical traditions, which it has superseded. Modern psychology's disdain for the teachings of the great moral traditions is an example of intellectual hubris. The diatribes against traditional religion and morality that one encounters in psychological circles reflect a superficial understanding of sin, vice, and virtue and other concepts in the moral vocabulary of the past. The deadly sins are not arbitrary, irrational restrictions on human behavior, imposed by a remote deity indifferent to human needs. On the contrary, most sins or vices, and the seven deadly ones in particular, concern the core of what we are, of what we can become, and most importantly, of what we should aspire to be. Amoral psychology is uncomfortable with "oughts"—it prefers to think that it can deal with facts about human nature, shunning values. But this is neither possible nor desirable for real, living humans, whose lives are an inseparable interweaving of fact and value. As long as secular psychology continues to avoid confronting the role that values play in everyday life—what is right and wrong for us to do to ourselves and to others—which is the focus of the religious and philosophical moralists, it will fail to ameliorate our anxieties. We need to reclaim the rich insights into human nature of earlier moral reflection if we want to lead more satisfying lives.[3]

Although I am critical of much of secular psychology's amorality and its arrogant disdain for past wisdom, I do appreciate its contributions to an improved understanding of man and to the treatment of his ills. We need not shun modern secular psychology and return exclusively to religion and philosophy for psychological knowledge and therapy. But we must recognize that secular psychology is seriously deficient in addressing problems associated with impulse control, selfishness, existential meaning, moral conflict, and ethical values which were so prominent in earlier psychological reflection. A first step in rectifying these deficiencies is for secularists to acknowledge them and to respectfully study the premodern traditions. It is my hope that this book will both convince and help them to do so.

Contemporary psychology is diverse and not all approaches are equally hostile or indifferent to traditional concerns. As the following brief survey of psychological therapies will show, some schools address traditional interests but their emphasis and attitude differ from that of the moralists. And frequently modern psychological jargon is little more than old wine in new bottles.

- Psychoanalysis shifts the burden of moral responsibility from the adult to his parents and childhood experiences. It recognizes the power of lust but sees greater psychological danger in overcontrolling rather than undercontrolling it.

- Behavior therapy focuses on what we do, not on whether or not we should do it. The fragmentation of our total personalities into bits and pieces of behavior responding to stimuli leaves most behaviorists coldly indifferent to broader concerns about the meaning and purpose of life. Behaviorists, however, have made notable contributions to our understanding of the mechanics of self-control.

- Adlerian, or individual, therapy appreciates the pull of pride. We are constantly striving, it says, to overcome feelings of inferiority, to achieve mastery, perfection, and superiority, in the sense of maximizing our potential. Adlerian therapy emphasizes the importance of social connectedness and responsibility for psychological health. However, because of its focus on overcoming feelings of inferiority it can err on the side of pride and fail to appreciate the value of humility.

- Existential therapy centers on the traditional sin of spiritual sloth—the meaninglessness, anomie, and despair of modern man. Some of its proponents, such as Viktor Frankl, the founder of logotherapy, and Martin Buber, were deeply impressed by the moral traditions of religion and philosophy. Their versions of existential therapy are explicitly concerned with moral values and responsibility. However, they do not make sufficient use of the specifics of the traditional teachings on sin, vice, and virtue. They also emphasize our existential freedom so much that they are reluctant to indicate specific values worth adopting, leading to an extreme, nondirective approach. However, a more morally directive approach can be justified.

- The same can be said of Rogerian client-centered therapy in which the therapist avoids any attempt to shape the values that his client will adopt in the process of personality change. Rogerian therapy also has a naive and unsubstantiated faith in the human tendency to develop ethically if only we are provided with a climate of respect and trust. This Rousseauian optimism is not shared by the moralists nor corroborated by man's cruel history. Client-centered therapy underestimates the powerful forces for evil in us, which erupt when we are impelled by our lusts or thwarted in satisfying them. The religious and philosophical moralists were much more realistic, which is why they spent so much time cataloging and analyzing our vices and teaching us how to overcome them.

- Gestalt therapy focuses on the present rather than harping on the past or worrying about the future. Its main concern is how we feel rather than what we think. It also encourages the overt expression of feelings, particularly anger and resentment. In these respects gestalt therapy is at odds with much of the traditional moral approach to dealing with our emotional problems and flaws of character. The moralists devote considerable attention to how our reflections on the future effects of our behavior, on ourselves, and on others are important means of influencing our present behavior. Gestalt therapy's preoccupation with the client's awareness of what he* is experiencing in the present discourages a longer-term view of the ultimate goals and meaning of life. The moralists also placed considerable emphasis on the power of reason to help us control our proclivities to sin and vice. Their approach combined the cognitive with the affective. What we think *is* important, and we should learn to think properly, about who we are, what we are doing, and why. The moralists also did not believe that we should

---

* Throughout this book, "he," "man," and "mankind" are used generically to refer to all human beings, male and female.

express all of our hostile feelings, even in a benign way. Although expression of feeling may be appropriate at times, such as when talking to God or confessing sin to a priest or other spiritual mentor, it is more important to eliminate (not suppress) feelings of rage, envy, greed, vanity, and lust than to cathart them.

• Rational-emotive and other cognitive therapies share many of the features of traditional moral analysis of sin and vice. Both emphasize examining underlying attitudes, changing our ways of thinking about experience, and exposing flaws in our logic. No better example of this approach in ancient or modern literature could probably be found than Seneca the Stoic's analysis of anger. However, many proponents of rational-emotive therapy, led by Albert Ellis, are egregiously amoral if not immoral in its application. Since, they say, our feelings of guilt and shame are basically our own doing, the results of our distorted thought and irrationality, we should learn how to get rid of them. The fact that there are many things we do or fail to do that rightly should awaken feelings of guilt and shame in us doesn't occupy a prominent place in rational-emotive therapy, but it is crucial to the traditional moralists. The rational-emotive (and the psychoanalytic) therapists say that we are overburdened with guilt. The moralists say that often we are more guilty than we allow ourselves to feel.[4]

• The shortcomings of these mainstream therapies have led thousands to search for help elsewhere. There are now dozens of self-help groups that shun the services of mental health professionals. Their lay members hope to find solace and support from a mutual sharing of weakness and pain. Every conceivable vice is represented by an association of devotees. Gluttons and lechers, thieves and the violent, the once arrogant but now fallen and those consumed by envy or in despair have their respective Anonymous meetings to attend. Some of these groups do succeed in helping their participants rise above their weaknesses. Others provide rationalizations for their members' behavior which keep them fallen where they are. All would be enhanced by careful study and application of the reflections of the moralists on the vices.

· Another approach of those unhappy with themselves but disillusioned with psychology is to look to New Age therapies. Perhaps happiness and self-mastery are to be found in martial arts or massage, in meditating over clay, or in Quantum Healing. Let us celebrate the summer solstice, the Earth Goddess, or our menstrual cycles, imbibe the universal life force and seek the holy grail of happiness in unlimited Reichean orgasm and Tarot cards. It is ludicrous and pitiful to see "mature" adults flock to every new New Age fad. But this is a symptom of the spiritual sloth of our age. These people are searching for something worth living for, and for some way to be at peace with themselves, to calm the inner conflicts and feelings of personal inadequacy that make them so dissatisfied with themselves. They are looking in the wrong place. The answers will not be found in magic and witchcraft and shamanism, or even in swimming with dolphins[5]—but in an honest grappling with their own inner natures. All of us must learn how to regulate our lives in accordance with right reason, to recognize and improve our flawed natures, to accept our obligations to meet the needs of others and make them happier, and not to worry exclusively about ourselves. If we do this conscientiously we will find reprieve from our anomie and self-loathing. The moralists can guide us to this goal.

The moralists maintain that man's happiness is not dependent upon physical or material pleasure, and indeed is often hampered by it. However, our culture teaches that pleasure and possessions *are* happiness, so that the pursuit of pleasure is often substituted for the pursuit of happiness and meaning. When secular man experiences an existential crisis which cannot be ameliorated by pleasure, he comes to the psychotherapist for help. But the psychotherapist's ability to help will be limited if he or the patient believes that pleasure is the necessary route to happiness. This is not to say that all psychological problems derive from a hedonistic philosophy, that pleasure is irrelevant to happiness, or that secular man will be happy only if he converts to religion. However, thoughtful secularists know that one can have an abundance of sex, food, and wealth and still be miserable. To the extent that secularism and a psychotherapy derived from it can formulate a vision of human purpose in which spiritual and moral values play a much greater role than they do now, secular man will be less prone to anxiety and despair.

Religious and philosophical moral reflection about sin, vice, and virtue, and the seven deadly sins in particular, has influenced the self-understanding and behavior of multitudes for centuries, and continues to do so for many today. But because it uses concepts foreign to the nonreligious it is necessary to translate its relevant teachings into an idiom that speaks to modern man while respecting his skepticism about religious dogma. This is my aim in the present book. Then the psychological insights and practical guidance of religious and philosophical moral reflection about sin and virtue will prove to be of value to all. Psychotherapists and patients will be able to apply them to many problems that impel the emotionally distraught to seek help.

Moral literature on pride, anger, envy, greed, gluttony, lust, and sloth does more than provide practical guidelines for controlling the vices. It is a fertile source of hypotheses about emotion and behavior that can be tested with the scientific methods of modern psychology. The seven sins directly relate to a host of problems addressed by clinical and social psychology. Low self-esteem, aggression, racial animosity, economic anxiety, executive stress, obesity, sexual dysfunction, depression, and suicide are among many problems directly related to the seven sins. Many other contemporary ills relate to the sins indirectly. The tree is a widely used medieval image for the seven deadly sins. The sins are its roots, trunk, or branches from which sprout innumerable evils and tragedies. The insidious effects of our vices extend far and wide. We may not at first recognize the connection between a deadly vice and its indirect effects but a deeper probing will often reveal it. Anomie, for example, the despair of finding meaning and purpose in life, is traceable in part to the materialism of greed, the spiritual apathy of sloth, and the narcissism of pride.

❧

We will draw on three great moral traditions, Judaism, Graeco-Roman moral philosophy, and Christianity. We will also cull the psychological insights of poets such as Chaucer, Dante, Shakespeare, and Milton. We will begin by surveying and comparing the teachings of the three great moral traditions on sin and vice.

The point of departure for Jewish reflection on sin is the Hebrew Bible. The Hebrew Scriptures, or Tanakh, includes many commandments, the decalogue being the most well known of them. However, it also contains narratives with religious and moral messages, exhortations, and advice for one who would obey God. Biblical stories were recorded in order to educate us about good and evil, and they dramatize the conflicts we all face between temptation and virtue. As the Jewish sages of later generations put it, the study of Torah is an antidote to our evil inclinations. In the following chapters we will look at several biblical stories that elucidate the deadly sins.

For the Hebrew Bible, sin is the violation of a divine command. Some commandments concern ritual and worship, and they are directed to the ancient Israelites. However, numerous laws and teachings of the Hebrew Bible are meant to be universal, applying to all mankind, and these deal with moral and ethical responsibility. From the biblical perspective, when we sin against our neighbor we also sin against God because He wants us to be compassionate towards one another.

Thus the injunction against murder was first addressed to Noah and his children as representatives of all mankind. Other ethical prescriptions and proscriptions are found in Job's self-justification before God (Job 31). Job, also a universal figure, argues that he has not committed deceit, adultery, or injustice, and that he has assisted the poor, the orphaned, and the widow, which is expected of everyone. Cain, symbolizing humanity too, is commanded to control his envy and the aggression it generates. The condemnation of Adam and Eve for eating the forbidden fruit teaches that we must not give in to temptation when we know that it is wrong, and that if we do so we will bring discord into the world and our relationships. God informs Abraham that there are no righteous in Sodom before He destroys it to prove that He is just and to remind us that we should be so too.

The laws in the Pentateuch, the first five books of the Bible, are primarily concerned with behavior. Some of the laws, however, and even more so the stories from Genesis through the historical books such as Samuel and Kings, are about sins of passion such as anger, envy, coveting, hatred, and hubris. The Book of Psalms, the Book of Proverbs, and the prophetic works contain even more explicit exhortations about sinful feelings and their opposite virtues, which are called purity of heart and righteousness.

From the Hellenistic period to the end of the fifth century, the biblical moral tradition was expanded upon by Jewish spiritual leaders whose teachings were collected in the Talmud and Midrash, known as rabbinic literature. Even more so than the Hebrew Bible itself, the rabbis analyzed human thoughts and feelings and how they relate to good and evil behavior. The rabbis vividly personified our evil inclination as a devious creature, ever conniving to induce us to disobey God. Our good inclination fights back. It reminds us of how much we owe to God, and of the punishments and rewards that await us in the hereafter.

The rabbis also teach us to channel our impulses so that they can be expressed in right behavior rather than in sin. For example, the sexual impulse should not, and indeed cannot, be eradicated. It should be directed towards procreation and the legitimate sexual satisfactions of marriage. Envy should be transformed into emulation of the wise and virtuous. Greed should be directed towards accumulating knowledge of Torah rather than money. The love of food should be sanctified by the appreciation of divine benevolence and by sharing what we have with the hungry.

Jewish reflections on human nature continued throughout the Middle Ages, in devotional guides and religious philosophy. Writers like Ibn Pakuda, de Vidas, and Luzzatto provide the most thorough Jewish analyses of sin and vice and how to overcome them. They build on material found in rabbinic literature but go beyond it, incorporating ideas from mystical and philosophical traditions. These moralists and their Christian counterparts were the equivalent of today's therapists. But they differ, by integrating psychology and morality into a harmonious system whose goal is both spiritual perfection and its correlate, true happiness. Only saints approach perfection—and even saints may falter—but the moralists believed that we can all elevate ourselves. In so doing we will become happier.

The second tradition we draw upon is that of Greek and Roman moral philosophy. Its most outstanding representatives include Plato, Aristotle, Plutarch, and the Stoics, especially Seneca. Each of these thinkers was as much a psychologist as a philosopher. For them philosophy (love of wisdom) seeks to learn what virtue and happiness are and how the two may be related. It incorporates psychology because only if we understand how and why we feel, think, and act can we choose the right kind of life.

According to Plato our "soul," which is "imprisoned" in our body, has three components: reason, desire (physiological drives or appetites), and emotion. The attainment of wisdom is the highest virtue for man, but this is impeded when desire and emotion go unchecked by reason. We should use our reason to guide and restrain our appetites and passions. When we do so, allowing each component of the soul its proper measure, we achieve psychological harmony.

There are similarities between Plato's goal of harmony and Freud's idea that through the insights of therapy the ego will be able to control the id and the superego.[6] However, the differences are greater than the similarities. Psychoanalysis often encourages acquiescence to id impulses and is starkly pessimistic about the power of reason to overcome desire.

Aristotle analyzes how our emotions relate to our personality traits, those towards whom our emotions are directed (for example, whom we tend to pity, to be angry at, or to envy), and which situations arouse those emotions. For Aristotle our character traits, or "dispositions of the soul," are either vices or virtues:

> It is possible, for example, to experience . . . desire, anger, pity, and pleasures and pains generally, too much or too little or to the right amount. If we feel them too much or too little, we are wrong. But to have these feelings at the right times on the right occasions towards the right people for the right motive and in the right way is to have them in the right measure, that is somewhere between the extremes; and this is what characterizes goodness. The same may be said of the mean and extremes in actions. ("Ethics," Book II, Chapter vi)

Aristotle's analyses of emotion and character suggest useful techniques for self-control. Taking into account individual differences in temperament, he offers a "vice therapy" by which we can minimize vice and cultivate virtue. For example, the individual who squanders money should practice miserliness, whereas the miser should practice squandering. Each will eventually achieve a moral balance and will thereby approach the mean of "liberality," or virtue with respect to acquiring and spending money. Continued practice will eventually make the mean a habit and a disposition of the soul. When that stage is reached the virtuous disposition will almost automatically produce morally correct feelings and actions.[7,8]

Aristotle cautions that because we are naturally inclined to pleasure we are prone to intemperance, or excessive indulgence in pleasures, particularly those derived from the sense of touch (which include sex, food, and drink).

Aristotle's theory of personality includes political and social values as well as individual ones. Happiness depends on the kind of society and political system we construct. Unfortunately, contemporary personality theory pays little or no regard to moral and social philosophy. Yet we need moral philosophy to help us decide how we should best live our lives as individuals and in community with others.

The terms *vice* and *sin* are often interchanged in medieval writings, but they are not identical. Vices and virtues were the concepts and terms of the Greek and Roman philosophers; sin of the Hebrew Bible and New Testament. Vices are character traits. Sins are specific acts of commission or omission. Once Judaism and Christianity adopted the concepts of vice and virtue from the Greek and Roman moralists, vices were often called sins and sins vices. The seven deadly "sins" are also called the deadly "vices," which is more accurate. They are basic, perhaps universal human tendencies, from which sins result. The vice of anger spawns the sin of violence against others and the vice of greed gives birth to the sin of theft.

Stoic ideas, synthesized by Hellenistic Jews with Hebrew Scripture, shaped Christian conceptions of sin and virtue. Among Stoic teachings were the virtue of living in accordance with the law of Nature, which is Reason, and the value of asceticism as a way of cultivating indifference to the vicissitudes of life. Stoics, such as Epictetus and Seneca, wrote lengthy treatises that combined moral philosophy with practical instructions in how to achieve these objectives. For the Stoics, the more capable a person is of divorcing himself from worldly pursuits and the better trained he is in controlling (and in some cases eliminating) emotions, the freer and happier he will be. Their essays on our emotions are masterpieces in the integration of philosophy, psychological theory, and cognitive therapy.

ॐ

The third tradition we use is Christianity. Jesus accepted the Hebrew biblical and Pharisaic tradition that thoughts and feelings, and not only behaviors, can be sinful, but went further than both. He emphasized almost exclusively faith, the ethical, and inner states and intention, making radical demands on our feelings:

> You have learned that our forefathers were told, "Do not commit murder; anyone who commits murder must be brought to judgment." But what I tell you is this: Anyone who nurses anger against his brother must be brought to judgment. . . .
>
> You have learned that they were told, "Do not commit adultery." But what I tell you is this: If a man looks on a woman with a lustful eye, he has already committed adultery in his heart. (Matthew 5:21–22, 27–28 NEB)*

Paul frequently addressed the question of sin and how to cleanse oneself of it. Paul's ideas about sin drew from both Jewish and Hellenistic sources, to which he added his own original contributions. His views markedly influenced all subsequent Christian understandings of human nature and sin.

Paul conceived of the struggle against sin as primarily one between the will and temptation. The body is the source of sin and we are impotent to overcome its temptations by exertion of our will alone. We must rely on faith in Christ as the means for freeing ourselves from sin.

Augustine, in his *Confessions*, describes his personal struggles with various temptations of the flesh and the spirit. The work, an account of the emotional and intellectual stages he went through in his spiritual transition from paganism to Christianity, is rich in psychological detail and nuance. Augustine wanted to get at the core of why we do evil. He

---

* NEB = New English Bible.

was guilt-ridden by the sins of his youth, when he indulged his sexual appetite and stole fruit from a pear tree for no apparent motive other than the sheer maliciousness of theft. With increasing age the sin of pride preoccupied him. Although in our post-Freudian era Augustine's obsession with sex, sin, and guilt seems extreme, his analyses of how we are influenced by our passions and egotism are enlightening.

Theologians such as Gregory the Great and St. Thomas Aquinas, and devotional writers such as Ignatius of Loyola and St. Francis de Sales, developed the Catholic moral tradition. They analyzed sin and vice from numerous perspectives, shedding light on our nature and how we can rise above our base instincts. Gregory, for example, distinguishes between sins of the flesh, such as gluttony and lust, and sins of the spirit or psychological sins, which include pride, anger, envy, greed, and acedia (sloth).[9]

Protestant thinkers, such as the Anglican bishop Jeremy Taylor and the American Puritan minister Cotton Mather, continued the tradition of moral-psychological analysis. Taylor's sermon on "The House of Feasting," his discussion of what it means for a Christian to lead a holy life, and Mather's treatise on the obligation of Christians to undertake social responsibility in the spirit of charity are examples of works well worth reading today. We rely on them in our analyses of gluttony, pride, and sloth.

In his *Summa Theologiae*, written for scholars, Thomas Aquinas provides the most systematic analysis of sin, vice, and virtue, combining theology, philosophy, and psychology. But it was the preachers and the authors of spiritual guides, the biographers of saints, the poets, and artists, who translated the abstract teachings of moral theology into popular language, visual imagery, and practical strategies for resisting temptation. In this way the teachings of the Church about sin and how to overcome it could be applied in everyday life. Popular medieval works dealing with the seven deadly sins have great aesthetic appeal and emotional immediacy. In sermons, literature, and art the sins are portrayed with vivid iconography.[10]

The temptation to sin engenders a desperate struggle between the person or a virtue, and the demon, or the sin or vice which he represents. In his poem *Psychomachia*, the fifth-century Prudentius personifies vices and virtues, and their sinful offspring, vividly describing the struggle between them in an elaborate battlefield metaphor which greatly influenced the art and the allegory of the Middle Ages. For example, the monster Greed, attended by Hunger, Fear, Anguish, Perjuries, Corruption, Treachery, Falsehood, and other diverse fiends, is confronted by the virtues Reason, Thrift, and Good Works. Greed fills her pockets and her money bags with plunder and booty which she conceals in her robe. Meanwhile, "Crimes, the brood of their mother Greed's black milk, like ravening wolves go prowling and leaping over the field."[11] Greed eventually succumbs to Good Works, who from Greed's dead body takes dirty pieces of gold and rusty coins which she distributes to the needy. Lust attacks Chastity, thrusting pitch and burning sulphur into her modest eyes. But Chastity disarms the harlot, exultantly declaring her victory with the words, "death to thee, harlot . . . be thou shut up in hell and thrust into the dark depths of night! . . . No more, thou chief of fiends, tempt thou the worshipers of Christ; let their cleansed bodies be kept pure for their own king."[12]

Other works represented the sins by different animals, whose behavior resembled that of people with the vice.[13] In Edmund Spenser's pageant of the seven deadly sins in *The Faerie Queene*, Pride calls for her coach. Normally it would be drawn by peacocks, whose magnificent outspread tails make them a symbol of Vanity. On the special occasion of Pride's visit to Jove, however, her coach is drawn by her "six sage Counsellor's," the other deadly sins, each riding on a beast that symbolizes it. Sloth rides an ass, Gluttony a swine, Lechery a goat, Avarice a camel, Envy a wolf, and Wrath a lion. The camel hoards food in its humps and the lion mercilessly attacks its prey.[14]

Another common motif was to compare the sins to wounds or diseases and the virtues to their remedies. Spenser combines the sickness motif with the animal one. Sloth, sleepy and sluggish, shakes with a raging fever. Gluttony, deformed, overweight, and sick with dropsy, brutishly spews up his gorge. Lechery, concealing his filthiness with fine clothes, suffers from rotting marrow and brain (the syphilitic consequences of his sins). Avarice is tormented by gout, Envy spews leprous poison from his mouth, and Wrath trembles, swelled with choler.

The greatest poetic use of the seven deadly sins was by Dante in *The Divine Comedy*. As he journeys through Purgatory Dante talks with souls he meets about the sins and crimes they committed in life. The souls of sinners can ascend to Heaven only after they are cleansed from the stains of their sins.

The seven deadly sins are purged in successive order on seven levels of Mount Purgatory. Each sin is assigned an appropriate penance. For example, the eyes of the envious who looked hatefully upon the good fortune of others are sealed with threads of wire. The proud bear heavy stones to lower their haughty spirit and the gluttonous starve. Then the sinners are given a meditation consisting of a whip (examples of the virtue which is the opposite of the vice), a bridle (deterrent examples of the vice), and a prayer. When the purgation is completed a guardian angel of a virtue recites a relevant benediction and receives the purified soul. Humility receives the Proud, Mercy the Envious, Peace the Wrathful, Zeal the Slothful, Liberality the Avaricious, Temperance the Gluttonous, and Chastity the Lustful.

The relationship between inner experience (thoughts and feelings) and deeds has important implications for psychotherapy, although it is not always fully understood. Why do some of us harbor hostile thoughts but not implement them, whereas others can barely restrain themselves from acting out their feelings? A psychological profile of serial killers notes that most of them are intensely angry individuals. They also are intelligent, systematic planners of their brutal crimes, and often avoid detection for years while they continue to murder and mutilate their victims. But somehow they have not learnt to control their evil impulses, and the transition from feeling to thought to deed proceeds without the inhibitory mechanism of conscience and guilt.

Sins can be feelings, such as envy or hatred; thoughts, such as planning criminal acts; speech, such as slander or insult; or actions, such as theft, murder, or adultery.

Aware that sinful acts are often the culmination of earlier malevolent ideas and desires, the moralists teach that just thinking about and wanting to commit evil can be vices or sins even if we do not take action. In contrast, some psychologists consider "sinful" thoughts and desires "healthy" and by implication good. Statements such as "there is nothing wrong with feeling angry or envious or lustful as long as you don't act upon your feelings in ways that injure others," or the even more extreme view that "it is desirable to experience, acknowledge, and verbalize hostile feelings, because in doing so you will feel less of an urge to act upon them," have become part of the common lore of the self-help literature. The idea of the Stoics, the rabbis, and Christian writers that we should purify our inner lives no less than our outer ones is alien to the modern temper.

Modern psychology is mainly interested in theology's sins against oneself, leaving sins against one's neighbor to the law, and sins against God to priests, ministers, and rabbis. The patient asks "Why am I so unhappy, self-destructive, or out of control? What am I doing wrong to myself?" With the assistance of the therapist the patient tries to discover the reasons for his unhappiness and to do things that will make him happier. But it is unwise if not impossible to divorce "sins against oneself" from "sins against one's neighbor." Consequently, the psychotherapist must be willing to address difficult moral issues with his patient. To do so effectively he has to be knowledgeable in moral literature and philosophy, and be morally sensitive himself.[15]

Jewish and Christian moralists analyze different sources of temptation to sin. Frequently the source is our bodies or minds, as in a sexual urge to masturbate or in ruminations about the benefits of crime. Sometimes the temptation is external, such as a person whom we envy, or pork for a Jew and meat during Lent for a Catholic. At other times, the temptation is ascribed to a direct act of God or the devil. God tests Abraham's faith by commanding him to sacrifice Isaac. The devil tempts Jesus or St. Anthony in the wilderness by exposing them to beautiful, seductive women. Whatever the source of temptations, theology considers human beings capable of resisting with their will as long as their reason is intact.

The similarities between the three moral traditions about vice, virtue, and human nature are greater than their differences. Medieval Judaism and Christianity both evolved from the same Hebrew biblical and Pharisaic religion.[16] Although Greek and Roman moral philosophy developed independently of Judaism and Christianity, the two religions assimilated much of it into their own moral thought. I shall, however, point out some of the differences between the three traditions in the course of analyzing each sin individually in the following chapters. Here let me note a few points on which Judaism, Christianity, and the classical traditions differ.

In the Hebrew Bible the enjoyment of physical pleasure is not considered sinful. In fact the rewards of virtue are material prosperity, longevity, and a large family. Although many biblical laws prohibit or restrict certain sexual behaviors and consumption of foods, it is not the pleasure that one experiences in them which is why they are prohibited. It is their connection to other sins, such as idolatry, disruption of the family unit and the social order, or disloyalty to the covenant. Life is not viewed as a continuous struggle between the flesh and some "higher" part of us. This attitude of the Hebrew Bible towards the body contrasts sharply with Plato, Paul, and Augustine's negative view. Many medieval Jewish moralists, however, were influenced by Plato and therefore valued asceticism although not mortification of the flesh.

A fundamental difference between Paul and the rabbis is in their assessment of man's ability to subdue his evil impulses. The rabbis, while acknowledging the need to be ever-vigilant, believed that such impulses can be overcome. Although God's assistance is sometimes necessary to strengthen the hand of the good inclination, the primary responsibility is ours. We are autonomous moral agents. Paul, on the other hand, despaired of our ability to control the evil within us, and so he opted instead for reliance on God's grace through faith in Christ.

Judaism and Christianity also differ in the degree to which they attribute temptation to malevolent, external powers. The idea of demons as evil spirits tempting man, and of a chief demon, such as Satan, is found in pre-Christian Jewish literature. Jesus as exorciser of demons is within this ancient Jewish tradition. In rabbinic and medieval nonmystical Jewish literature, however, there are few references to Satan as a real being who as God's antagonist regularly tries to induce man to sin. It is the inner *yetzer ha'ra*—the evil inclination—which is the main tempter. The absence in mainstream Judaism of belief in original sin and a real, powerful devil contributed to the Jew's strong sense of freedom and responsibility.

In Christian theology the devil is not a direct and sufficient cause of sin. He can only tempt man but not coerce him to sin. However, the popular belief that the devil compels a person to sin can make a Christian feel guiltless (or use his belief in the devil to deny his guilt) if he believes that he was powerless against such a strong adversary:

> Recently a man murdered a number of coeds on Long Island and, when he was apprehended and charged with the crimes, he used as his defense a form of the insanity plea so old that it seemed ingeniously new. He claimed that he was in the power of the devil when he committed those crimes and was, therefore, not in control of his actions. The court seriously entertained the case but finally the scientific skepticism of our age prevailed and the defense was dismissed. The murderer was, in fact, only taking advantage of the current recrudescence of demonology in our country, but he had tapped an interesting historical connection between innocence and guilt, loss of free will, temporary insanity and possession by the devil, a complex of ideas which still flourishes in more minds than we like to admit. The folk expressions that we are "full of the devil" or in a "diabolic rage" or "bedeviled" or looking "haunted" merely mask vague concepts about the loss and invasion of the self and self-control.[17]

The court could have cited Aquinas to the defendant to deny the validity of his claim that the devil controlled him. If the defendant's claim was being made in earnest and if he was amenable to reason, citing Aquinas might have helped him control his future homicidal impulses. But his belief that the devil controlled him when he committed the murders for which he was being tried, might have discouraged him at the time from trying to overcome his urge to kill. This is an extreme psychological effect of belief in the devil, but lesser though important effects most probably exist too. Researchers have discovered that people who believe that what happens to them and how they feel are determined by things external to themselves are less inclined than others to take initiatives to change themselves or their life situations. Belief in the devil as an external force probably has a similar effect.

The moralists teach that not all sins are of equal gravity. The malicious intention of the sinner, the strength of the temptation he faced, the extent of the injury he caused, and mitigating circumstances such as illness or drunkenness all enter into the equation that determines the gravity of a sin. Catholicism, for example, distinguishes between more serious mortal sins and lesser, venial sins. One factor in determining whether a sin is mortal or venial is the motive for it. If, for example, it was done out of malice towards man or God it is mortal. If it was done out of negligence or addiction it is venial. Venial sins are more easily forgivable than mortal ones. Mortal sins result in the death of the sinner's soul if he doesn't confess them and perform the sacrament of penance, whereas death of the soul is not an automatic consequence of venial sin.[18]

Now that we have considered sin and vice in general we will look at the concept of "seven deadly sins" in particular.

The seven deadly, capital, or cardinal sins are especially dangerous. Why the number seven? What is meant by cardinal or capital? Why do pride, anger, envy, greed, sloth, gluttony, and lust merit special attention in Catholic moral thought?

The expression "seven deadly sins" is actually a misnomer that resulted from popular confounding of mortal sins with capital or cardinal sins. The seven deadly sins can be mortal or venial. The correct designation of them is the seven cardinal, capital, or chief sins, but we retain the popular usage.

It was a widespread practice in the ancient world to compile lists of sins and vices, and groupings of seven were particularly common. The number seven was considered special and sometimes sacred in the ancient world. In the Hebrew Bible we find it in the story that God rested on the seventh day, in the seven-day week, and in the seven branches of the candelabra in the Temple. Noah brought seven of each pure animal into the Ark, and many sacrifices consisted of seven animals. Postbiblical Jewish tradition taught of seven chambers of Gehenna (Hell) and seven firmaments leading up to the uppermost celestial abode of God. It is not surprising, therefore, that the number seven also played a role in classifications of sin and vice.

In the Book of Proverbs (6:16–19, NEB) we have an early example:

> Six things the Lord hates,
> Seven things are detestable to him:
> A proud eye, a false tongue,
> Hands that shed innocent blood,
> A heart that forges thoughts of mischief,
> And feet that run swiftly to do evil,
> A false witness telling a pack of lies,
> And one who stirs up quarrels between brothers.

In the *Testament of Reuben*, a work of Hellenistic Judaism, Reuben, the son of Jacob, who according to the account in Genesis had illicit sexual intercourse with his father's concubine Bilha, is exhorting his sons on the evils of promiscuity. In the course of his last testament to them, he speaks of seven spirits of error or deceit of which they should beware:

> And now give heed to me, my children, concerning the things which I saw during my time of penitence, concerning the seven spirits of deceit. . . . First, the spirit of promiscuity [lust] resides in the nature and the senses. A second spirit of insatiability [gluttony], in the stomach; a third spirit of strife, in the liver and the gall [anger]; a fourth spirit of trickery and flattery [vainglory], in order that through excessive effort one might appear to be at the height of his powers; a fifth spirit of arrogance [pride], that one might be boastful and haughty; a sixth spirit of lying, which through destructiveness and rivalry, handles his affairs smoothly and secretively even with his relatives and his household. A seventh spirit of injustice, with which are thefts and crooked dealings, in order that one might gain his heart's desire [greed]. (pp. 782–783)

These seven spirits of deceit are similar though not identical to the Christian seven deadly sins.[19]

Aristotle and the Stoics also classified vices and virtues and the Roman poet Horace, in one of his Epistles (I.1.33–40) has a list similar to our seven, which require special expiation.

Jesus, as exorciser of demons, teaches that:

> When an unclean spirit comes out of a man it wanders over the deserts
> seeking a resting-place; and if it finds none, it says, "I will go back to the
> home I left." So it returns and finds the house swept clean, and tidy. Off
> it goes and collects seven other spirits more wicked than itself, and they
> all come in and settle down; and in the end the man's plight is worse
> than before. (Luke 11:24–26, NEB)

In Deuteronomy, the Israelites are told by the Lord that when He
delivers into their hands the seven powerful Canaanite nations, they
should put them to death. This passage, and numerous other biblical
ones, was interpreted allegorically by Christian writers to refer to the
spirit's battle against the flesh and the seven vices. Thus, by the early
centuries of the Christian era there existed a well-established tradition
about seven evil spirits which induce man to sin.

Another reason for seven sins was its parallelism to Christianity's
seven virtues: prudence, fortitude, temperance, justice, faith, hope,
and charity. Only some of these virtues, though, are the opposites of
deadly sins.

In rabbinic and medieval Jewish literature no authoritative group of
"seven" sins emerged as being distinct from other sins. However, because of their intrinsic psychological and moral significance, the seven
on the Christian list are of great interest to Jewish moralists too.

A rabbinic midrash enumerates seven sins that are linked in a causal
chain, each one in the sequence producing the next, a feature also
common in Christian explanations of the cardinal sins as we shall see
shortly in the case of John Cassian. One who (1) does not preoccupy
himself with the study of Torah will (2) cease to perform the commandments. He will then (3) despise others who observe the Torah
and (4) eventually hate the sages who expound it. This will lead him
(5) to prevent others from observing the commandments. The next
step in his spiritual deterioration will be (6) to deny that the commandments were divinely revealed and ultimately he (7) will deny the
very existence of God.[20]

The designation of certain sins as cardinal, capital, or chief began in
ascetic and monastic communities established in the first centuries of
the Christian era in the Egyptian desert. Evagrius, a fourth-century

monastic, lists eight chief sins: gluttony (*gula*), lust (*luxuria*), avarice (*avaritia*), sadness (*tristitia*), anger (*ira*), spiritual lethargy (*acedia*), vain glory (*vana gloria*), and pride (*superbia*).

The desert fathers usually considered sin to be an external, objective power, which is why they often referred to sins as demons. This idea survived well into the Middle Ages, particularly in the popular mind, where the sins were in the service of the devil. St. Anthony, the founder of Christian desert monasticism, is often depicted in legend and art as heroically overcoming various temptations of the devil, in the tradition of Jesus himself.

According to John Cassian, a student of Evagrius, each cardinal sin generates the one that follows, so, for example, gluttony will lead to lust which will lead to avarice. He also shows how each one of the cardinal sins spawns many other specific sins—its "children," so to speak. This was the most important notion associated with the seven deadly sins tradition and generated the wide use of the tree with many branches as a symbol of the deadly sins and their progeny.

Gregory the Great modified Cassian's list. He considered pride to be a category by itself, the root of all sins, added envy, and merged spiritual lethargy with sadness. The tradition continued to evolve, culminating in the popular version we use today—pride, anger, envy, greed, sloth (the combination of spiritual lethargy and sadness), gluttony, and lust.

The existence of different versions of the seven sins and of their order was due in part to different opinions about the theological and psychological importance of each one. In an ascetic and monastic environment, gluttony and lust were more threatening than pride. In the ordered medieval society the exaggerated individualism of pride—a rebellion against authority and God—was most dangerous. In the later Middle Ages we find an emphasis on avarice as the worst of the seven. This was because the significant increase in merchants, commerce, and money provided greater opportunities for greed and its "off-spring."[21]

Cardinal or capital has several senses according to Aquinas.[22] Pride, which for Aquinas is contempt for God and the refusal to obey Him, is the "head" (*caput* in Latin) or "root" of all sin. A sin is also "capital" if it is the reason for committing other sins. Greed is a capital sin because we steal, cheat, and lie to satisfy it. Sloth is a capital sin

THE SEVEN DEADLY SINS

because we ignore the dictates of charity out of our apathy to spiritual matters. Envy will induce us to harm others. A sin is also called capital if it enables us to commit many other sins. The money we accumulate through our greed empowers us to be gluttons or lechers, and to do other evil things.[23]

We have now completed our brief survey of the tradition of the seven deadly sins and in the following chapters can look at each of the seven in depth. The moralists' reflections on the sins and their practical suggestions for mastering them will be useful to all who want to become better and happier people. They are also of especial importance to mental health professionals and their patients, who often face the challenges of vice and sin with particular intensity.

CHAPTER TWO

Pride

Of all the causes which conspire to blind Man's erring
judgment, and misguide the mind,
What the weak head with strongest bias rules,
Is pride, the never-failing vice of fools.
—ALEXANDER POPE, *An Essay on Criticism*

The passions evoked by the Gulf crisis of 1990–91 between the United States and Iraq remind us that pride and humiliation are among the most powerful motives for behavior and a major cause of conflict between nations. Throughout the crisis, emotions related to pride were most frequently mentioned by antagonists and analysts to condemn or justify actions. Iraqi and American leaders accused each other of arrogance. Saddam Hussein claimed to be fighting to restore Arab dignity. President Bush wanted to humiliate Hussein. The outcome of the war presumably restored America's pride and national honor which had been diminished when our forces departed from Vietnam in shame and humiliation. According to one issue of *Newsweek*, for example:

A combination of pride and insularity led Saddam Hussein to overplay an otherwise strong hand. . . . The Iraqi president's pride is easily injured. From his youth as a fatherless peasant, it was all he had. In this war with a superpower, it is the last thing he is likely to sacrifice. . . . Iraqi pride, Saddam's pride, would be worth [a million deaths]. If there is going to be peace . . . his honor will have to be respected, and a way found to save face.

The columnist George Will wrote:

> A peculiar kind of patriot today says that by this war America "will get its pride back" . . . since when has American pride derived primarily from military episodes? A nation that constantly worries about its pride should worry. It is apt to confect military occasions for bucking itself up, using foreign policy for psychotherapy. (February 25, 1991, pp. 34–35, 70)

At the personal level, inappropriate pride can cause considerable emotional distress. The psychologist Gordon Allport writes:

> Any neurotic is living a life which in some respects is extreme in its self-centeredness . . . the region of his misery represents a complete preoccupation with himself. The very nature of the neurotic disorder is tied to pride. If the sufferer is hypersensitive, resentful, captious, he may be indicating a fear that he will not appear to advantage in competitive situations where he wants to show his worth. If he is chronically indecisive, he is showing fear that he may do the wrong thing and be discredited. If he is over-scrupulous and self-critical, he may be endeavoring to show how praiseworthy he really is. Thus, most neuroses, are, from the point of view of religion, mixed with the sin of pride.[1]

A patient of mine was bitter and resentful because she had been denied a promotion at work. She envied her co-worker who had been appointed to the position she coveted. One dimension of therapy was to make her examine the bases for her expectation that she was entitled to the promotion. She had believed herself to be the brightest and most competent member of her group. She had to eventually accept the fact that she wasn't as bright and competent as she had thought herself to be. The experience was very painful but edifying. Similarly, freshmen at prestigious universities, used to being the stars of their class in high school, often experience the humbling realization that they are less outstanding than they had assumed. Some react to this jarring awakening with anxiety and depression.

Pride

૨૭

Pride or arrogance—exaggerating our worth and power, and feeling superior to others—has been recognized since ancient times as a root cause of cruelty and evil. The sin of pride, particularly man's attempt to transcend human limits, is condemned in both Greek and Biblical thought.[2] In Greek literature man's hubris, his overweening pride, is punished by nemesis, his downfall. As much as the Greeks admired and cultivated human wisdom, skill, and talent, they also felt that man must always remember his mortality. The myth of Daedalus illustrates this idea. Daedalus, a master craftsman, made a pair of wings for himself and for his son Icarus, whose feathers were held together with wax. Daedalus warned Icarus not to fly too high, lest the sun melt the wax. But Icarus ignored his father's warning and ascended towards the sun. The wax melted and Icarus plunged into the sea. Icarus aspired beyond his reach and was punished with death.

Turning now to the Judaic tradition in the Bible, the story of Adam and Eve conveys a similar message. God places Adam and Eve in the Garden of Eden and instructs them not to eat from the Tree of Knowledge. They disobey, are expelled from the garden, and punished by a life of toil. Adam and Eve's sin is not only that they disobeyed God, but that they aspired to be like Him. Their punishment fits their crime. God is immortal, human life is brief. God creates effortlessly, man must sweat to eke out his food from the earth. God is sovereign over all. Man is threatened by serpents and beasts, and woman is ruled by man.

Commenting on the passage in Isaiah "For my thoughts are not your thoughts and your ways are not my ways. This is the very word of the Lord" (55:8), a Jewish preacher contrasted God and man's attitudes towards their possessions. Man is happy when he has a utensil that remains whole and is saddened when it breaks. God, on the other hand, whose most cherished possession is man's heart, delights when it is broken in humility, as Scripture teaches "The Lord is close to the brokenhearted, those crushed in spirit he delivers" (Psalms 34:19) but "Proud men, one and all, are abominable to the Lord" (Proverbs 16:5). God himself exemplified humility when He chose to speak to Moses from a lowly bush rather than a lofty tree, and to reveal His

Torah at Sinai, an unimpressive mount, rather than from some majestic peak.

Isaiah's dirge against a haughty Babylonian tyrant mocks his proud insolence and rejoices in his humiliating downfall:

> You said in your heart,
> "I will ascend to heaven;
> above the stars of God
> I will set my throne on high;
> I will sit on the mount of assembly
> in the far north;
> I will ascend above the heights of the clouds,
> I will make myself like the Most High."
> But you are brought down to Sheol,
> to the depths of the Pit.
> Those who see you will stare at you,
> and ponder over you:
> "Is this the man who made the earth tremble,
> who shook kingdoms,
> who made the world like a desert
> and overthrew its cities,
> who did not let his prisoners go home?"
> And the kings of the nations lie in glory,
> each in his own tomb;
> but you are cast out, away from your sepulchre.
> (14:13–19, RSV)*

A common secular form of the Greek and biblical sin of hubris is expressed in the lives of individuals who strain themselves beyond reason in order to prove that there are no goals they cannot achieve, no obstacles they cannot overcome. Not only may they do themselves considerable psychological and physical harm, but in their drive to demonstrate their brilliance or ability, they often injure family members or subordinates.

---

* RSV = Revised Standard Version.

Pride

Our culture is understandably and perhaps even justifiably ambivalent about hubris. We value the quest for knowledge through free inquiry. We encourage our children to dream of conquests in space or of solving nature's mysteries. We try to reach distant galaxies, peer into black holes, discover secrets about the origin of the universe, and map the genome. Yet we are painfully aware of the inadequacies of our political and social structures, our inability to solve the human problems of war, poverty, drug dependence, violence, and prejudice. We may be able to unravel many complexities of the brain, but we are far from being able to cultivate the wisdom that will shape attitudes and behavior so as to make our personal and interpersonal lives more satisfying, ethical, and meaningful. Thus, while we do not identify with either the Greek or the biblical constraints on our uninhibited exploration of the cosmos, we do sense that our pursuit and attainment of power and knowledge do not suffice to guarantee the peace which we need. Indeed, we sometimes feel that too much of our attention is being diverted to our quest for scientific and technological achievements and too little to social, psychological, and spiritual ones. In the personal sphere too, it is important that the individual who is driven by the achievement goals of our culture, and deceived into believing that nothing is beyond his ken or grasp, should temper his hubris by reflecting upon his personal inadequacies and vices, and how they are often exacerbated by his pride. Too many a successful father, uncritically proud of his own achievements, has destroyed the spirit of a less able son by insisting that he aspire to goals too difficult to master or of no interest to him. In my practice I have seen a successful husband break the spirit of a devoted wife and destroy his family because he constantly disparaged her for not being able to meet his standards of achievement. She was never bright, sophisticated, or witty enough for him. These qualities are of questionable value, but he was too egocentric to see that.

Nevertheless, we should not avoid challenge and attempts to extend ourselves beyond the constraints we feel because of excessive fear or lack of self-confidence. The Greeks and the Hebrews, though denigrating hubris, extolled man's reason, skill, and courage. We, too, must find a proper balance, an Aristotelian mean, between hubris on the one hand and a sense of impotence on the other. But in calling attention to sinful pride we want to focus on our failure to recognize our deficiencies and temper our ambitions with humility.

Judaism's reverence for the scholar carried with it the danger of intellectual arrogance. Devotional writers never ceased warning the learned that if their knowledge is tainted with pride it is not valued by God and is subject to distortion by base motives. The scholar who thinks too highly of himself is not open to constructive criticism or to learning from the wisdom and experience of others. In our society, where knowledge is power and experts shape public policy in every field, intellectual arrogance is common and can be dangerous. The economist, military strategist, or physician who, so sure of himself that he neglects to solicit information and advice from others, can be responsible for events that can bring harm to many.

Jewish and Christian theologians and devotional writers analyzed the various manifestations of pride and their consequences.[3] They differentiated between inner and outer aspects of pride, the objects of its different subtypes, and the diverse effects they can produce on the sinner himself and on those around him.

In his analysis of pride, St. Thomas Aquinas[4] juxtaposes several definitions of it that had been given by his predecessors, with the aim of including all of them in a comprehensive understanding of the vice. Gregory the Great spoke of four species of pride. Some people consider themselves to be the cause of their achievements and talents. Others, though acknowledging that these qualities are from God, believe that they deserve them. Then there are those who boast of qualities they do not even possess. The fourth group despise others who lack the qualities they possess—they want to call attention to their uniqueness. Other Scholastic schoolmen saw ingratitude, justification of one's faults, and presumption (aspiring to that which is above one's legitimate grasp) as forms of pride. Anselm says that pride rears itself in three ways, in will, in speech, and in deed; Bernard includes, in his twelve degrees of pride, such qualities as licentiousness and habitual sinfulness. The sin of vainglory, though sometimes considered separate from pride, was frequently merged with it. Vainglory, the desire for glory and praise, can be vain in three senses. Some people seek praise for a quality or object that is unworthy. In some instances the source of the praise is worthless, such as being praised by someone of unsound judgment. Where the praise is being sought to enhance the reputation of the person rather than God's honor or his neighbor's salvation it is also considered vain. St. Thomas says that these varied descriptions of pride are neither contradictory nor mutually exclusive. Any individual may manifest all or part of them to different degrees.

Although some people's arrogance and feelings of superiority may extend to almost all aspects of their personality, frequently pride is delimited to a few qualities. One can be conceited about one's looks without presuming to be very knowledgeable, or one can be vain in seeking recognition for one's wealth without expecting praise for a nonexistent talent. The pride that people find most offensive in others is that which affects them, and this is the pride that is reflected in the proud sinner's speech and behavior. However, the source of that vice is in our inner selves—our craving for superiority and our beliefs about ourselves that fuel that craving. Medieval literature and iconography provide many elaborate descriptions of the external physical features and demeanors of the proud sinner, but the more reflective moralists emphasized that the fundamental criteria for ascribing the sin of pride to someone are how he thinks, feels, and behaves towards others. Appearances alone can be deceptive—the moralists repeatedly emphasize that people may assume the external signs of humility while being proud in their hearts.

Some of the medieval descriptions and definitions of pride refer not so much to various kinds of pride, but to its antecedents and consequences. Thus, Aquinas says that one may consider vainglory a consequence of pride. The pride is in the inordinate craving for excellence, the vainglory in its display. Indeed, Gregory did not include pride as one of the seven cardinal sins, but rather considered that it breeds the seven, which in turn breed a multitude of other vices. It is not difficult to see how pride leads to the other sins. The arrogant person who thinks so highly of himself believes himself entitled to what his heart desires, whether in the social or in the material sphere. Since he expects deference he is easily angered when he doesn't receive it. Assuming himself superior to others, he is especially prone to envy, which is a response to threats to one's self-esteem.[5] Being self-satisfied, the proud person does not feel compelled to activate himself in the pursuit of spiritual goals, and so commits the sin of sloth. Believing his "eminence" to be an entitlement, he will easily trample over the rights of others, as is so frequently done by the greedy, the gluttonous, and the lustful. It is not that pride inevitably leads to these vices, or that all manifestations of these vices are effects of pride. However, since these are frequently the case, Gregory accorded pride a separate status, designating it the mother and Queen of all vices.

Medieval artists and poets depicted pride with a variety of symbols which capture the many facets of the proud sinner. Pride was a queen or king (lord of the vices), helmeted with spear in hand, mounted on a white steed, attacking the virtues. Pride was a lion, king of the beasts, an eagle, flying above all others in the sky, a peacock arrogantly calling attention to its glorious feathers, and a woman vainly admiring her reflection in a mirror.

One of the most powerful dramatic presentations of the psychological dimensions of pride is Milton's portrayal of Satan in *Paradise Lost*. Being too proud to pay homage to God, he leads a rebellion of angels. God casts Satan and his followers from heaven into hell, and Satan's revenge for his defeat and punishment is to tempt Adam and Eve to sin in the Garden of Eden by eating the forbidden fruit:

> Who first seduced them to that foul revolt?
> The infernal Serpent; he it was, whose guile
> Stirred up with Envy and Revenge, deceived
> The Mother of Mankind, what time his pride
> Had cast him out from Heaven, with all his Host
> Of Rebel Angels, by whose aid aspiring
> To set himself in Glory above his Peers,
> He trusted to have equaled the most High,
> If he opposed; and with ambitious aim
> Against the Throne and Monarchy of God
> Raised impious War in Heaven and Battle proud
> With vain attempt.   (Book I, 33–44)

Satan, barely recovered from the effects of being thrust from the celestial sphere into the fiery furnaces of the underworld, regains his composure and addresses his second-in-command, Beelzebub:

P r i d e

>   . . . What though the field be lost?
> All is not lost; the unconquerable Will,
> And study of revenge, immortal hate,
> And courage never to submit or yield:
> And what else is not to be overcome?
> That Glory never shall his wrath or might
> Extort from me. To bow and sue for grace
> With suppliant knee, and deify his power.
>   (Book I, 105–112)

So saturated with pride and insolence is Satan, so ambitious for supremacy, that even defeat and damnation do not humble him. What he began in Heaven he now resumes in Hell with full vigor, enlisting the support of his fellow travelers in sin:

>   . . . Farewell happy Fields
> Where Joy for ever dwells: Hail horrors, hail
> Infernal world, and thou profoundest Hell
> Receive thy new Possessor: One who brings
> A mind not to be changed by Place or Time
> The mind is its own place, and in it self
> Can make a Heaven of Hell, a Hell of Heaven.
> . . . .
>   . . . Here at least
> We shall be free; . . .
> Here we may reign secure, and in my choice
> To reign is worth ambition though in Hell:
> Better to reign in Hell, than serve in Heaven.
>   (Book I, 249–263)

Milton here presents the inner life of pride, the thoughts and attitudes of the proud sinner. Satan's pride makes him envious of God's sovereignty. He believes that God's greatness depends on his submission—if he will not submit to God he can replace God. He becomes sinfully ambitious in that he attempts to grasp more power and authority than is due him as an angel created by God to serve Him. When Satan is punished his pride makes him even more insolent, stubborn, vengeful, hateful, and treacherous. With guile and cunning he revenges himself against God by enticing God's creatures into sin. Milton's Satan can be considered a personification of pride, which he depicts as a sin not easily corrected and as a mother of many other vices.

૨૦

Pride is unique among the seven deadly sins in that we are frequently unaware of our arrogance, whereas we tend to know when we are angry, greedy, gluttonous, and so on. Moreover, unlike the other six sins, when our pride is pointed out to us we often do not even realize that it is a vice. This is because it is difficult for us to admit that we are of less worth than we imagine ourselves to be, and because our culture values high self-esteem and fails to appreciate humility or even modesty.

In our society the most desirable assets are wealth, power, social status, physical attractiveness, and intelligence. Many arrogant individuals are indeed superior to others in a socially desirable way. As Aquinas said, a person who possesses more of these than do other people may believe that this entitles him to special privilege, or that he is exempt from behaving with respect and empathy toward others. It may make him contemptuous of human weakness and indifferent to the needs of others. His arrogance can lead him to unethical and illegal behavior. It frequently takes a dramatic reversal of his good fortune to make him aware of his own vulnerability and inherent human weaknesses—some humbling experience to remind him that he shares with all a common existential lot that includes pain, sorrow, sickness, and death.

૨૦

Contemporary Jewish and Christian moralists find themselves in a quandary when they discuss pride, which in traditional religious thought is the worst of the deadly sins. The proud sinner does not submit to God, and so his pride is the root of most other sins. In contrast, modern psychologists claim that high self-esteem is good for us, while low self-esteem is harmful. Devotional works provide antidotes to pride and try to cultivate humility. Psychologists offer workshops on overcoming inferiority complexes and building self-esteem. Indeed, the very connotation of "pride" has been reversed from a reprehensible to an admirable trait in the transition from traditional religion to contemporary secularism. In hundreds of references to "pride" in psychological papers published during the last decade, the vast majority use the word in a positive sense. In general discourse as well, it is proper to be proud of one's achievements, to take pride in our work, to stand tall and proud. There are English terms for personality traits closely related to the traditional sin of pride, which still retain their negative sense, such as *arrogant, haughty, conceited, egocentric, narcissistic, insolent, presumptuous,* and *vain.* The classical word itself, *pride,* has, however, been transformed from a vice into a virtue. This is indicative of the profound cultural changes our society has undergone as it has shifted from a God-centered to a man-centered orientation.

Unfortunately, some therapies are so weighted towards nurturing high self-esteem as defined by secular criteria of worth that they often neglect the vice of self-love. They reiterate the importance of our feeling good about ourselves and that we are entitled, first and foremost, to be happy. At its worst, the human potential movement, which peaked in the 1970s but whose influence is still felt in popular psychology and self-help manuals, justified and encouraged selfishness, a core element of pride. According to this movement, personal growth is to be our priority. We should focus on becoming the most that we can be—ignoring in the process our responsibility to others. If you are unhappy with your spouse then pick up and leave him or her, regardless of the effect it will have on your children. If you are enamored of your neighbor's wife and want to embark on an affair, by all means don't let moral strictures or ethical considerations be obstacles to experiencing your life to its fullest. The fact that your egocentricity will bring pain and injury to others need not deter you. Each of us is entitled to look out for his own interest because each of us is the center of his own world, which is the world which should count most for us.

In theory our culture advocates an egalitarian ethos. All men are created equal, and no group or individual should dominate or serve another. Humility suggests submission to authority, a sense of being low in a hierarchy of merit and power. Such feelings go against the grain of equality and so we undervalue humility as a virtue. Such an ethos also makes arrogance towards others a serious breach of our egalitarian social contract. However, wealth, power, and aggressive individualism, which our ethos also values, easily generate pride, and so we are ambivalent about the moral status of this sin.

Can the traditional derogation of pride and advocacy of humility be reconciled with the contemporary advocacy of high self-esteem and derogation of feelings of inferiority? Some religious writers maintain that sinful pride and high self-esteem refer to different attitudes. One can have high self-esteem without being "proud" and one can be humble without feeling inferior. One writer goes even further, para-doxically maintaining that high self-esteem is a prerequisite for hu-mility. The proud sinner actually suffers from feelings of inferiority. There are other religious thinkers, however, who maintain that it is disingenuous to try to reconcile pride as a sin with high self-esteem as a psychologically desirable character trait. They say that the two are indeed inherently incompatible, based upon fundamentally different premises about the nature of man and his responsibilities, and the proper relationship of man to a Creator.[6] It seems to me, though, that in some ways they are contradictory, in others, compatible, as is also the case with humility and feelings of inferiority.

Social psychologists have pointed out that one determinant of prej-udice is the psychological need of the prejudiced group to feel that it is socially superior to the group it despises. The sense of ethnic or national pride is enhanced to the extent that the victimized group is considered inferior. Frequently, the psychological need to feel superior is actually produced by an underlying feeling of inferiority. This is why some of the bitterest manifestations of ethnic prejudice are to be found in groups relatively low on the social scale, as illustrated by the poor whites in South Africa, who were some of the strongest supporters of apartheid.*

The same mechanism operates at the individual level. Overt mani-festations of pride and arrogance can often reflect covert feelings of

---

* Of course, aristocratic pride, felt by groups highest on the social scale towards "lower" ones, is even more common.

inferiority. This insight into the relationship between manifest pride and latent low self-esteem, although noted by some of the medieval religious writers on pride, plays a much more prominent role in contemporary psychological analysis of personality as a result of the influence of Freud and Adler. The medievalists tended to view the arrogant sinner at face value, rather than as engaging in compensatory psychological defenses. Pride as actually believing oneself to be superior and pride as a compensation for feeling inferior require quite different therapeutic approaches and moral evaluations. The former's exaggerated self-esteem has to be deflated, whereas the latter's underlying low self-esteem has to be bolstered so that it will no longer be necessary for him to feel better about himself by putting others down. Whereas devotional writers were less sensitive to the inferiority behind the facade of some proud sinners' airs of superiority, contemporary therapists are more prone to explain all sinful pride as a defense against an inferiority complex, ignoring the fact that many of their patients are "sincerely" arrogant.

On the other hand, with respect to the virtue of humility, the devotional writers discussed at great length and with subtle insight the possibility that what appears to be humility could really be disguised pride. In a society which rewards humility with social esteem, some people may mimic behaviors typical of the authentically humble. More spiritually dangerous, however, is the temptation of the person who was truly humble to be caught in the snare of sin by, paradoxically, becoming proud of his very humility. Finally, the proud person, living in a society that condemns pride as a sin, might seek to conceal his pride by simulating humility. The person who honestly aspires to extirpate his pride and cultivate his humility must engage in frequent introspective analyses in order to ferret out any of these impure motives.

᳕᳕

We can better understand pride and how to remedy it by considering in greater depth its contrasting virtue, humility, since the sin of pride begins with the absence of humility. Most Jewish and Christian moralists consider humility to be the moral virtue which is the prerequisite for attaining any of the other virtues. The devout Christian and Jew share a sense of utter dependence on God for all of the natural and material gifts with which they have been endowed. Even those achievements which appear to be primarily the results of one's own efforts, the religious person attributes to God's will and goodness or grace. In the moral sphere too, he holds himself responsible for the evil which he does, but considers God to be the source of most of the good which he performs. From such an attitude follow other characteristics of the humble person, manifested in thought, feeling, and action.

For example, he avoids praise and is not bothered by insult or contempt. He is not ashamed of his origins, his social status, or his occupation, low as they may be on the conventionally acceptable social scale. The humble person never engages in behavior in order to achieve honor or glory, but is motivated by benevolence or the glory of God. When praise is given him he reacts with indifference and thanks God for having made him an instrument for the benefit of others. Rather than envying the advancement of his brother, he delights in it.

Another way in which religious humility has been construed is as the utter lack of self-consciousness. As Thomas Merton puts it,

> How can you be humble if you are always paying attention to yourself?
> . . . If you were truly humble you would not bother about yourself at
> all. Why should you? . . . A humble man can do great things with an
> uncommon perfection because he is no longer concerned about inci-
> dentals, like his own interests and his own reputation, and therefore he
> no longer needs to waste his efforts defending them.
>
> (*New Seeds of Contemplation*, pp. 189–190)

The secularist may not accept the theocentric premises upon which the devotional writers build their case against pride and for humility. Yet, many of the prescriptions for humility and proscriptions against pride which they elaborated are quite sensible. They bespeak a wisdom and human sensitivity which the nonreligious person will also find attractive and useful.

Jeremy Taylor, the seventeenth-century Anglican divine, offers reflections on pride and humility which help us avoid the vice and acquire the virtue.[7]

P r i d e

Taylor points out that humility is a uniquely Christian value, not taught by the pagan philosophers.[8] When Jesus instructed his disciples to imitate him, he said, "Learn of me, for I am meek and humble, and ye shall find rest unto your souls," indicating thereby that "humility is the great ornament and jewel of Christian religion" (p. 105).

Taylor maintains that pride is essentially foolish whereas humility is wise. Are we proud of our bodies? Let us remember the orifices of our bodies which send out so many disgusting odors and excreta. Of our strength? Let us consider how dependent we are on stronger beasts such as horses and asses. Of our beauty? Our color is much less beautiful than the flowers and many animals are better proportioned than we are. Illnesses easily transform our outward beauty into yellow pallors, hollow stares, and wrinkles of deformity.

Our culture is obsessed with physical attractiveness and athletic prowess, and elevates to fame and fortune those who possess these qualities. Taylor reminds us of an important truth which we too often forget. Both those who feel superior because of their beauty or strength and those many more who feel inferior because of their lack of them, are foolish, because both ascribe undue importance to that which is deceptive, fragile, and transient.

Other common sources of pride are one's knowledge, wealth, or inherited social status. "To be proud of learning is the greatest ignorance in the world," says Taylor,[9] because no matter how much we know, it is only a minute amount compared to all of which we are ignorant. People naturally evaluate their intellectual or scholarly achievements by comparing themselves to others in their field. When they perceive themselves as being superior in their attainments, they may become arrogant and condescending to others. The outstanding lawyer, doctor, or scholar, particularly when his interests are narrowly focused on his field of specialization, can become so enamored of the praise and recognition that he receives from those whose professional opinion he seeks and values, that he comes to believe in his "general" superiority. Two patients of mine, a lawyer and a doctor, had great difficulty relating to others. They realized that they were disliked by colleagues, acquaintances, and even close family members. Their arrogance was partly to blame for their social maladjustment. I assigned them readings in a field about which they had no knowledge, but which commanded no less social respect than their own. The lawyer was assigned *The New England Journal of Medicine*; the doctor, *The Harvard Law Review*. It didn't take long for each to realize that for all his expertise in his field he was quite ignorant in the other. This experience tempered their feelings of superiority and helped improve their social interactions.

Some people are proud because they possess wealth, even if they acquired the wealth without working hard or ingeniously, as if wealth per se confers status and privilege. The ultimate source of this feeling is the fact that our culture worships money and people often do behave towards the wealthy individual as if he is more important than someone who isn't rich. The wealthy man may internalize these social attitudes and come to believe that he is indeed more significant than those less well off materially. Taylor mocks such a proud man with the argument that "if he be exalted above his neighbors because he has more gold, how much inferior is he to a gold mine?"[10] In fact, were he to reflect upon how fast this respect would evaporate if he lost his wealth, he would be chagrined at how he foolishly convinced himself that people respected him for who he is rather than for what he has. Many wealthy people who have suffered reversals of fortune lament the fact that nobody remembers them now when they are down and out.

For those proud of their aristocratic birth or the fame of their parents, Taylor suggests that they reflect that they had no role in their parent's nobility, and that it is rather common that he who boasts of his ancestors is in effect admitting his own lack of virtue or honor.

In order to acquire humility, says Taylor, one must subject oneself to constant and severe self-examination and self-criticism. One should highlight one's deficiencies and focus upon them. This can be facilitated by making frequent confession of our sins to God. We should also make it a practice every day to reflect upon one of our foulest sins or most shamefully disgraceful actions. By reminding ourselves of our vices through confession and reflection we will prevent the swelling of our self-regard. Taylor's advice goes counter to the prevailing tendencies of our culture and our child-rearing practices. We are inclined to deny our faults or to justify them with rationalizations. We are attracted to psychological theories that encourage us to focus primarily on our goodness while ignoring the darker elements of our personality. But humility requires us to be brutally honest with ourselves even if we are unhappy with what we see. We must recognize our selfishness, our viciousness, our deceptiveness.

Although Freudian personality theory and its therapeutic offshoot, psychoanalysis, are in many respects incompatible with and hostile to Judaism and Christianity, they share with them a view of man as essentially egocentric, with a proclivity to evil. Like the religions, Freudianism tries to tear away man's veil of self-deception and reveal his aggressiveness and narcissism. Freud claimed that opponents of psychoanalysis denied the truth of his revelations about the dark side of our unconscious impulses, the irrational forces that influence us without our being aware of their power, because to acknowledge the bestial in us rather than the divine shatters our self-esteem. Freud considered himself an opponent of religion. It is ironic, therefore, that his pessimistic view of man, and his call for greater insight into our dangerous potential for evil, are compatible with the teachings of the devotional writers of the religions he was attacking. Indeed, the religious call to humility is based, to no small extent, on similar views. The first step in the traditional remedies for pride is to subject ourselves to a self-examination that does not selectively notice only those traits we would prefer to see.

Although many people suffer from feelings of inferiority, it is not usually because of their sense of moral or spiritual inadequacy. They don't typically ruminate about how unkind, dishonest, or insensitive they might be, but about how incompetent, ugly, or professionally unsuccessful they are. They do not aspire to greater virtue but to greater recognition. This sense of inferiority and self-deprecation is not what the moralists want to cultivate as the basis for humility. On the contrary, the person who feels inferior about his social status, wealth, or looks is accepting values which from the religious point of view are inappropriate as criteria for evaluating true self-worth. What the moralists want us to feel inferior about are our ethical, moral, and spiritual faults.

Taylor artfully develops the argument for honesty in appraising our own faults by reminding us of how ready we are to see the faults of others. If we would only apply the same standards of criticism to ourselves as we do to our neighbors, our pride would be deflated. We usually disparage others on slight grounds. Even a person who until

now has been highly commended, will become demeaned in our eyes
with the revelation of only one of his sins or infirmities. When the
tendency to accentuate our neighbor's evil is combined with our opposite tendency to give greater weight to the good in our selves while
ignoring our own evils, we have a formula for sinful pride. We should,
says Taylor, be fair and just in our evaluations. Were we scrupulously
honest with ourselves, we would see that the base and unworthy in us
outweighs the good.

It has often been observed that in forming opinions of a person we
usually ignore his overall behavior and consider only whether or not he
is kind to us. This is unfair since the person's relationship with us
might constitute but a small percentage of his life activity. My employer might be charitable, a devoted father, and a person of integrity.
He might also be insensitive to my needs as his employee, about which
I may justifiably have a right to feel aggrieved. What we often do,
however, is magnify the fault that affects us and minimize or ignore
the virtues that affect numerous other people. While it is wrong to do
this with respect to others, it is a good antidote against pride for us to
do it in forming opinions of ourselves. After all, says Taylor, we cheat
ourselves with pretenses and lies, and fail to exercise our power of
choice to do good. Were others to do these things, we would look
down upon them. Let us then not flatter ourselves with too high an
opinion of who and what we are.

Taylor advises us to meditate upon the effects of pride and of humility. Among them is that "humility is the most certain way to real
honor, and pride is ever affronted or despised."[11] An excellent if pathetic example of the self-deceptive quality of pride is the case of a
distinguished scientist and church lay leader I know. She expected and
received a regular stream of praise and deference from the members of
her congregation. On matters of controversy within her congregation
she expected her views to prevail, and they often did because of the
aura of superiority which she projected. Yet the woman, whose behavior was pompous in the extreme, was very much disliked and
resented. She was regularly mocked in the private conversations of the
people who were publicly catering to her pride through flattery and
fawning. Because of her inflated sense of her worth and her belief that
she was indeed entitled to the "respect" which she received, she was
incapable of realizing how false and superficial was the deference being

accorded her. The very respect which she demanded was itself the cause of lack of respect. She, though, was oblivious to the true feelings that lay behind the veneer of "honor" which she received. This example points to another feature of pride. Although the arrogant individual is the primary sinner, for his pride to be fed and sustained requires the collusion of those around him.

Humility requires honesty and integrity, which are incompatible with the shifting roles and facades we assume in our daily lives. We seek to make favorable impressions on others so that they will think we are better or more talented than we really are. Taylor admonishes us to refrain from these play-acting games. If you were resting or sleeping or engaged in some other unimpressive activity when someone unexpectedly comes to visit you, "snatch not up a book to seem studious, nor fall on thy knees to seem devout, nor alter anything to make him believe thee better employed than thou wert."[12]

People do not go to psychologists in order to obtain guidance on how to avoid pride and acquire humility. In fact they rarely consult anyone, even a clergyman, for that purpose. Taylor tells us, however, that in order to cultivate humility we should seek out a spiritual confidant to whom we should reveal our sins. Self-revelation will serve as an antidote to pride. By honestly confiding our thoughts and behaviors to a trusted mentor, we will become aware of those which derive from or lead to pride and vanity. The spiritual mentor does not listen in order to forgive, but to facilitate self-observation. In confessing sins the shameful inclination to pride is exposed. Often, this alone suffices to set us on the path to humility. Moreover, the spiritual mentor can also offer advice and disciplines that help overcome pride. Sometimes he will discern motives for the confessant's behavior of which the confessant is unaware. Since vice breeds unhappiness, if we were to follow Taylor's advice to confide in a spiritual mentor, and more of us were willing to be mentors to others, fewer of us would find it necessary to consult with mental health professionals.

According to moralists like Taylor, one who wishes to be humble should compare himself to others only for the purpose of advancing them and denigrating himself, but not the reverse. He should reflect on his vileness and their virtues. This one is more learned than I am, that one more charitable, the third less arrogant. When the sins of others are transparent he should consider that perhaps theirs were performed out of illness or ignorance whereas his own were committed willfully and knowingly. This instruction of the moralists to weigh the balance in favor of others and against ourselves appears to us to be unfair. Most probably, though, it is dictated by their awareness of our tendency to do the opposite. Training ourselves to think this way acts as a corrective to our inclination to accentuate our virtues but not those of our neighbors and to minimize our vices while highlighting theirs.

The proud person rationalizes his faults, since to acknowledge them would threaten his sense of superiority. The humble person, on the other hand, readily admits guilt and patiently listens to the reproofs and anger even of his enemies. Our enemies do not seek to protect our self-image with falsehoods and often monitor our behavior more accurately than does many a friend. Therefore, our enemies' admonishments are often of greater value to us in exposing our faults than are the kind and soothing words of a friend.

This last insight can be applied to intergroup relations, particularly where different cultures clash. We in the West are often arrogant and condescending towards less technologically or industrially sophisticated societies. We ignore the spiritual and social costs of our exaggerated materialism and individualism. Were we to read critiques of our culture penned by outsiders we would become more aware of the flaws in our system, such as weakened family ties, high crime rates, and the sacrifice of humane values to greed. This would temper our pride.

Does humility require that we blind ourselves to the real differences that exist between ourselves and others? Does it mean that the scholar believe that he is an ignoramus, the beautiful woman ugly, or the benevolent man selfish? If these were the demands of humility then it would be predicated on falsehood. Since truth is a virtue, humility would, paradoxically, be incompatible with virtue. If, on the other hand, we are bound by truth to recognize those areas in which we excel relative to others, how do we prevent arrogance? At first sight it would appear that many of the prescriptions for humility do indeed require us to ignore reality.

In addressing this question the moralists argue that humility is not an exercise in deliberate self-deception but is compatible with truth. Authentic humility requires that we recognize our "gifts" and it is sinful to deny them, whether they are innate or acquired. Whether we are humble or proud depends on how we view and use these gifts and what we believe they imply for our attitudes towards God, ourselves, and others.

St. Thomas Aquinas, in his analysis of humility,[13] teaches that it is a virtue only insofar as it reflects our consciousness of our shortcomings. However it is not a virtue when man, "mindless of his dignity, compares himself to senseless beasts, and becomes like to them." Many pathological criminals consider themselves and mankind to be of no greater worth than vermin and feel no remorse in treating their victims with callous indifference to their pain. This is also a feature of nihilistic terrorism. Nothing is of value so nothing matters. If I am worthless then the morality of how I act is insignificant. If my neighbor, too, is worthless, who cares what I do to him. The religious teachings on pride and humility emphasize that though we must be self-critical to the extreme, we must also bear in mind that we and our fellow men are created in the divine image, crowned with reason, freedom, responsibility, and potential for virtue. Awareness of this acts as a corrective to the self-deprecating aspects of humility.

St. Francis de Sales points out that some people who have a mistaken understanding of true humility avoid reflecting on their talents and achievements, out of a fear that this will bring them to the sins of vainglory and self-complacency. On the contrary, St. Francis says, the true means to attain a love of God, which is the goal of the life of devotion, is by considering the benefits with which God has graced us. The more we are aware of them, the more we will come to love Him. Since our special talents, those which set us apart from others, have a greater effect on us than those we share with others, we must pay especial attention to them. Rather than inducing vanity or complacency, proper contemplation of them will make us humble. "There is no need to fear that knowledge of his gifts will make us proud if only we remember this truth, that none of the good in us comes from ourselves. What good do we possess which we have not received? And if we have received it why do we glory in it? On the contrary, a lively consideration of graces received makes us humble because knowledge of them begets gratitude for them."[14] Joseph, when he wisely deciphers Pharaoh's strange dreams and is appointed viceroy over Egypt, attributes his wisdom and power to the Lord rather than to himself. Similarly, Handel said of his musical genius, "Not I, but a power beyond me" is responsible for it.

A humility, in which protestations of unworthiness fail to reflect one's true abilities, is not only false but malicious as well, says St. Francis. It is often used as an artifice and excuse to avoid responsibility. We should use our talents in the service of God and of our neighbors. If we deny our talents we will not energize them for proper service. Such false humility is often a pretext for sloth.

One of the arguments of modern psychology in defense of high self-esteem is that in its absence we are not motivated to self-improvement. Our feelings of inferiority generate high levels of anxiety about possible failure and the ensuing shame, and so we avoid striving for challenging goals. St. Francis presents a paradoxical reversal of that argument, at least for the authentically religious individual, who sees God's hand in all. "The proud man who trusts in himself has good reason not to attempt anything. The humble man is all the more courageous because he recognizes his own impotence. The more wretched he esteems himself the more daring he becomes because he places his whole trust in God."[15] Thus, humility need not be a deterrent to an active life of challenge and achievement. On the contrary, it can empower rather than inhibit. However, it empowers only when it energizes the humble person to use his talent for service rather than for self-aggrandizement.

In our secular, materialistic, and competitive culture, major spurs to achievement are social recognition, prosperity, and surpassing others. In such a culture, low self-esteem is deemed deleterious to personal growth and high self-esteem advantageous to it. However, the religious culture reflected in devotional literature uses alternative mechanisms to energize people to challenging and worthwhile actions. As we said, alongside its denigration of pride and its espousal of humility, it reminds us of our uniqueness. Our reason, moral capacity, and aesthetic talent must be used to the utmost for proper ends. The religious worldview which reiterates how ignorant, sinful, and dependent upon God's grace we are, produced great scholars, ethical saints, and masters of art, music, and literature who were devout and humble. Humility is compatible with creativity and fulfillment. We today too should adopt morally and socially sensitive ways of encouraging achievement and rely less on pride and greed.

In psychotherapy for low self-esteem, fear of failure, and social anxiety, I include a reassessment of the patient's premises about what confers worth on him as a person and of the standards against which he should measure his achievements. The more he can separate his sense of personal worth from social recognition, wealth, attractiveness, or intelligence, the better will he be able to cope with feelings of inferiority. A very successful businessman who enjoyed running his own company was forced into bankruptcy. He was depressed and gnawed by feelings of shame and failure. He felt there was little for him to live for, since all his life he had built his self-image around his high income, independence, and control. The bankruptcy deprived him of all three. In therapy he decided to undertake a new business venture. His motives for success, however, were no longer to be pride, vanity, control, or greed, but benevolent use of whatever income he would earn this time around. As long as his motives were virtuous, and he was honest and doing his best, he could feel good about himself. Another client, a graduate of a prestigious Ivy League law school, considered himself a failure in life because he hadn't advanced professionally as far as some of his classmates. He implicitly defined his worth in terms of income and status relative to fellow attorneys. Through a value-oriented therapy he came to appreciate that if he were to provide several hours per week of pro bono services to the indigent, he would be doing something of greater worth than if he were a successful corporate lawyer, oblivious to the needs of the unfortunate. This approach should not be used merely as a palliative "sour grapes" defensive mechanism. One who sincerely internalizes the value that our worth as humans is defined by our service to man, will be gratified to see others do the same. He would have great respect and appreciation for peers more "successful" than he, who are also concerned about the poor and vulnerable.

Psychoanalysts have identified the "narcissistic personality."[16] Like Narcissus, who fell in love with his reflection in a spring and eventually died of frustration because his self-love could never be consummated, the narcissist is totally enamored of himself to the exclusion of interest in the welfare of others. According to Karen Horney, he has an unrealistically idealized self-image which temporarily enhances his self-esteem but which ultimately leads to dissatisfaction when he fails to live up to his glorified vision of himself. The narcissist behaves in ways harmful to both self and society. Many of his features, such as exploitativeness, self-absorption, and dominance, are similar to those of the proud sinner described by the moralists. Unlike the psychoanalyst, who in therapy concentrates on formative experiences from the narcissist's childhood, the religious moralist tells the sinner that irrespective of his childhood experiences, which helped shape his arrogance and self-absorption, he is now free and obligated to choose the path of humility. If evoking and resolving early emotional conflicts will make it easier for him to better himself, that should be done. But he should abandon pride even if childhood conflicts remain unresolved.

૨�

The sense of "success" is among the most important determinants of self-esteem in our society. Success is generally experienced in four different ways, through power, significance, competence, and virtue. Power refers to the ability to influence and control others and significance to the acceptance, attention, and affection of others. Competence refers to successful performance in meeting demands for achievement and virtue to adherence to moral and ethical standards.[17] Power and competence include feelings that one is in control of events. The person feels that he is primarily responsible for his social and occupational attainments, that what he does determines what will happen to himself and to others with whom he interacts. But this sense that "my strength and might have wrought me all this" is a characteristic of pride and the antithesis of humility. The religiously humble person sees himself as God's instrument or agent. Indeed, had God not willed his "successes" they would not have occurred, regardless of how hard he worked or how talented he was. Although such a belief by itself could lead to passivity, Judaism and Christianity provide other motives for action, primarily the belief that God has commanded man to engage in activities that sustain himself and society. The theologians were aware of the contradiction between believing that everything is determined by God's will and the common observation that there frequently is a causal relationship between what we do and what we accomplish. However, there are many exceptions to our apparent effectiveness, as when natural disaster destroys our hard-earned wealth or our social standing is reversed by forces beyond our control. These exceptions, together with belief in an omnipotent God and the denigration of pride, produced a compromise which, however logically tenuous, simultaneously denied human efficacy while affirming the obligation of human activity.

Whatever the philosophical or theological resolution of the question of who or what controls events and determines social and material "success," from a psychological perspective the religious teachings on pride and humility provide a valuable perspective even for a nonbeliever. Paradoxically again, the religious teaching that "man proposes, God disposes" is similar in its psychological implications to the secular psychological and sociological view that to a great extent our life situation is determined by events and causes over which we have little or no control. We are what we are because of a series of accidents: the circumstances of our birth, the kinds of parents we have, the particular culture in which we were socialized, and the political and economic environment in which we found ourselves by chance or luck but not by choice. True, within the parameters defined by these social and cultural molders, our own efforts can affect to some extent what our lives will be like. However, the range of our personal influence on what happens to us, as important as it definitely is, is considerably narrower than we tend to imagine. This is a humbling realization and one that can be very important in therapy. Both he who blames himself unduly for his perceived failures and he who praises himself unduly for his perceived successes are guilty of pride to the extent that they fail to acknowledge that their power is considerably more limited than they assume.

We need to take responsibility for our own thoughts, feelings, and behaviors, to realize that the passions and self-injurious behaviors like envy and anger which make us unhappy are, to a considerable extent, of our own doing. At the same time, though, we must also be realistic about how limited we are in our ability to control events external to ourselves. This is one of the most important of the teachings about the sin of pride and the virtue of humility. Just as it is necessary to be humble without being impotent, it is necessary to feel responsible and effective without being arrogant.

If pride is essentially a failure to accept God's sovereignty and humility is submission to him, can the religious teachings speak meaningfully to an atheist or agnostic who does not stand in awe before God? Many nonbelievers in the God of Judaism or of Christianity believe in a power which transcends our humanity and mortality and is responsible for our existence. They can feel humble before such a power although their humility will not be as intense and all-encompassing as that which is religiously inspired.

I once had a young patient who was raised as a devout Jew and who had studied many years in a rabbinical seminary. The school's spiritual environment was imbued with the intensely pietistic teachings of the great nineteenth-century moralist Rabbi Israel Salanter, who emphasized pride as a grievous sin and humility as a saving virtue. This client, an outstanding Talmudic scholar in a religious-academic setting and social environment which honored intellectual achievement, had worked hard to curtail his pride and to cultivate his humility. The worldview which supported and sustained his struggle with pride was that of traditional Judaism and its God-centered values. He considered his intellectual talents to be gifts of God; he felt a deep responsibility to use his knowledge to teach and illuminate the ways of Judaism, particularly to adolescents groping for spiritual meanings. He regularly examined his thoughts, feelings, and behaviors to see if they conformed to the radical expectations of the devotional writers. Although he was to a limited extent motivated by fear of punishment for sin and expectation of spiritual reward for piety, his main motive for shunning evil and doing good was his belief that sin is inherently bad for his soul and virtue inherently good for it. He believed that God had created him with a mission and purpose in life and that pride would deter him from accomplishing that mission, whereas humility would direct him towards its fulfillment.

In his early twenties he experienced a deep crisis of faith, a crisis whose result was the rejection of his religious beliefs and his adoption of an agnostic philosophy of life. In addition to having to cope with the psychological and emotional turmoil that his loss of faith engendered, he faced an additional problem of reestablishing a system of moral and ethical values. The issue was not simply the formulation of an abstract

P r i d e

or theoretical system that would be intellectually satisfying, but one with which he would be emotionally comfortable as well. Interestingly, notwithstanding his intellectual rejection of the ideological bases of his religious values such as humility and forbearance, he still felt that these values were valid and appropriate for him even in his agnosticism. Given his intellectual bent, however, he wanted to find a new rationale that would be consonant with his present views. In the course of therapy one of the issues which we considered in depth was whether elements of religiously motivated humility could be justified in the context of a nonreligious worldview. Several arguments denigrating pride and favoring humility emerged from our discussions (some of which we have already mentioned). The one closest to the traditional religious view was that, at the most basic level of existence, all mankind are equal. We all revert to dust and ashes after a very brief life. Therefore feelings of superiority over others belie the most fundamental truth about who we are. In addition, in the broad scheme of history and of the universe, each of us is of minute importance and ephemeral. Therefore to ascribe any unique importance to ourselves is blind and foolish. Moreover, no matter how marvelous our attainments or high our status, when we take the time to think about our dependence on so many others of lower social status or achievements for our survival and happiness, we realize our indebtedness to those we do not normally appreciate and may even denigrate.

Apropos of this last idea I told him of a young acquaintance of mine who had quickly reached the top of the ladder in her profession, with the concomitant wealth, status, and adulation of friends and colleagues. Her life successes clearly went to her head and were evident in the way she behaved. One day she was nearly killed in a freak automobile accident. This experience humbled her considerably. As she confided to me later, she had had a eureka-like insight as she lay on the road, bleeding, weak, and losing consciousness, waiting for a police officer and a paramedic to save her from death. This was a moment of truth for her. Here she was, the executive to whom presidents and chairmen of leading corporations turned for advice and assistance, now helplessly hovering on the margins of death. She was utterly dependent on two people with whom but moments before she would have considered it beneath her dignity to interact in any but a most perfunctory way. She begged them to alleviate her pain, to save her not only for her own sake but for the sake of her children. She, who was used to commanding, was now beseeching; she who was always dominant was now passive; she who believed in her superiority was now made aware of the more important social function than hers that was filled by these two men who were less educated, culturally sophisticated, and economically well off. They saved lives. They alleviated pain and suffering. She never did these things. This lesson was a powerful corrective to her pride.

These reflections enabled my client to retain a commitment to humility notwithstanding his loss of faith. Given the personal and social costs of pride and arrogance and the rewards of humility, many people who do not perceive themselves as religious or pious could agree that pride is a pernicious vice to be avoided and humility a virtue worth cultivating. The humbler we are, the more humanely will we relate to one another, as individuals, groups, and nations.

Envy

Envy is so shameful a passion that we never dare acknowledge it.
　　　　　　　—FRANÇOIS DE LA ROCHEFOUCAULD

Political scientists maintain that a major cause of international conflict is the envy and resentment felt by poorer nations towards wealthier
ones. This was one reason why Iraq invaded Kuwait in August 1990.
Saddam Hussein tried to capitalize on this envy and hatred and transform it into violent street protests by impoverished Arab masses against
the oil-rich Gulf states and prosperous America.

Civil strife, too, is often an expression of the envy of one social class
by another. Envy, along with other nobler motives, lurks beneath the
surface of the heated demands for affirmative action. Some ethnic
hostility, such as the antisemitism of black extremists or attacks on
academically or commercially successful recent Asian-American immigrants, are fueled by envy.

Envy affects our interpersonal relationships as well, and can be a
cause of great misery. Consider the following episode. A man is happily married to a woman whose physical and emotional companionship he enjoys. He is pleased with his job as a college professor and
earns a respectable if modest salary. The neighborhood in which he
lives is a good one and his children attend quality public schools. He

55

has several close friends and many acquaintances. All in all, if he were asked to reflect upon his life he would say that it has treated him well.

Then he receives an invitation to the twentieth annual reunion of his college graduating class. Curious about how time and events have dealt with his former classmates, he decides to attend.

At the reunion the professor discovers that many of his former classmates earn considerably more money than he does. Their jobs sound more exciting and respectable than his, and they live in more prestigious neighborhoods. Their children attend select private schools. Moreover, many of his peer group are married to spouses more educated and more attractive than his wife. Clearly, a good number of former school chums who didn't outshine him in academic or social achievement during those college years have attained a higher social, economic, and professional status than he has.

How might the professor feel when he returns home after the weekend reunion? Inferior? Gnawed by a sense of failure? Questioning his worth as an individual? Resentful towards his spouse for not being more than she is and regretful that he settled for less than he deserved to get? Critical of the education he is providing for his children? Dissatisfied with the monotony and lack of influence of his job, and the modest income he earns? Harboring a secret animosity towards his successful fellow alumni, coupled with the hope, perhaps barely conscious, that some setback befall them?

What has happened over the weekend? Has anything actually changed in the professor's life during the three days he spent at the reunion? Is his spouse uglier now than last Friday morning? Did he get a salary reduction? Are his activities as a teacher, researcher, and scholarly author any different this Monday morning from what they were before he left for his trip? Has there been any deterioration over the past seventy-two hours in the quality of instruction being provided at the schools his children attend? Has he himself suddenly blossomed into a more intelligent and stimulating person, so much so that his spouse, whose social and physical companionship he enjoyed before his trip, is now, relative to him, a dull and unexciting bore?

Objectively, absolutely nothing in his life on Monday is different from what it was just a few days earlier. What has changed, of course, is the new way in which the professor thinks about himself. His envy of his former classmates has become a source of ongoing psychic pain which affects the way he feels about many different things. But why does he feel envious? What are the components of this powerful, debilitating, and dangerous emotion?

かる

First we need to examine what envy is. Envy is the pain we feel when we perceive another individual possessing some object, quality, or status we do not possess. But why is the disparity between what we and others possess so painful? It is because when we compare ourselves unfavorably to others our self-esteem is impugned and envy is our response to this hurt. It is related to our pride and our quest for recognition, or, for some of us, for fame, glory, and power. When the envious person is unable to get what he desires, he usually hopes that the person he envies will lose the desired thing and he may even conspire to make that happen. These envious feelings often exist even when they have no moral justification. In other words, envy is often experienced in situations where the envied person is not the cause of the envious person's lack, and where the envied person possesses what he has for very good reasons, such as having worked hard to attain it. Envy is particularly malicious when the envious person seeks to deprive the envied person of what he has, even though if he succeeds in doing so, the desired object, quality, or status won't thereby be transferred to the envier.

The roots of envy begin early in life. From childhood we are compared to others. Our value as individuals is measured by how much dumber or smarter, uglier or more beautiful, weaker or stronger, poorer or richer we are than our peers. In our more rational moments we may reject these criteria of worth as unfair and irrational. However, they have been so deeply ingrained in us by family and society that we automatically react with painful envy when we believe that others surpass us in these attributes. Envy also results from greed and lust, for it is only because we value the things that money can buy or the gratifications of sexual indulgence that we covet them in others. Although not all coveting is envious, coveting lays the groundwork for much envy.

Shakespeare's Iago envies Othello's success and his beautiful wife,

Desdemona. He is also disgruntled that Othello, whom he despises as a black, pagan Moor undeserving of honor in white, Christian Venice, did not appoint him as his lieutenant. He deviously conspires to make Othello suspect that Desdemona is unfaithful to him. Iago succeeds in driving Othello mad with jealousy to the point that Othello murders Desdemona, who truly loved him. Thus his envy is satisfied. Iago has deprived Othello of the objects of his envy, although he does not acquire Desdemona or honor for himself but rather brings about her death as well as Othello's and his own punishment. Shakespeare, the master psychologist, lays bare the goal of the most malicious envy. If I, Iago, can't possess the desired objects, then, Othello, neither will you.

Another characteristic of envy is the way in which it permeates our entire consciousness. Although to an outside observer the object of our envy may appear to be petty and insubstantial, as indeed it often is, it affects us as if it were central to our very being. Many a student has experienced pangs of envy at seeing a classmate receive a grade on an exam only a few points higher than his own. A person I know once suffered several sleepless nights when he learnt that one of his friends was invited to a party given by another friend, while he was left out. His envy of the invited friend (and his anger at his host) disrupted his inner emotional life for many days and to a degree far beyond the significance of the event which precipitated it.

I once had a client who would constantly compare herself with her more successful sister. Nothing she ever achieved satisfied her because in her mind it was still less than what her sister had attained. Her envy impacted on all areas of her life, constantly gnawing at her, giving her no peace, and affecting her behavior in many perverse ways. Her predominant motive in life was not to do what she really enjoyed but to overtake her sister. How distorted a life-style it produced! Yet try as she might she could never reach her goal. What was even more pathetic was her self-denial of what her true motive was. It took many hours of therapy to make her aware of her envy and of how it was totally dominating her life—producing unhappiness for herself and her family.

The reason for envy's intense and all-pervasive effect is because, as we have said, we interpret our lack of what another person possesses as somehow indicative of our lessened worth in general. My client (before therapy) didn't think to herself "My sister was admitted to Harvard Medical School whereas I wasn't because she was more conscientious about her studies in undergraduate school than I was. I preferred participation in the social and athletic scene to long hours of study and to earning good grades." No, her thoughts were global in nature. "My sister is better and smarter than I am." Period. And to compensate for her feelings of lessened self-worth which were essential components of her envy, she spent two years at arduous study of premed courses after college and was finally accepted to and enrolled in a medical school. All of this she did only to "prove" that she was "as good as" her sister. She spent years in medical school doing something which provided her with little real satisfaction and considerable frustration. She spent a lot of money in the process. The long and tiring hours at school alienated her from her husband and deprived her of opportunities for enjoying her child. Yet even after acquiring her medical degree she continued to envy her sister!

Because secular psychology does not challenge the prevailing materialist and hedonist values and our culture's nonspiritual and amoral criteria for evaluating human worth, it cannot provide radical remedies for envy. Some psychologists have suggested strategies for coping with it, such as focusing on one's positive attributes, working harder to achieve what one envies or, alternatively, discounting the importance of what you envy.[1] These, however, fall far short of what the religious and philosophical moralists would prescribe. Secular psychology does not emphasize the immorality of envy and its incompatibility with compassion, love, and justice as they do.

ॐ

In contrast to secular values, Judaism and Christianity teach that our worth is not measured by things that are external to us but only by our moral and spiritual virtues. We should compare ourself with others only on these and if we find ourselves wanting, rather than envy the other, we should work on improving ourselves. It may be pleasant to be beautiful, rich, successful, and bright and unpleasant to be ugly, poor, unsuccessful, and dull. However, our self-esteem should not depend on these attributes, and comparisons made along these lines can only be morally harmful. They will result either in pride or in envy.

This is not to suggest that religious people are free of envy. If that were the case religious writers would not have had to expend so much energy teaching about its danger and how to overcome it. However, individuals who internalize the moral values of Judaism or Christianity are able to minimize their feelings of envy and to the extent that they do so the happier they are.

Envy has been compared by various religious authors to hissing hot coals, to poison spreading throughout the body, to boomeranging arrows, or to a fire raging within. Some people are "consumed by envy"—an apt expression to describe the psychic pain suffered by those whose envy dominates their lives and consciousness. These and similar picturesque descriptions of the inner effects of envy point to two of its most pronounced features. Most of us are not as evil as Iago nor are we as "effective" as Iago in depriving others of the object which excites our envy. It is we who suffer most from our envy. Generally, envy causes more unnecessary pain to the envier than it does to the envied. An ancient Greek poet put it nicely—"Envy slays itself by its own arrows."[2] After the reunion which the professor attended he probably won't do anything that will in any way harm his former classmates whose seeming success outshone his achievements. He probably won't even make any major changes in his life-style. What he will do is ruminate about his deficiencies, perhaps become obsessed with them. These envious and self-deprecating thoughts will make him unhappy and sour his relationships with family, friends, and co-workers.

In commenting upon envy the Jewish eighteenth-century moralist, Luzzatto, points out its irrational and even masochistic quality:

Envy is nothing but want of reason and foolishness, for the one who envies gains nothing for himself and deprives the one he envies of nothing. He only loses thereby. . . . There are those who are so foolish that if they perceive their neighbor to possess a certain good, they brood and worry and suffer to the point that their neighbor's good prevents them from enjoying their own. (*Path of the Just*, p. 165)

Another Jewish devotional work relates the parable of a greedy man and an envious man who met a king. The king said to them, "One of you may ask something of me and I will give it to him, provided I give twice as much to the other." The envious person did not want to ask first for he was envious of his companion who would receive twice as much, and the greedy man did not want to ask first since he wanted everything that was to be had. Finally the greedy one pressed the envious one to be the first to make the request. So the envious person asked the king to pluck out one of his eyes, knowing that his companion would then have both eyes plucked out. This illustrates the masochistic form that extreme envy can take. The pathologically envious are willing to suffer great injury as long as those they envy suffer even more.[3]

The ubiquity and danger of envy made it a central sin in all of the moral and religious traditions. Indeed, one of the very first accounts of human interaction in the Hebrew Bible is a story about envy and its effects:

> Abel became a keeper of sheep, and Cain became a tiller of the soil. In the course of time, Cain brought an offering to the Lord from the fruit of the soil; and Abel, for his part, brought the choicest of the firstlings of his flock. The Lord paid heed to Abel and his offering, but to Cain and his offering He paid no heed. Cain was much distressed and his face fell. And the Lord said to Cain:

> > "Why are you distressed
> > And why is your face fallen?
> > Surely, if you do right
> > There is uplift.
> > But if you do not do right
> > Sin couches at the door;
> > Its urge is toward you,
> > Yet you can be its master."

> . . . And when they were in the field, Cain set upon his brother Abel and killed him. (Genesis 4:2–8, JPS)*

This brief narrative is illuminating in many ways. Cain murders Abel because he is envious of the fact that God accepted Abel's gift but

*JPS = Jewish Publication Society.

not his own. In other words, God preferred Abel to Cain. The first homicide is a result of envy. But who was responsible for the Lord's positive response to Abel and His negative response to Cain? Was God justified in preferring Abel? Cain himself was to blame. Look carefully at the text again. Cain's offering was from the fruit of the soil—not the choicest of the fruits. He only grudgingly acknowledged his debt to God for providing for his needs. Abel, on the other hand, brought the choicest of his flock. He was deeply appreciative of God's provisions. Cain envied Abel's status before God even though it was deservedly earned, it could have been earned by Cain himself had he so willed it, and it was not acquired at Cain's expense. Furthermore, the biblical story makes it clear in the Lord's warning to Cain before he murders Abel that it is within his ability to control his envious passion. In effect the Lord is telling Cain—"Don't try to avoid responsibility for your emotion of envy and for the dastardly actions you might perform in order to satisfy it."

The biblical story demonstrating Solomon's wisdom also reveals the nature of envy.[4] A woman whose infant died was envious of the mother of a live baby, and so she falsely claimed that the child was hers. When Solomon offered to cut the child in half and distribute it between the two, the woman agreed whereas the true mother was horrified at the thought and preferred to lose her child to the imposter as long as it would live. By their different reactions to his proposal Solomon discovered which was the real mother and which the imposter. Here we see the cruelty of envy. Not only did the envious woman try to deprive a mother of her child, she preferred the child dead rather than allow someone else to enjoy what she lacked.

According to Christian mythology, Satan, the devil, tempts man to do evil and to disobey the will of God. Who is this malicious creature who opposes the forces of good in the universe? Where does he come from and what is the source of his evil character?

Christian mythology, based upon Jewish legends, answers that originally Satan was an angel. However, he was envious of God and so led a rebellion against him. As a punishment he and his followers were cast from heaven into hell. The devil expressed his envy and hatred of God by tempting Adam and Eve (who represent all of mankind) in the Garden of Eden to sin. In the passage on pride from *Paradise Lost* which we cited on pages 34–35, Milton uses this myth to reflect on envy too as a source of sin and sorrow. He tells us that envy, which comes from the distorted sense of self-worth of pride, leads to folly, sows the seeds of discord, and fans the flames of hatred.

One of the paradoxes of envy is that it is related to what appear to be two opposite senses of the self. Benedict Spinoza analyzes the proud man and the despondent man. Pride, he says, is joy which arises from the false opinion that we are superior to others. Despondency is sorrow that arises from the false opinion that we are inferior to others. Surprisingly, both of these emotions produce envy. The proud person is envious since, thinking he is superior to others, he cannot tolerate that they should possess something which he doesn't. The despondent person is envious since, feeling sorry for himself for being of lesser worth than others, he constantly searches for ways to reduce the disparities he perceives. Most often this takes the form of finding fault with others who have more than he has and rejoicing in their loss or misfortune, both being classic symptoms of envy.[5]

As powerful as envy is we are not helpless before it. There are many strategies that can be used to deal with envy, which can be summarized in "ten commandments." Some of these are in the spirit of religious values, others are derived from the reflections of moral philosophers:

1. Reconsider the underlying assumptions you have about what makes you a worthy individual.
2. Deemphasize the value of the envied objects either for yourself or for the person who possesses them.
3. Think about positive and valuable things you have that the envied person does not.
4. Compare yourself to those less fortunate than you rather than to those more fortunate than you.
5. Consider that the person you envy deserves the object or quality which he has as his just reward and that there may be good reasons why you do not.

6. Reflect upon the irrationality of your envy. It hurts you without improving your situation.
7. Think about the potential danger of your envy. It could lead you to do certain things which will harm others and yourself.
8. Consider that your envy is inconsistent with the kind of person you would really like to be.
9. Associate your envy with negative qualities.
10. Cultivate feelings and thoughts that are incompatible with envy and the emotions it evokes.

Considering some of these ideas in depth will preoccupy us for most of the remainder of the chapter. As we have indicated, moralists emphasize that envy results from greed, lust, vainglory, and pride. Since we envy others because we value material possessions, sexual experiences, honor, or power, a basic remedy for envy is to develop disdain for or at least an indifference to these objects of envy.

Thomas Hardy describes how envy may be overcome by maintaining a proper perspective on what is worth valuing:

A PRIVATE MAN ON PUBLIC MEN

When my contemporaries were driving
Their coach through Life with strain and striving,
And raking riches into heaps,
And ably pleading in the Courts
With smart rejoinders and retorts,
Or where the Senate nightly keeps
Its vigils, till their fames were fanned
By rumor's tongue throughout the land,
I lived in quiet, screened, unknown,
Pondering upon some stick or stone,
Or news of some rare book or bird
Latterly bought, or seen, or heard,
Not wishing ever to set eyes on
The surging crowd beyond the horizon,
Tasting years of moderate gladness
Mellowed by sundry days of sadness,
Shut from the noise of the world without,

E n v y

Hearing but dimly its rush and rout,
Unenvying those amid its roar,
Little endowed, not wanting more.
                                   (*Selected Poems*, p. 252)

The poem's speaker compares himself to his contemporaries who have chosen to engage in professions that are public, prestigious, and wealth producing. Some are highly successful businessmen, others bright lawyers, a third group famous politicians or statesmen.

The speaker himself is a very private man. He has spent his life in isolation, appreciating nature and the world of books. He lives a modest, quiet existence, with little social status. Moreover, he doesn't seem to have any "achievements," at least from society's point of view.

Although the speaker is well aware of the attainments of his contemporaries he is somewhat critical of them. In order to reach their goals they had to "strain" and "strive" (which suggests not only hard work but fighting against others). They didn't just earn a lot of money, but in a greedy way "raked" it into heaps. They worked late into the night (at what expense to their family life and mental health?) in order to become famous. But their fame is partly due to "rumour," which, of course, often exaggerates the truth about their achievements. Their world is one of a "surging crowd," pushing and shoving one against another. It is a stressful state of wild confusion, filled with "noise," "roar," "rush," and "rout."

The speaker comforts himself by pointing out the "costs" paid by his contemporaries for their apparent successes in life which he has not had to pay. Furthermore, for all its quiet and humble character, his own life has provided him with many benefits. He has enjoyed reflection and tranquility, and experienced years of gladness, even if they were only moderate rather than intense. Although he has been endowed with little, it doesn't bother him since he never wanted more. He wasn't even interested in seeing, let alone becoming a part of, the "surging crowd" and he did not envy those caught up in its roar.

Through Hardy's poem we can open ourselves to a new perspective on what constitutes "the good life." We might discover that we have been neglecting sources of fulfillment that are readily available, such as reading and enjoying the beauties of nature. We should also think about the negative aspects of the lives of those with whom we have tended to compare ourselves unfavorably while we reflect upon the positive aspects of our own life-style. A teacher or social worker on a modest salary might envy a brother, friend, or classmate who is a highly paid senior corporation executive. Is it true, as the envious sibling might believe, that corporation executives are happier than teachers or social workers? Precisely the opposite might be true! I know of many "highly successful" executives whose lives are plagued by depression and anxiety, by marital and family discord. These men and women, who project an image of having "made it" in the world, often yearn for precisely the kind of life-style that a teacher might have. Ironically, while the less "successful" sibling is envying his more "successful" brother, the latter is envying the former.

Aristotle points out that we tend to be envious of those similar to us and with whom we are competing. Ambitious individuals, in particular, are susceptible to envy. Moreover, we are envious of even very slight differences in achievement between ourselves and our competitors.[6] If we consider the combined effects of these characteristics it comes as no surprise to find that many "successful" people are caught up in an unending cycle of envy.

Most of us earn considerably less than $150,000 a year. We are certain that if we made $200,000 annually for the rest of our lives (adjusted for inflation) we would never envy anyone for their money. Unfortunately, envy dictates otherwise. As soon as the ambitious go-getter reaches the $200,000 mark he forgets where he was a short while before and looks at those he has now reached. But, of course, there will always be someone out there, among his competitors, who is ahead of him, if only by a few thousand dollars or by being one step above in the corporate hierarchy. The gnawing of envy resumes with an internal dialogue along these lines: "Why is he ahead of me? I'm as competent as he is, aren't I? After all, I brought myself up by my own bootstraps. Well, aren't I? You mean maybe I'm not really that good! I'll prove (to others and to myself) that I am! If I've gotten this far I can surely go a little beyond where I am now, just to catch up to him." So he never really rests, he's never really satisfied, envy has him in its grasp and he is forever in a race he can never win.

The technique Hardy describes of devaluing the benefits of what one envies can be applied to many things besides financial success, influence, or power. For example, a major source of envy, particularly in our lust-full culture, is the perceived sexual happiness of others. A patient of mine had a friend and next-door neighbor whose wife was more beautiful and physically enticing to him than his own wife. Every time he saw her sunning herself on her lawn he would immediately begin to imagine what an exciting sex life her husband must enjoy. Much as he cherished his own wife as a companion, he could not help but feel that he was being deprived nightly of sexual pleasures that could only be provided by someone with the attractiveness and mystique of his neighbor's wife. Surely, he imagined, the couple next door must engage in sex frequently and in most interesting ways. My sex life, by comparison, is monotonous and minimally enjoyable. The more he harped on those thoughts, the more frustrated he felt. He wondered why his wife wouldn't wear the kind of suggestive clothing and carry her body the way his neighbor's wife did. Had she done so, he was sure that this would add some of the spice to his nighttime activities that he was certain enlivened the long evenings of play enjoyed only one house away. These envious ruminations persisted for several months, making him miserable. They begin to affect his relationship with the friend he envied. He harbored a secret wish, difficult for him to admit to himself, that some misfortune befall his neighbor or that the beauty of his neighbor's wife be marred in some way.

My patient became increasingly irritable with his own wife, blaming her for his frustrations. He began to pressure her to lose weight, to dress in a more sexually provocative way, and to study manuals of sexual technique, things which she had little interest in doing.

In this case my patient's envy stemmed from his lust. It was a classic case of coveting a neighbor's wife. Although he had no pretensions of seducing her, the lust became an intense envy which made him unhappy and created serious friction with his wife. Therapy involved several strategies. The most obvious and easiest one was for the patient to avoid looking at the neighbor's wife when she was outside. The less his lust was stimulated, the less it would arouse his envy. However, another component of therapy was to get my patient to overcome his envious thoughts and feelings by applying the method of minimizing the "desirability" of the object of desire.

We examined the assumptions he had about his neighbors' presumed sexual pleasure. How true were they? How certain could he be that what he imagined reflected reality? The two main assumptions were that physically attractive women always make exciting sexual partners and that the neighbor's wife was as physically attractive to her husband as she was to my client.

I pointed out that both assumptions are often wrong. Many beautiful women and handsome men suffer from sexual dysfunction or incompatibility with their spouses. In fact, the sexual pleasure actually enjoyed by couples bears very little relationship to the appearance of the body, but has much to do with the feelings that a man and a woman have towards each other as companions and friends who respect and care for one another. My client was allowing his envy to ruin his emotional relationship with his wife. Furthermore, sexual pleasure is subject to habituation. The neighbor's wife was especially attractive to my patient because she was forbidden and inaccessible. But because she was permitted and accessible to the neighbor, his sheer physical pleasure with her was less than my client was imagining it to be. Moreover, since my patient didn't really know what took place in the private lives of others, it was to his advantage to assume that his experiences were no less fortunate than those of others, where there is no objective way of it being proven otherwise. The purpose in educating my patient as to the incorrectness of the premises which sustained his envy was not to denigrate the physical beauty of his neighbor's wife or the pleasures of their marital bed. It was to give him a more realistic perspective on the object of his envy, a perspective which made the envied pleasure considerably less attractive than it had been prior to his consideration of these facts. It was to correct his erroneous exaggerations about other people's happiness and good fortune.

ॐ

Another remedy for envy is the well-known adage to count our blessings. When we begin to dwell on someone who seems to be better off, we should remind ourselves how much more fortunate we are than are many others in the world. A teenage patient I had was envious of her girlfriend who was asked out for a date an average of three times a week while she was asked out only once a week. She dwelt on this comparison, feeling sorry for herself and hostile towards her girlfriend, so that the friendship between the two was cooling. Failure to control such envious thoughts may cause a cherished relationship to deteriorate. I instructed her to stop comparing herself to her girlfriend and start comparing herself to other girls she knew who hardly get asked out once a month. And what about all those girls who are so shy or uncomfortable about themselves that even when they do go out with boyfriends they find the experience so stressful and unpleasant that they regret going out in the first place. Compared to their social life, hers wasn't bad at all. The more one dwells on comparisons of this sort, the less one will feel sorry for oneself and antagonistic towards more popular individuals. I am not suggesting that we should feel good that others feel bad. Indeed, this itself is a form of envy, and is contrary to the humane values necessary for happiness. But given the fact that there are almost always individuals worse off than we are in some way, even within our narrow social frame of reference, we should learn to view our life from a broader and more realistic perspective. We shouldn't focus our sights only in the direction of those who have more than us. We should at least be honest enough with ourselves and with life as it really is to look also in the direction of those who have less.

I know an individual who made it a practice of visiting with his children the most sordid slums of the city in which he lived. He had several purposes in exposing his upper-middle-class children to the poverty, helplessness, and despair that were evident in the run-down neighborhoods they would walk through. He wanted his children to be aware of others' suffering and to cultivate in them a sense of compassion and social responsibility. He wanted them to be acutely aware of the fundamental human similarity between themselves and people who live in squalor and who appear to be so different from them. Many years after his children had grown up and left home, this wonderful man told me that these childhood excursions had an unintended side benefit. They had made his children much more appreciative of what they did have in life, so that as adults they are much less prone to envy as an emotion and motive for behavior than was typical of their childhood friends with whom they had grown up in affluent suburbia. It seems that they learnt to look beneath as well as above them when assessing themselves and what they had in life.

Too often we forget what is really worth valuing in life and so we envy others, deprecate ourselves, and become depressed, all the while ignoring what we have which should more than compensate for what we lack. In one of his sonnets Shakespeare reminds us that to be loved by someone we love is the most precious gift we can hope for and if we appreciate this gift we will have no cause for envy or despair:

> When in disgrace with fortune and men's eyes,
> I all alone beweep my outcast state,
> And trouble deaf Heaven with my bootless cries
> And look upon myself, and curse my fate,
> Wishing me like to one more rich in hope,
> Featur'd like him, like him with friends possessed
> Desiring this man's art, and that man's scope,
> With what I most enjoy contented least;
> Yet in these thoughts myself almost despising,
> Haply I think on thee. And then my state
> (Like to the lark at break of day arising
> From sullen earth) sings hymns at heaven's gate;
> For thy sweet love remember'd such wealth brings,
> That then I scorn to change my state with kings.
> (Sonnet 29)

Another strategy to adopt when envious, which in many instances can help overcome the emotion, is that of "just reward" or merit. One of my patients was very unhappy at his job. As we probed for the sources of his job-related depression we discovered that the kind of work he was doing was actually quite satisfying to him. He got along well with his co-workers and was highly respected by those he supervised. What then was the cause of his depression which was clearly work-related? After searching for clues over several sessions of psychotherapy he finally admitted to me and, much more importantly for his eventual improvement, to himself, that he deeply resented his immediate superior. The resentment derived from his envy of his boss. This superior was the same age as my client and only two years earlier had been at a lower management level. During a two-year period he had progressed so rapidly in the firm that now my client was answerable to him. It was evident that the best way to alleviate my client's depression was to address the envy and resentment at its root. I approached the issue by asking my client whether he believed that people who are conscientious and work hard should be rewarded for their efforts and accomplishments. Wouldn't he want his achievements to be acknowledged and rewarded? Did he feel that those in charge of allocating responsibility and authority to employees should ignore demonstrated ability and dedication to the goals of the organization? Would he himself, in the long run, benefit from a society in which excellence was ignored and mediocrity reinforced?

After due reflection my client agreed that effort and excellence deserved reward. In fact, it was through such a system of rewards that he himself had managed to reach his present position. He wasn't being discriminated against by the company. The fact was that his superior did invest more time and effort on the job than he did. As unpleasant as the reversal of roles vis-à-vis his present boss had been, he had to honestly admit that it was fair and just. Moreover, the existence of such a reward system still could work in his favor, since it left open many opportunities for future advancement in his career.

In essence the treatment consisted of a rational discussion of the irrational and unjust assumption underlying my client's envy. Once he became aware of the contradiction between what he genuinely believed was fair, just, and proper and the assumptions on which his envy was based, which were unfair, unjust, and improper, he was better able to cope with the situation. As he learned to reconsider his attitude towards his boss and focus on the justness of both of their present positions, the envy diminished and along with it so too did the depression.

One reason why this very "rational" approach to resolving an "emotional" problem was effective was because in this particular case the envier, when confronted with the facts, had to admit that no one had committed any injustice against him by rewarding the envied person. Neither did the envied person himself do anything unfair or antagonistic. If, however, his boss had been promoted for reasons other than merit or if the boss had flaunted his new position of power in a condescending way, then cultivating this new way of thinking about the situation might not have been successful in reducing the envy.

St. Basil, an early church father, wrote a lengthy discourse on envy, which illuminates many aspects of the vice, in particular how it hurts the envier:[7]

> No vice more pernicious than envy is implanted in the souls of men. . . . Now, envy is pain caused by our neighbor's prosperity. Hence, an envious man is never without cause for grief and despondency. If his neighbor's land is fertile, if his house abounds with all the goods of this life, if, its master, enjoys continual gladness of heart—all these things aggravate the sickness and add to the pain of the envious man . . . like so many blows and wounds piercing . . . to his heart's core. The worst feature of this malady, however, is that its victim cannot reveal it to anyone, but he hangs his head and is mute . . . . not choosing to reveal these sentiments, he confines in the depths of his soul this disease which is gnawing at his vitals and consuming them. (pp. 463–464)

In this passage St. Basil emphasizes the pain that envy causes the envious person. To allow ourselves to succumb to this emotion goes against all logic and reason. Awareness of this is the first step in coping with our envy.

There are two ways in which envy can harm the envious person himself. The most obvious way is that it makes the envious person feel unhappy. The second, and more important harm that envy causes is in the kind of person into which it transforms us. From a moral, ethical, and spiritual point of view, our envy both reflects and produces negative character traits. Envy is not just a psychological "problem" but a moral one. In his essay on envy St. Basil goes on to examine this second effect of envy by which envy distorts and perverts our personality in many ways. For one, it makes us hypocrites and liars, shedders of crocodile tears:

> The sick [envious] man awaits only one alleviation of his distress—that, perchance, he may see one of the persons whom he envies fall into misfortune. This is the goal of his hatred—to behold the victim of his envy pass from happiness to misery, that he who is admired and emulated might become an object of pity. Then when he sees him weeping and beholds him deep in grief, he makes peace and becomes his friend. He does not rejoice with him when he is glad, but he weeps with him

when he is in sorrow. The reversal in the condition of the envied one, his fall from such great prosperity to such bitter misfortune, he pities, and he speaks in glowing terms of his former state. This he does, not animated by humane sentiments or from sympathy, but that the misfortune may appear in a more calamitous light. He praises the envied man's son after he is dead and extols him with a thousand encomiums— How fair he was to look upon! How quick to learn! How versatile! Yet, while the boy was living, he did not favor him with even a word of praise. (pp. 464–465)

Another perverse effect that envy has on us is ingratitude. It is most natural that we should appreciate and be thankful for kindness that others do to us. But the envious person reacts very differently. Again we turn to St. Basil:

Envy is the most savage form of hatred. Favors render those who are hostile to us for any other reason, more tractable, but kind treatment shown to an envious and spiteful person only aggravates his dislike. The greater the favors he receives, the more displeased and vexed and ill-disposed he becomes. . . . When dogs are fed, they become gentle; lions become tractable when their wounds are dressed; but the envious are rendered more savage by kind offices. (p. 467)

Envy and hatred often go hand in hand, as they did with Iago, who repeatedly declares "I hate the Moor." Yet the two emotions are not identical. Envy usually leads to hatred whereas not all hatred is a result of envy. In "On Envy and Hate," Plutarch differentiates between envy and hatred by the way these emotions can be assuaged:

Men forgo hostility and hate either when convinced that no injustice is being done them, or when they adopt the view that those they hated as evil are good, or thirdly when they have received from them some benefit. . . . Now the first of these circumstances does not wipe out envy; for men feel it though persuaded from the first that no injustice is being done them. The other two actually exasperate it: for enviers eye more jealously those who enjoy a reputation for goodness, feeling that they possess the greatest blessing, virtue; and even if they receive some benefit from the fortunate, are tormented, envying them for both the intention and the power. . . . It [envy] is therefore quite distinct from hate, if what soothes the one torments and embitters the other. (pp. 105–107)

St. Basil uses the biblical story about David and King Saul to illustrate this feature of envy. When Saul was king of Israel, young David slew Goliath, the Philistine giant who was instilling terror in the hearts of the Israelite army. During the victory march the dancers attributed a tenfold greater share in the achievement to David than to Saul, saying: "Saul slew his thousands and David his ten thousands." This made Saul envious of David and he repeatedly tried to kill him, pursuing him in the wilderness and forcing him to live the life of a fugitive. On two occasions David found Saul asleep and could have easily slain him. However, out of love and respect for Saul, David spared his life. Did David's benevolence towards Saul alleviate Saul's envy and hatred of David? By no means. He continued to pursue David and to try to eliminate him.

A third, morally despicable feature of envy according to St. Basil is the way in which it makes us focus on the negative aspects of experience. We are always seeking to find fault in others, to minimize their virtues and positive achievements, and to call attention to their weaknesses and faults. We become bitter and venomous. St. Basil uses very picturesque imagery to depict the distorted "bitchiness" of the envious individual:

As vultures are attracted to ill-smelling places and fly past meadow and pleasant, fragrant regions; as flies pass by healthy flesh and swarm eagerly to a wound, so the envious avert their gaze from the brightness in life and the loftiness of good actions and fix their attention on rottenness. . . . Envious persons are skilled in making what is praiseworthy seem despicable by means of unflattering distortions. . . . The courageous man they call reckless; . . . the clever man, cunning. . . . In general, all forms of virtue they invariably supply with a name taken over from the opposite vice. (pp. 470–471)

Another way one can cope with envy is by cultivating feelings and thoughts that are incompatible with it and with the emotions it evokes.

E n v y

A mother who deeply loves her child delights in his good fortune. When the child of a poor and uneducated mother graduates from a prestigious college or becomes a successful businesswoman, the mother rejoices and takes pride in his success. She doesn't envy the privileges the child has enjoyed in life. If we truly love someone we want to see that person flourish—even, at times, at our own expense. A most beautiful example of this is in the biblical story about the relationship between Jonathan, the son of King Saul, and David. We have already noted how envious Saul was of David. Actually, if anyone's self-interest was threatened by David it was Jonathan's. Jonathan was heir to the throne and David's growing popularity with the Israelite people made him an obvious rival for the kingship. And the course of events proved that Saul's fears were quite justified, for when Saul and Jonathan died together on the battlefield, it was David rather than Jonathan's child who became king of ancient Israel. Yet Jonathan did everything in his power to protect David from his father Saul's wrath. Why, then, did Jonathan take pride in David's achievements rather than envy and hate him for them, seeing that they were at his own expense? The biblical explanation is crystal clear. Jonathan loved David deeply. He loved him as a friend, as a courageous soldier, as a man of God, as a charismatic leader of the Israelites. David describes Jonathan's love for him when he eulogizes him:

> How are the mighty fallen
> In the midst of the battle!
> Jonathan lies slain upon thy high places.
> I am distressed for you, my brother Jonathan;
> Very pleasant have you been to me;
> Your love to me was wonderful,
> Passing the love of women.
> (II Samuel 1: 25–26, RSV)

It was because of Jonathan's passionate (but not physical) love of David that Jonathan did not, indeed, could not, experience envy towards David.

What might be some practical application of the fact that love and envy cannot live together? How might one control envy by cultivating feelings of love towards someone? One approach, at least for certain relationships, would be to focus on positive qualities of the person that is envied, qualities that make him lovable.

Can one really "convince" oneself to love someone, just in order to eliminate envious feelings? Doesn't love come "naturally" or else not at all? Not necessarily. In many instances, if we think the proper thoughts and cultivate the proper feelings, we can honestly come to like or on rare occasions even love, certain people whom we formerly disliked or envied. The goal of this envy-inhibiting technique is to engender enough warm goodwill towards the envied that one will be glad at their prosperity rather than saddened by it.

Let us consider a hypothetical but common example. Martha envies her older sister Joyce for her charm, good looks, and talent. Joyce was always the center of the family's attention, the one the parents spoiled. They always bragged about her talent in ballet, dance, and music, whereas Martha's talents were ignored or belittled. Every sacrifice was made to pay for Joyce's private lessons, but Martha wasn't worth the extra expenditure. Joyce always wore the new clothes, while Martha got her hand-me-downs. Years of such unfair treatment have bred in Martha a deep resentment of Joyce. Now, as an adult, Martha cannot bear to hear anything good about Joyce. Each reference to some achievement or good fortune of Joyce's re-arouses in Martha a painful, resentful envy.

However, when Martha thinks objectively, she knows that Joyce wasn't responsible for the favored treatment that their parents gave her. They might have been insensitive but Joyce isn't to blame. And so Martha knows that her envious resentment of Joyce is really mis-directed. She would very much like to have an affectionate sisterly relationship with Joyce, even a loving one. But her envy is a barrier to love and affection. On every occasion that calls for mutual sharing of experiences and close family ties, Martha's feelings of envy intervene to sour the opportunity. She becomes resigned to her impotence in the face of envy's might. She believes, erroneously, as do so many other people, that her emotions are forces over which she can exercise no control, that she is indeed a slave to her passions. In truth, though, she can change her feelings towards her sister and create a new and better relationship with her. She can replace her envy and resentment with caring and affection. In so many cases like this one the potential for love exists, if one is only willing to try hard enough to work at it.

The Hebrew Bible teaches and Jesus reiterates, "Love thy neighbor as thyself." Paul elaborates on the qualities and powers of love:

> Love is patient; *love is kind and envies no one.* Love is never boastful, nor conceited, nor rude; never selfish; not quick to take offense. Love keeps no score of wrongs; does not gloat over other men's sins, but delights in the truth. There is nothing love cannot face; there is no limit to its faith, its hope, and its endurance. Love will never come to an end. (I Corinthians 13: 4–8; emphasis added)

The biblical assumption is that one can and should induce oneself to love others. Let us return to the hypothetical example of Martha and her envy of Joyce and see how this might be applied. Martha should focus on several thoughts that could considerably minimize her envy by cultivating a positive appreciation of her sister. She could begin by formulating a written list of all of the kindnesses and good deeds that Joyce has done for her and for others over the years. To this can be added all of the compassion and concern that Joyce has expressed for those in need or less fortunate than she. Assuming that Joyce is like most people, there are probably many commendable things she has done during her lifetime. In therapy I have often seen how beneath the surface of many seemingly unsympathetic personalities there exists a considerable degree of compassion and goodwill towards others. So even if "objectively" Joyce may not be so easily likable, Martha can still compile a "goodness" file on her. In doing so Martha need not deny Joyce's negative qualities; she is simply affirming and paying attention to the positive ones, which were previously ignored because of her envy. Martha should review the "goodness" file periodically. The more Martha becomes aware of Joyce's "likability" and the more she reflects upon it, the more she will find herself actually getting to like her better and the less envious she will feel.

The real challenge of loving another human being is when the person isn't naturally lovable. To love someone who is saintly or who gives us pleasure is proper but not all that difficult. It isn't necessary to be commanded or instructed to do so. A "duty" to love—as in the biblical commandment "You shall love your neighbor as yourself"—teaches us that our "loving" often has to be directed at people we might even dislike. It therefore implies that one must acquire skills and strategies for loving. One of the most important of these is training ourselves to look for the positive dimensions of people. Surely we would want to be appreciated for our admirable human qualities, with less attention directed at our ethical or moral weaknesses. We should apply that same standard in relating to others. Just as you would want to be loved notwithstanding your faults, love your neighbor in the same manner. Once we become adept at this way of thinking about others, we will find that the feelings that are incompatible with love, such as envy, will eventually succumb to love's power.

Another emotion that is incompatible with envy is pity or compassion. Whereas envy is sorrow at another's good fortune, pity or compassion is sorrow at another's bad fortune. It is very difficult to envy and pity the same person at the same time. Therefore, if one envies someone, it is useful to try to think about ways to feel compassion for him. As the compassion becomes stronger, the envy will become weaker. A patient of mine, also a psychologist, who was writing a book on how to cope with suffering, confessed his envy of a rabbi who had written a very successful book on the same theme. The financial success of the book made him a millionaire (or at least so my client imagined, for he had never read the rabbi's contract). Every time my patient saw the book on the best-seller list or heard the rabbi discussing it on a TV or radio talk show, he would be upset by his fame and fortune. It was a classic case of envy.

Finally, he realized that his envy was only hurting him and that it was totally unjustified and quite irrational. After all, the rabbi had written the book, not he, so why shouldn't the author reap since he was the one who had sowed. But my therapeutic strategy for helping my client overcome his envy went beyond this, and I had him reflect as follows: You know that the rabbi's book on how to cope with suffering was based upon a profound and prolonged personal tragedy which he had experienced. One of his children had been born with a debilitating genetic disease that entailed slow, progressive deterioration. Eventually the child died of the disease when he was a teenager. It was these long years of helplessly watching the physical and emotional pain suffered by his own child which provided him with the life experience of coping with apparently meaningless suffering and inspired him to write his book. The fact that it became a best-seller testified to the sensitivity and wisdom that he had acquired and his ability to pass it on to others in need of solace. Now you, in your personal life, have never experienced suffering in any way comparable to the torment that the rabbi went through for so many years of his life. Can you really envy this man and his success as a writer? Would you be willing to undergo what he experienced even for a million dollars? Don't think about his fame or fortune. Think rather of his pain and suffering. Even as a rich man now, can his money bring his child back to life or erase the memories of his child's suffering from his consciousness? As my client began to focus his thoughts on the rabbi's misfortune in life, which engendered compassion, his envy subsided.

Moreover, I suggested to him—shouldn't you be happy that this author wrote a book that has helped alleviate so much mental and emotional anguish throughout the world? After all, as a psychologist you should view this man as a companion and co-worker in a common, humane goal. He isn't your competitor, someone against whom your own achievements will be measured unfavorably, but rather a partner in good works. Your envy is incompatible with your true self and the ideals you have set for yourself.

Probably the most powerful of all antidotes to envy, and one of the most difficult to apply in our competitive, materialistic culture, is "contentedness." This means being satisfied with what one has in life. Such an attitude can derive from a religious belief in the operation of a Divine Will in the universe. Whatever one's lot in life and the lot of others might be, the existing state of things is attributed to God's divine wisdom and to God's goodness. Based upon his belief in an all-wise and all-good God, the religious believer accepts life as it is even though it remains a mystery to him. A second source of contentedness is a belief in Fate. Things are the way they are because that is how they were destined to be, by the laws of nature that operate in the universe. The third source of contentedness is rooted in the Stoic philosophical belief that ultimate happiness is a result not of externals such as material acquisitions, power, status, or family, but of our feelings about ourselves. Happiness is a state of mind and we control our states of mind. No matter what we have or do not have, no matter where we stand relative to others in the scheme of life, we have the capacity to make life meaningful and ourselves happy by adopting certain inner values. Since, ultimately, happiness is a function of our attitudes and our ability to use reason to regulate our emotions, it really becomes irrelevant to true happiness whether I possesses or do not possess something which another person has. To thc extent that one adopts a worldview of being content with what one has, he will have gone a long way towards conquering envy.

ટ

Finally, we will consider three emotions that are often confused with envy: jealousy, indignation, and emulation. Although jealousy is often used as a synonym for envy, it is probably best to consider them as different emotions.[8] We have defined envy as a feeling of pain that a person experiences when he sees that someone else possesses something which he does not. Jealousy arises when a person possesses something of great value and significance to himself and fears that someone else will deprive him of it. Threats to self-esteem are usually involved in both envy and jealousy, but the situations that provoke them are different and the jealous person will probably be more ready to take overt action to protect what he believes is rightfully his. Overt crimes of passion motivated by jealousy are frequent, whereas crimes of envy tend to be secretive. In general it is shameful to be envious but more acceptable to be jealous in protecting what one rightfully possesses.

Aristotle contrasts envy with indignation:

> Indignation is pain at unmerited good fortune . . . it is our duty . . . to feel indignation at unmerited prosperity; for whatever is undeserved is unjust. . . . It might . . . be thought that envy is closely akin to indignation, or even the same thing. It is true that it also is a disturbing pain excited by the prosperity of others. But it [envy] is excited not by the prosperity of the undeserving but by that of people who are like us or equal with us. (*Rhetoric*, Book II, Chapter 9)

Thus, although the subjective quality of the emotions of envy and indignation may be similar, the former is unjustifiable while the latter is just.

Because envy and indignation are so similar and because determinations of "just" and "unjust" are subject to debate, it is often difficult to establish whether envy or just indignation is the true motive in social animosity and conflict. Deprived social groups sometimes mask their envy of more privileged groups as righteous indignation, and some privileged groups falsely accuse oppressed groups of envy when the oppressed are justifiably indignant.[9] One psychologist explains the dynamics and the ideological "justifications" of intergroup conflicts in the following way:

Many intergroup conflicts in the world—between countries, races and religious groups, for example—may begin with envy. One group is better off economically, for example, than another, and the "inferior" group feels envy as a result. But if they're just envious no one is going to give them any sympathy. So they tend to see their situation as unfair and unjust. In this way, envy becomes righteous resentment, which in turn gives them the "right" to protest and conduct hostile—or even terrorist—activity.[10]

Iago did the same when he convinced himself that Othello had an affair with his wife, thus justifying his envy-induced hatred of the Moor.

Aristotle also contrasts envy with emulation:

Emulation is pain caused by seeing the presence, in persons whose nature is like our own, of good things that are highly valued and are possible for ourselves to acquire; but it is felt, not because others have these goods, but because we have not got them ourselves. It is therefore a good feeling felt by good persons, whereas envy is a bad feeling felt by bad persons. Emulation makes us take steps to secure the good things in question, envy makes us take steps to stop our neighbor having them. (*Rhetoric*, Book II, Chapter 11)

One of the wisest ways of dealing with envy is, where possible, to transform it into emulation. Instead of harboring resentment at the achievements of others we should undertake actions that will bring us closer to attaining those things.

The focus of this chapter has been on envy as a negative, potentially destructive emotion and sin. If envy can be changed into emulation it can have remarkably positive individual and social consequences. But even when envy remains envy, some social theorists, such as Helmut Shoeck,[11] argue that its positive consequences have been insufficiently appreciated by moralists. Envy, for him, is a necessary fuel for social and economic progress. If we didn't envy one another's possessions or achievements we would be fatalistic or lethargic about our station in life. Another positive role of envy that some psychologists discern, is its power to make us aware of what is important to us. It isn't until we feel ourselves becoming envious of someone that we are fully conscious of what we really consider of value. The enhanced self-awareness, and the rising of unconscious attitudes and values to the surface via the operation of envy, are psychologically useful.

Envy does sometimes serve these useful functions. However, there are other, more benign means for encouraging individual and social progress and inducing self-awareness, and these rather than envy should be cultivated. Let envy, so malicious and malignant as it usually is, continue to be considered a sin which we should condemn and control.

Anger

Anger is a short madness.
                    —HORACE, Epistles

Of all the emotions, anger is one of the most common and most powerful. It assumes various forms designated by terms such as *fury, wrath, ire, rage, resentment, vengeance,* and *indignation.* Hardly a day goes by without most of us experiencing some measure of anger— either our own or that of someone with whom we interact, often a family member. The news regularly reports acts of violence unleashed by long-festering anger, a hidden desire for revenge, or a sudden, impetuous fit of rage. Anger plays a central role in assault, child abuse, murder and many rapes, and in interethnic and international violent conflict. Of the seven deadly sins, anger is the most pervasive, injurious to self and others, and most responsible for unhappiness and psychopathological behavior. It is also inextricably linked to the other cardinal sins, particularly pride and envy, as well as to hatred, and it is regularly aroused by frustrated greed and lust. As a psychotherapist I spend more time helping clients deal with their anger than with any other emotion.

One family in therapy with me was entangled in a web of anger. Each parent and child was angry at the others for a different reason and no two of them expressed their anger in the same way. The family was on the verge of dissolution because the husband, a successful lawyer and loving and devoted father, in recurring fits of anger slapped and pushed his wife, a small, frail woman. She threatened to leave home if he hit her one more time and insisted that he see a therapist. He realized that he was too easily angered and irritated, and dreaded a divorce. He was a perfectionist, obsessive about completing tasks without delay, and expected every member of the family to be the same. Although his wife was, by any reasonable standard, a conscientious housewife and mother, in addition to working thirty hours a week, he perceived her as a procrastinator. At the outset of therapy he was unaware that he was trying to impose an irrational trait of his own on her. Furthermore, he hardly helped with chores around the home and his wife was simply overwhelmed by the demands of her three roles. Another deep source of resentment that flared up in outbursts of rage was his wife's lack of interest in sexual relations. He interpreted this as a malicious use of sexual denial as a way of getting even with him. He failed to understand that for his wife sex without affection was an unpleasant, mechanical activity, even physically painful, and since he was harsh to her she did not have the positive feelings she needed in order to make love. When the wife declined to join him and the children at dinner, he interpreted it as another hostile act on her part. She, however, saw it as a way of avoiding his frequent criticism of her in front of the children at the dinner table and the quarrels that would ensue.

Overall, the husband was unable to see events from his wife's perspective and was unaware of the depth of her anger and resentment, which she rarely communicated openly. Some of his anger also stemmed from the fact that his mother used to beat him as a child, and though he hated his mother for this, he never told her how he felt. Once his wife interrupted him during a television program in which he was absorbed, to tell him that she was disturbed to have found condoms in the drawer of their twelve-year-old daughter. She also made a critical comment about a facial gesture of his. He blew up at her, for

A n g e r

the comment, the interruption, and the invasion of their daughter's privacy. They started shouting, and the wife inadvertently or in a protective gesture swiped his hand. He slapped her in the face, making her fall to the ground. He told me that when she had hit his hand he "saw" her not as his wife but as his mother abusing him as a child.

It was this episode that was the straw that broke the camel's back for the wife and which brought him to therapy. His habit of ascribing malicious intent and insult to events that could be understood more benignly extended even to his coming to me. He perceived his wife's statement that unless he see a therapist she would leave him, as a humiliating threat. Actually, it was a desperate desire on her part to save their marriage. What she was telling him was that she could no longer live in constant fear of being struck by him, never being able to anticipate his next outburst, and that if he saw a therapist the marriage and family might be preserved. For her part the wife too was responsible for some of the tension in the household. She was irrationally insecure about money and preoccupied with it. Even though her husband was earning $120,000 a year, she insisted on working long hours at a low-paying job, since "every extra dollar counted." She was constantly tired as a result. Unlike her husband, she was also reluctant to spend money on vacations and entertainment. Her fears were grounded in her history—her father had been a gambler who had squandered the family's money, leaving her and her mother in a state of constant financial anxiety. The anger of both husband and wife was linked to their unhappy experiences as children and adolescents. But what they ultimately had to learn was that their anger was in the present and was threatening their future, and they needed to master it before it destroyed them. We cannot allow the ghosts of our past to frighten us forever.

જ⁀

B. F. Skinner, in his novel *Walden Two*, describes a utopia based upon a science of human behavior and the conscious design of cultural environments. One of the goals of Frazier, the Master Planner, is to develop in the children of this utopian community the capacity for self-control over anger in the face of frustration. Explaining his procedure Frazier says:

I began by studying the great works on morals and ethics . . . looking for any and every method of shaping human behavior by imparting techniques of self-control. Some techniques were obvious enough, for they had marked turning points in human history. "Love your enemies" is one example—a psychological invention for easing the lot of oppressed people. The severest trial of oppression is the constant rage which one suffers at the thought of the oppressor. What Jesus discovered was how to avoid these inner devastations. His technique was to *practice the opposite emotion*. If a man can succeed in "loving his enemies" and "taking no thought for the morrow" he will no longer be assailed by hatred of the oppressor or rage at the loss of his freedom and possessions. He may not get his freedom or his possessions back, but he's less miserable. It's a difficult lesson. It comes late in our program. (pp. 105–106; emphasis in original)

Jesus, in preaching "Love your enemies," was primarily concerned with the spiritual rather than the psychological import of his teaching, as were most of the religious and philosophical writers to whom we will turn for insight into anger.[1] Yet, with Skinner, one cannot but be impressed with the psychological wisdom they articulate in their analyses of the the sin or vice of anger. Moreover, there are fundamental differences between the way in which the moralists would have us deal with our anger and current popular, secular assumptions about how to express and manage it.

The fact that anger is so often a cause of violence, aggression, and destruction as well as of psychosomatic disorder and unhappiness made it an important topic for study by Greek, Roman, Jewish, and Christian moralists. The central theme of *The Iliad* is the nature and consequences of Achilles' anger, and many stories and laws in the Hebrew Bible and the New Testament deal with man's or God's anger.[2] Moses was denied entry to the Promised Land because he lost his temper when the thirsty Israelites wandering in the wilderness complained of their plight. In another episode it was Moses who placated God's anger when the Israelites built and worshiped the golden calf. Anger is worthy of neither man nor God.[3] The moralists' analyses of anger focus on its nature and causes, its moral status, and how to control it.

The most thorough analyses of anger in Graeco-Roman literature

Anger

are by Aristotle, Seneca, and Plutarch,[4] who essentially define it as follows:

Anger is aroused when a person suffers a real or perceived injury. Usually the angered person directs his actions towards punishing the real or perceived offender. The feelings of anger are an intermingling of pain and pleasure—pain at the injury and pleasure at the expectation of vengeance and the overt expression of the anger.

Anger is thus not only a strong and complex emotion, but includes thoughts and actions. This multidimensional understanding of anger can help us develop strategies to control it.

In addition, the ancients and medievals speculated on the physiological basis and effects of anger, but assumed that whatever these might be man could still control his anger. Recent psychiatric studies have linked some violent outbursts of rage to brain damage, particularly of the frontal areas of the cortex which, according to one theory, are the areas that ordinarily control and inhibit aggressive impulses. These findings suggest that it might be useful to differentiate between "neurological rage" and "ordinary anger," and the psychiatrist Stuart Yudofsky has summarized the major differences between the two. Rage which results from neurological impairment is usually triggered by what appears to be a very trivial event, unlike ordinary anger which is a response to some provocation or frustration. Neurological rage seems to have no purpose, whereas typical anger is usually justified by the angry person on some psychological grounds. Neurological rage explodes instantly and unexpectedly as if from nowhere, whereas ordinary anger usually builds up gradually. Neurological rage seems to be atypical of the pre-brain-damage behavior of the individual who manifests it. Ordinary anger, in contrast, is usually a fairly predictable behavior, consistent with a person's previous patterns of response to provocation or frustration. Finally, people who manifest neurological rage are upset about it afterwards, whereas many angry people, feeling that their anger was justified, are not remorseful.[5]

The establishment of a relationship between specific brain injuries and rage has made some researchers question whether certain angry behaviors, long considered sins or vices because they are assumed to be under our control, are indeed voluntary. Within the psychiatric, psychological, and legal communities the validity of the neurological rage–ordinary anger distinction and its moral and legal implications are still being debated.[6] In this book we are concerned with the kind of anger that can be assumed to be voluntary and hence controllable.

෧

Does the association of anger with violence and injustice make it always an undesirable emotion? Seneca the Stoic unequivocally says yes. He argues that anger serves no legitimate moral purpose that cannot be achieved equally well, if not more effectively, by the dictates of reason alone, or by reason in combination with desirable emotions. Bravery in battle, chastisement of children, the prevention of crimes and evil deeds, or their just punishment do not, according to Seneca, require the arousal of feelings of anger. This consideration, together with the fact that anger, once aroused, is fraught with danger and is humanly debasing, make it desirable that anger should be completely extirpated form the range of human emotions. If that is not feasible, then every effort should be made to suppress all manifestations of anger, regardless of circumstance. Seneca believes that it is within man's power to do this even under extreme provocation and provides examples to prove his contention. Harpagus, who was served the flesh and heads of his children by the king of the Persians, responded to the king's inquiry about what he thought of the meal, with the remark "at the king's board any kind of food is delightful." Praexaspes urged his dear friend the king Cambyses to drink more sparingly, since drunkenness is disgraceful for a monarch who must be ever ready to command. Cambyses, to prove that even when intoxicated he was in full mental and physical control of himself, drank recklessly, and when besotted with wine ordered the son of Praexaspes to stand at a distance with his left hand raised above his head.

> Then he drew his bow and shot the youth through the very heart—he had mentioned this as the mark—and cutting open the breast of the victim he showed the arrow-head sticking to the heart itself, and then turning toward the father he inquired whether he [Cambyses] had a sufficiently steady hand.

A n g e r

How did Praexaspes respond to this brutal provocation? He said to the king that Apollo himself could not have made a more unerring shot.

> The point . . . is clear, . . . it is possible to suppress anger. He did not curse the king, he let slip no word even of anguish, though he saw his own heart pierced as well as his son's.[7]

The Stoic view, though Seneca presents it most persuasively, remains a minority one. Aristotle had already set forth the doctrine of justifiable anger that was later accepted, with significant modifications, by most Christian and Jewish moralists. Aristotle's views seemed to the religious thinkers to possess the virtues of inherent plausibility, psychological realism, and compatibility with the predominant tenor of biblical thought. He states:

> A person is praised who is angry for the right reasons, with the right people, and also in the right way, at the right time and for the right length of time. . . . It is a slavish nature that will submit to be insulted or let a friend be insulted unresistingly. (*Nichomachean Ethics*, IV: 11)

Catholic moral theology, while including anger as one of the seven capital sins, maintains that it is not always sinful. It may be righteous when it is aroused against evil or for the sake of justice.[8]
Jeremy Taylor, the Anglican, agrees:[9]

> Such an anger alone is criminal which is against charity to myself or my neighbor; but *anger against sin is a holy zeal*, and an effect of love to God and my brother, for whose interest I am passionate, like a concerned person; and if I take care that my anger makes no reflection of scorn or cruelty upon the offender, or of pride and violence . . . anger becomes charity and duty. (p. 333; emphasis added)

Rabbi Elijah de Vidas, the Jewish mystic,[10] maintained that ethical and moral perfection are prerequisites for attaining the highest goal of the mystic, communion with the Divine. Inasmuch as anger is a grave sin and an obstacle to the mystic's quest for communion, de Vidas discourses at length on its evils. However, at the conclusion of his discussion he briefly and almost reluctantly notes that there are limited

THE SEVEN DEADLY SINS

instances when anger is appropriate. Thus, for example, a parent or teacher would be justified in becoming angry if that were necessary to create an atmosphere of reasonable fear and reverence in the household or classroom. He considers too little fear of authority as detrimental to obedience and to diligence in studies, while too much can lead to the rupture of domestic harmony or rebelliousness. Students, children, and wives, though, should respect and obey those in authority over them, and when they fail to do so, anger is a legitimate means of chastising and reestablishing control. *

Although most Jewish and Christian moralists agree that anger is sometimes justified, their primary concern is its danger and abuse. Recall how Taylor, though allowing "holy zeal," is careful to enumerate cautions, such as that no scorn or cruelty be associated with it. De Vidas too suggests that even where a situation calls for anger, an individual should try to deal with it by simulating the exterior behaviors of anger while remaining calm in thought and feeling. The moralists were aware of the very fine line dividing moral from immoral anger in two respects. First, we are easily prone to rationalizing our immoral behavior by attributing moral motives to it. Sometimes, we ourselves aren't even aware of our true motives for anger. This clouds our ability to objectively evaluate the appropriate response to an alleged offender's actions. Second, even where the perpetrator of an injury behaves in an unequivocally sinful or criminal way, and anger is therefore morally appropriate, it is in the very nature of anger, once aroused, to easily get out of control.

These considerations actually impel St. Francis de Sales[11] to adopt Seneca's view rather than that of his fellow Catholic St. Thomas Aquinas. Following Aristotle, Aquinas had stated that "if one is angry according to right reason, then to get angry is praiseworthy."[12] But Francis says otherwise:

> We must not be angry with one another . . . but rather we must march
> on as a band of brothers and companions united in meekness, peace and
> love. . . . Do not accept any pretext whatever for opening your heart's

---

* This is not to accept de Vidas's notions about the proper distribution of power or the desirability and effectiveness of even moderate anger and fear in the home and school, but only to illustrate his exception to the general rule that anger is a sin.

door to anger. . . . "The anger of man does not work the justice of God."

Constantly and courageously but meekly and peacefully we must resist evil and restrain the vices of those under our charge. Nothing so quickly calms down an angry elephant as the sight of a little lamb, and nothing so easily breaks the force of a cannon ball as wool. . . . "It is better" says St. Augustine, "to deny entrance to just and reasonable anger than to admit it, no matter how small it is. Once let in, it is driven out again only with difficulty. It comes in as a little twig and in less than no time it grows big and becomes a beam." . . . It is nourished by a thousand false pretexts; there never was an angry man who thought his anger unjust. (pp. 120–121)

Henry Fairlie,[13] discusses the psychology of terrorism in extremist liberation movements as a manifestation of the vice of anger at its most heinous.[14] These angry terrorists develop an ideology that justifies their anger, and then commit atrocities in the name of justice. They direct their terror against innocent victims who are in no way responsible for the "oppressions" that the terrorists claim to be opposing. Jews praying in a synagogue in Turkey or Rome, and their infant children, are massacred in cold blood because a Palestinian is angry at the State of Israel, and shoppers in Harrods department store in London are blown to bits because the IRA is angry at the British government. Having justified any means of venting their anger they feel no guilt at the suffering they unleash. They are not even deterred by the fact that their terrorist acts inflict greater harm on their cause than on their enemy. Once anger and a thirst for revenge are aroused, it is very difficult to restrain them by appeals to reason, particularly when they are "nourished by false pretexts."[15] However, even those who like Aristotle consider justifiable anger to be moral, do not absolve the justifiably angry individual from the requirement of expressing that anger in morally acceptable forms.

૪ં

We live in a very angry society, with the highest rate of violent crime in the West. Our courts are clogged with the litigation of angry spouses embroiled in disputes over divorce and custody rights, and claimants bitterly suing each other for pain and injury. We have lost the ability to solve differences calmly and amicably. Why are we so angry? Perhaps it is because our culture espouses pride, standing up for one's rights, and combative competitiveness. Although we know that thousands of murders are committed by enraged people, we tolerate such behavior, lacking the national will to ban the weapons of their wrath. We enjoy violent sports and support violent media entertainment. Were our society to denigrate anger and the use of force, and encourage compromise, forgiveness, and stoic resignation, it would have a much lower incidence of anger and assault.[16] A central problem of anger is how to control it, a subject that will preoccupy us in various guises for the rest of this chapter.

Since the moralists consider most, if not all, anger to be immoral, they teach us how to control our anger and how to cultivate its opposite virtues, such as love, forbearance, and forgiveness. They derive the remedies for the vice of anger by careful analysis of its nature, causes, and effects. Many of their strategies for managing anger can be effective today for individuals who come to therapists deeply troubled by the anger which disrupts their inner life and their relationships with others. It is often the case, too, that people in therapy for a problem other than anger, such as depression, discover that their misery is caused in part by repressed anger. Usually they are angry on an unconscious level at a parent or other person with whom they had a particularly close but difficult relationship. During the course of therapy the anger, of which they were hardly aware, is brought to the surface and can then be addressed.

Certain basic values must be inculcated in people if anger is to be controlled. For example, Seneca remarks:

> That you may not be angry with individuals, you must forgive mankind at large. . . . The wise man will have no anger towards sinners. Do you ask why? Because he has fully grasped the conditions of human life, and no sensible man becomes angry with nature . . . and so the wise man is not the foe, but the reformer of sinners. ("On Anger," pp. 186–189)

Seneca is not arguing that sinners be allowed free rein to engage in evil. He is saying that it is better to accept human frailty in a spirit of forgiveness and understanding than to harbor anger and punish offenders in a spirit of hatred. Our responses to insult and injury will then be directed to reform rather than revenge.

Seneca's views are similar to Jesus' teachings on anger and to those of his Jewish spiritual compatriots in first-century Palestine. Catholic and Protestant writers saw the affinities between Seneca's moral philosophy and Christianity, citing both him and Plutarch extensively in theological treatises, devotional guides, and sermons that deal with anger.

Seneca tells us that there are two general rules for dealing with anger. The preferred one is to avoid becoming angry in the first place. The second is, once angry, to restrain our anger so as to avoid doing any wrong as a consequence of it. How can we avoid becoming angry?

Proper child rearing, says Seneca, is one of the surest methods of immunizing against anger in adulthood.[17] He suggests guidelines for child rearing which will decrease the probability of our raising irascible adults. The child, says Seneca, should "gain no request by anger; when he is quiet let him be offered what was refused when he wept"—in modern terms, reinforce the child's mild behavior and never his angry responses or tantrums.

Envy, pride, and high material and status expectations make one particularly susceptible to anger since they lower the threshold for real or perceived injuries. Therefore, Seneca says, let the child's food and clothing be simple and his style of living like his companion's: "The boy will never be angry at someone being counted equal to himself, whom you have from the first treated as an equal." The child's good deeds should be encouraged, but he should not be allowed to develop too high an opinion of himself. The child, even of wealthy parents, must never be pampered "for there is nothing that makes the child hot-tempered as much as a soft and cuddling bringing up," and he must have experience with being denied things since "prosperity fosters wrath." Presumably, the child who is used to getting whatever he wants will become arrogant and unrealistically expect all of his desires to be fulfilled. In his adult years his frustration will be exacerbated since he has more desires to be thwarted, and his inflated sense of worth will be the more easily pricked, leading to outbursts of anger.

Finally, Seneca informs us of the powerful role that models play in the development of personality. Parents should be careful to provide their children with teachers and guardians of quiet disposition. "Every young thing attaches itself to what is nearest and grows to be like it; the character of their nurses and tutors is presently reproduced in that of the young man." He tells of a boy who had been brought up by Plato; when he returned to his parents and saw his father in a blustering rage, he remarked: "I never saw this sort of thing at Plato's." Seneca wryly comments, "I doubt not that he was quicker to copy his father than he was to copy Plato." Angry behavior is unfortunately more readily imitated than mildness.

Plutarch tells us that "he that wishes to come through life safe and sound must continue throughout his life to be under treatment [for anger]." This is because a temper will not submit to reason unless "we acquire far in advance the reinforcements which philosophy provides against temper and convey them to the soul."[18] In other words, whatever attitudes and strategies philosophy recommends must be regularly reviewed, practiced, and thoroughly assimilated in order to be used successfully as a remedy for anger.

Some therapists assign readings to their clients that explain the underlying rationale and procedures of a treatment program. Yet rarely does a therapist tell a patient to review such material on a weekly basis for the rest of his life. However, patients who have experienced success with an anger-control program may well be responsive to such a suggestion. Although a dry statement of principles and procedures would be quite boring to read, even if only once a week, the classical authors demonstrate that such statements need not be dry.

The moralists try to weaken anger by cultivating a variety of dispositions that are incompatible with it, preaching the virtues of love, humility, patience, forgiveness, compassion, empathy, aversion to cruelty, and domestic tranquillity. If these dispositions are consistently reinforced by society and the individual who adopts them is rewarded, there is a greater chance that when they come into conflict with anger, they will prevail over it. Joy and humor are also incompatible with anger and can be employed to minimize it. Seneca recommends that hot-tempered people listen to soft and gentle music and tells how Socrates turned offenses into a farce or jest—"when once he received a box on the ear [he] merely declared that it was too bad that a man could not tell when he ought to wear a helmet while taking a walk."[19]

Anger

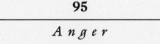

The classicists and devotional writers, though well aware of the power
of emotion, were firm believers in the ultimate ability of reason to
control passion. This is an important aspect of control over anger to
which we will now turn. They constantly appeal to our rationality and
capacity for enlightened self-interest. The primary goal of their essays
and sermons is to enhance our skills at self-control. They assume that
in order for us to be able to regulate our behavior we must understand
how external events, bodily states, and our attitudes influence us. Only
after we are aware of the factors that induce us to react emotionally and
behave in undesirable ways can we be expected to avoid or alter them
on our own.

Thus Seneca tell us "we are not all wounded at the same spot;
therefore you ought to know what your weak spot is in order that you
may especially protect it."[20] We should not undertake activities that
are too difficult and will almost inevitably lead to frustration; when ill
or fatigued we should avoid situations that have a potential for frustration.

Seneca and Plutarch attempt to convince us by appeals to both our
reason and our emotions, that anger is neither wise, nor virtuous, nor
in our self-interest. Most of us, when we are in a thoughtful state of
mind, will agree that we do not want to behave savagely, insanely,
impotently, or self-destructively; nor would we wish others to perceive
us as behaving in such a manner. The problem of the anger-prone
person is that he often does not realize that this is what happens to him
when he becomes enraged. Even if he does realize it, knowledge alone
usually isn't enough to prevent his outburst of anger. One objective of
Seneca's and Plutarch's anger-therapy is to educate us to associate
anger with highly aversive images, thoughts, and feelings. We need to
be made vividly aware that angry people are indeed bestial, mad,
impotent, and ridiculous.

We often perform cruel acts when angry, acts that repel us when we
reflect upon them after our anger has subsided and for which we suffer
remorse (even in ordinary anger or rage and not only in neurological
rage). I had a patient who vaguely realized that at times he unjustly

hurt his wife and children when in a rage. However, he was not aware how much pain he inflicted or the potential for even greater cruelty in a future outburst. He didn't perceive himself as a cruel person, nor did he associate anger with cruelty, because he always justified his anger. Furthermore, he considered forbearance to be a sign of weakness. In order to sensitize him to the harm his anger was doing to others and to himself, I had him read the essays of Seneca and Plutarch. They fuse reason, vivid imagery, appeals to emotion, anecdotes, behavior techniques, aphorisms, and self-instructions in order to create negative attitudes towards anger and positive ones towards its opposing virtues. Repeated perusal of these essays helped him respond less angrily when he encountered anger-provoking situations than he was wont to do.

Plutarch, for example, says: "We, who tame wild beasts and make them gentle . . . under the impulse of rage cast off children, friends and companions and let loose our wrath, like some wild beast, on servant and fellow citizens."[21]

Seneca provides several examples of acts of extreme cruelty performed by enraged kings. "My purpose," says Seneca, in recounting these tales of anger-induced ferocity and cruelty, "is to picture the cruelty of anger, which not only vents its fury on a man here and there but rends in pieces whole nations."[22] And in a passage remarkable for its imagery and dramatic impact, he literally paints with words a picture of anger-inspired cruelty:

Moreover, if you choose to view its results and the harm of it, no plague has cost the human race more dear. . . . Behold the most glorious cities whose foundations can scarcely be traced—anger cast them down. Behold solitudes stretching lonely for many miles without a single dweller—anger laid them waste. Behold all the leaders who have been handed down to posterity as instances of an evil fate—anger stabbed this one in his bed, struck down this one amid the sanctities of the feast, tore this one to pieces in the very home of the law and in full view of the crowded forum, forced this one to have his blood spilled by the murderous act of his son, another to have his royal throat cut by the hand of a slave, another to have his limbs stretched upon the cross. And hitherto I have mentioned the sufferings of individual persons only; what if . . . you should choose to view the gatherings cut down by the sword, the populace butchered by soldiery let loose upon them, and

A n g e r

whole peoples condemned to death in common ruin . . . ("On Anger,"
p. 111)

After associating anger with destructive cruelty, Plutarch instructs us
to carefully observe it in others and to address it in ourselves with words
such as "you [anger] are able to overturn and destroy and throw down,
but to raise up and preserve and spare and forbear is the work of
mildness and forgiveness and moderation in passion."[23] Seneca, as a
counterpoint to descriptions of despotic cruelty to avoid, provides models to imitate of royal forbearance in the face of provocations. Philip of
Macedon once asked an envoy of the Athenians what he could do to
please them, to which Demochares replied "Hang yourself." "All the
bystanders flared up in indignation at such brutal words, but Philip
bade them keep quiet and let [Demochares] withdraw safe and unharmed. But you, he said, "you other envoys, go tell the Athenians
that those who speak such words show far more arrogance than those
who listen to them without retaliation."[24]

The classical and religious writers were aware that behavior is, to a
large extent, influenced by its anticipated consequences. They therefore reiterate the theme that anger is self-injurious. Loss of temper has
deleterious effects on our health, our economic well-being, and on our
most significant human relationships. Since anger provides intrinsic
pleasure and immediate gratification, it is necessary to remember these
less obvious consequences if we are to control it:

> This rather, is what we ought to realize—how many men anger in and
> of itself has injured. Some through too much passion have burst their
> veins . . . and sickly people have fallen back into illnesses . . . many
> have continued in the frenzy of anger, and have never recovered the
> reason that had been unseated . . . these all call down death upon their
> children, poverty upon themselves, destruction upon their house . . .
> they become enemies to their closest friends and have to be shunned by
> those most dear . . . it conquers the most ardent love, and so in anger
> men have stabbed the bodies that they loved and have lain in the arms
> of those whom they have slain. ("On Anger," pp. 249–251)

As in Seneca's day so in ours, anger and the failure to control it are
a major cause of wife battering and child abuse. Recent studies also

find a correlation between angry, hostile personalities and shorter life spans.

Jeremy Taylor, too, prescribes various remedies for anger, including a consideration of some of its effects:[25]

> He that would not have . . . his family be a den of lions, his marriage a daily duel . . . or his feasts bitter . . . he that delights not to . . . be himself, brutish as a bear or peevish as a fly, or miserable upon every accident . . . must mortify his anger. . . . [Moreover, anger] makes a man's body monstrous, deformed and contemptible; the voice horrid, the face pale or fiery, the gait fierce, the speech clamorous and loud . . . it turns friendship into hatred; it makes a man lose himself and his reason, and his argument, in disputation . . . it turns justice into cruelty and judgment into oppression. (p. 442)

Seneca and Plutarch also suggest that when we become angry we look in a mirror where we will see ourselves as hideous, ferocious, and absurd. A modern variant has been used as part of a self-control treatment program for loss of temper, when psychologists have their patients view video feedbacks of their own angry demeanor during therapy sessions.

Elijah de Vidas says that anger should be inhibited and, if possible, extirpated, because it is an obstacle to the attainment of important values of Judaism. Among these are study and teaching of Torah, prayer, spiritual-ethical growth, deeds of loving kindness, and peaceful interpersonal and domestic relationships. A teacher who becomes unjustifiably angry discourages his students from asking questions. Even if they overcome their fear of his temper and do ask for clarification, his anger prevents him from explaining adequately. The easily angered person is disliked and thought to be a fool. Thus, even an otherwise pious scholar will not be considered worthy of emulation or accepted as a teacher if he is easily angered. Anger generates quarrels; it deprives the angry man of opportunities to perform beneficent deeds since compassion and pity are incompatible with anger. De Vidas continues that anger, which is agitating, prevents us from praying with devotion. The scholarship of the anger-prone individual will be deficient since when angry he doesn't respond intelligently, provide adequate proof for his assertions, or acknowledge his errors. If an anger-prone person responds irately when criticized, it will discourage others from reproving him and pointing out his deficiencies, thus depriving him of an important stimulus for spiritual advancement. If he reproves others in a spirit of anger, it will have precisely the opposite of its desired effect, since men tend to harden and resist when attacked. Anger is particularly unfortunate in the family. A man who terrorizes his family with his anger will cause them to sin out of fear of him. His wife, for example, will desecrate the Sabbath in order to attend to some task that had not been done, as it should have, prior to the beginning of the Sabbath, such as lighting the Sabbath candles. His children will come to disrespect him and rebel, violating the commandment to honor and respect parents.

Another important issue in the arousal and control of our anger is how we interpret the motives for a provocation, insult, or injury and their implications. In treating anger, the classicists and medievals emphasize what contemporary psychologists call "cognitive reappraisal" of apparent injury. When provoked we should reappraise our assumptions about all the elements in the anger-arousing situation. We should reevaluate our own characteristics and those of the perpetrator, of the event around which our anger is centered, and of mankind in general. There are many conciliatory thoughts which can prevent or dissipate our anger. St. Thomas, basing himself on Aristotle, describes how important ascribed intent is to whether or not we become angry:

> One can injure another in three ways: out of ignorance, from passion, and by deliberate intent. The greatest injustice is to injure someone by deliberate intent or effort, with conscious malice. . . . That is why we are especially angry at those whom we believe have made a deliberate effort to injure us. If we think the injury was done out of ignorance or emotion we are not angry with them, or at least not violently so. The injury is not as serious . . . and in a sense calls for mercy and forgiveness. But those who do injure deliberately seem to be guilty of contempt, which is why they anger us so intensely. (*Summa Theologiae* 1a2ae, Question 47, Article 2)

Herein lies the major key to controlling our anger. If we could only convince ourselves that the harm we suffered was not done out of malice or contempt, or that the injury was only apparent but not real, our anger would disappear or at least diminish. For Seneca, the primary idea we should consider in appraising ourselves when injured is that the harm we experienced may be justified. This can be on two grounds. First, some behavior of ours could have been an instigating factor. Second, even if we were completely innocent in this particular instance, we merit punishment for other injustices we have committed that have gone unpunished. Furthermore, we should consider that it is our own undesirable personality traits and values that make us prone to anger. For example, in some cases the source of our bitterest anger is the distorted and unreasonable expectations we have of others. Seneca tells us to say to ourselves, "I may have less than I hoped for, but perhaps I hoped for more than I ought."[26]

The relevance of Seneca's advice to my patient, the angry lawyer, is apparent. His perfectionist demands were unfair to his wife. He misinterpreted her rejection of his sexual advances. He was not empathetic enough to appreciate her anxieties. In treatment we focused on these issues and the irate lawyer underwent a reappraisal of himself, acquiring a better understanding of his wife and greater sympathy for her in the process.

In Judaism and Christianity self-criticism as a way of restraining anger is especially compelling since we are expected to consider ourselves constant sinners before God. According to de Vidas, a fundamental, if indirect way of coping with anger is to cultivate humility before God. We should reflect that we have little right to be so easily angered by insult and injury, given the extent to which we ourselves insult and injure God and other human beings. Jeremy Taylor uses a similar approach in *Rule and Exercises of Holy Living*:

> Humility is the most excellent natural cure for anger in the world; for he that by daily considering his own infirmities and failings makes the error of his neighbor or servant to be his own case, and remembers that he daily needs God's pardon and his brother's charity, will not be apt to rage at the levities . . . or indiscretions of another . . . (RE, p. 327)

Anger considered from this perspective is a daughter of pride, self-righteousness, and a double standard of justice. By becoming angry I am implying that it is acceptable for me to be insensitive to others, but I will not tolerate their behaving that way towards me. How true it is that we are often angry at someone for doing the very things to us which we do to others without considering ourselves guilty of wronging them!

Since attribution of malicious intent to one who harms us is a major factor in making us angry at him, we must always be on guard against our tendency to suspect malicious behavior or intent in others in the absence of any evidence for it. Plutarch instructs us to "avoid anger by removing as far as possible the act that arouses wrath from any suspicion of contempt or arrogance and by imputing it to ignorance or necessity or emotion or mischance."[27] To assist us in acquiring these skills of rethinking our assumptions, Seneca provides us with examples of how to ascribe benign rather than malicious intent to the actions of others. These motives for injurious or insulting behavior can be considered levels on a finely discriminating scale of intentionality, somewhat analogous to distinctions of degree of intent in criminal law. Each step on the scale is a reason to excuse the perpetrator from malicious intent and hence remove grounds for anger:

> Let us consider, I say, that some are not doing us an injury but repaying one, that others are acting for our good, that some are acting under compulsion, others in ignorance, and even those who are acting intentionally and wittingly do not, while injuring us, aim only at the injury; one slipped into it allured by his wit, another did something, not to obstruct us, but because he could not reach his goal without pushing us back; often adulation, while it flatters, offends. ("On Anger," p. 227)

Other mitigating circumstances we should think about when evaluating the motives of a perpetrator of insult or injury against us, are his weaknesses due to age, ill health, or a stressful life situation, and his regret at having hurt us. As Taylor puts it, to prevent our anger we should "use all reasonable discourses to excuse the faults of others; considering that there are many circumstances of time, of person, of accident, of inadvertency, of infrequency, of aptness to amend, of sorrow for doing it."[28]

Bishop Joseph Butler,[29] an eighteenth-century Anglican moralist who believed that Christian morality is rational and in harmony with human nature, offers a penetrating insight into the psychology of anger:

Anger may be considered as another false medium of viewing things, which always represents characters and actions much worse than they really are. . . . Thus in cases of offence and enmity, the whole character and behavior is considered with an eye to that particular part which has offended us, and the whole man appears monstrous, without any thing right or human in him: whereas the resentment should surely at least be confined to that particular part of the behavior which gave offense: since the other parts of a man's life and character stand just the same as they did before. (p. 137)[30]

Few modern psychologists try to help patients control their anger by teaching them compassion, empathy, forgiveness, or philosophical tolerance. One notable exception is the work of Richard Fitzgibbons. He describes the psychological benefits of forgiveness as a response to anger:

Forgiveness is a powerful therapeutic intervention which frees people from their anger and from the guilt which is often a result of unconscious anger. Forgiveness helps individuals forget the painful experiences of their past and frees them from the subtle control of individuals and events of the past; [it] facilitates the reconciliation of relationships more than [does] the expression of anger; and decreases the likelihood that anger will be misdirected in later loving relationships and lessens the fear of being punished because of unconscious violent impulses. Forgiveness . . . expedites the resolution of depressive episodes, and leads to a decrease in anxiety as anger is released.[31]

❧

Another useful means of controlling our anger is to examine the objects or events that tend to make us angry. Perhaps a reassessment of their true worth will alter our perceptions that we have suffered injury. Seneca shows us the triviality of those things that most frequently incite our rage:

From this I say, from the fact that you attach great value to petty things, come your anger and your madness. ["On Anger," p. 337] . . . Most of

the outcry is about money. It is this which . . . pits father against son
. . . it is daubed with our blood; because of it husbands and wives make
night hideous with their quarrels . . . it is a pleasure you say, to see
money bags lying in the corner. But these are what men shout for until
their eyeballs start; for the sake of these the law courts resound with the
din of trials, and jurors summoned from distant parts sit in judgment to
decide which man's greed has the justest claim . . . with what laughter
should we attend the things that now draw tears from our eyes! (p. 335)

External symbols of honor are ludicrous and it is absurd for us to be
aroused to anger because of them:

Because you are given a less honorable place at the table, you began to
get angry at your host, at the writer of the invitation, at the man himself
who was preferred above you. Madman! What difference does it make
on what part of the couch you recline? Can a cushion add to either your
honor or your disgrace? (p. 343)

The devaluation of materialistic and egotistic goals plays at best a
minor role in modern anger-treatment programs, since so many psychologists are sympathetic to the prevailing values of our culture in
which altruism and spiritual ends are rare.

Finally, there are several useful techniques for controlling anger which
we will consider in turn. In their reflections on anger, the classicists
and medievals discovered several techniques for anger control that
focus more on overt behavior than on feelings and thoughts. One of
them is the anger diary. At the end of each day we should ask ourselves
the following questions about specific incidents which provoked us to
anger and our responses to them:

• Could I have avoided the provocation?
• Was my response to it justified?
• Was my response too intense? Did it accomplish its goal?

- What unfortunate side effects did my response have?
- What alternative response could I have made?
- Would I react otherwise if the incident were repeated?
- Am I to be blamed or praised for my behavior?

"Anger," says Seneca, "will cease and become more controllable if it finds that it must appear before a judge every day."[32] Anger diaries have been incorporated into therapeutic anger-management programs by contemporary clinical researchers such as Raymond Novaco.[33] The diary encourages the patient to monitor his anger reactions and provides a means for him and the therapist to discriminate different levels of his anger responses to various provocative situations.

An old and widely used technique for self-control is the vow. Although in our culture it is no longer very effective in inducing or preventing behavior, it was important in ancient and medieval times. People regarded vows with utmost seriousness and would not lightly violate them. Plutarch made a vow that he would

> first pass a few days without anger . . . then I would do so for a month, or so, and so making trial of myself little by little, in time I made some progress in my forbearance, continently observing and keeping myself courteous in speech, placid and free from anger, and pure of the tint of evil words and offensive actions and of passions, which at the price of a little unsatisfying pleasure, brings great perturbations of spirit and a most shameful repentance."[34]

Jewish moralists generally discouraged vows, which were often made in God's name. Violation of one's vow was fraught with danger, because it meant that God's name had been taken in vain, one of the prohibitions of the Ten Commandments. Moreover, failure to live up to one's vow was akin to blasphemy since the violater was in effect saying that he did not fear God's punishment which he had called upon himself at the time of the vow if he did not keep it. However, the moralists realized the power of vows, as instruments of commitment and control. Recognizing that vows could serve a useful function in acquiring mastery over anger, in this case they made an exception to their general advice that they be avoided. Thus *The Book of the Pious*, a Jewish religious-ethical tract of twelfth-century medieval Germany, tells of an individual who was prone to violent temper tantrums which brought great distress to others and himself. After consulting a sage for advice, he made a solemn vow to donate a substantial, predetermined sum of money to charity for each future irresponsible outburst of anger. Such a technique can be very effective in therapy. It may be even more effective if the commitment is to an organization whose activities are anathema to the patient. If I know that every time I lose my temper my therapist will send a presigned $100 check of mine to the Ku Klux Klan, I will have a very strong incentive to control my anger. [35]

In addition to including self- or externally administered rewards and punishments, the vow usually produces two other important results. When the individual successfully abides by his vow, the realization that he is indeed controlling himself strengthens his will to continue to do so. Furthermore, the psychological and social benefits he derives from substituting adaptive for maladaptive responses sustain his resolve to resist anger.

Plutarch, citing Aristotle, tells the story of Satyrus, a lawyer who had the professionally damaging weakness of reacting to insult in the courtroom with a loss of temper. His friends solved this problem for him by stopping up his ears with wax before he was to plead his case. Thus, Plutarch advises, if circumstances prevent one from actually leaving a provocative situation, an attempt should be made to avoid it. Skinner, in *Walden Two*, describes a higher-level avoidance, that of developing psychological barriers that help "tune out" offensive or frustrating stimuli. Seneca says "the mark of true greatness is not to notice that you have received a blow,"[36] referring to the even more demanding psychological "tuning out" to insult and injury so that one will never become angry when provoked.

The well-known tactic of delay, by counting to ten or some other diversionary behavior, is frequently recommended by the moralists. Delay is not only a useful technique to save us from impulsive acts we will later regret, but is essential to the just punishment of the offender. It is not only in immediate individual self-interest but is mandated by our vision of a just social order. We must never punish when angry but must hold off until the emotional arousal has subsided, because offenses always seem greater when we view them through a "mist of rage." Plutarch, in discussing responses to those under our authority

who have provoked us, deftly combines a specific technique of delay
with four rationales for it:

> I try to get rid of my anger, if possible, by not depriving those who are
> to be punished of the right to speak in their defense, but by listening to
> their plea. For both the passage of time gives a pause to passion and a
> delay which dissolves it, and also the judgment discovers a suitable
> manner of punishment and an adequate amount; furthermore, the man
> who suffers punishment has no pretext for opposing the correction if
> punishment is inflicted, not in anger, but after the accused has been
> proved guilty; and finally, the most shameful thing is avoided—that the
> slave should seem to be making a juster plea than his master. ("On the
> Control of Anger," p. 133)

How frequently do some of us vent our anger and frustration on our
children without first giving them an opportunity to explain their
behavior! Their view of right and wrong may be different (sometimes,
justifiably) from ours or there may have been mitigating circumstances
of which we were not aware. King Lear's behavior towards his daughter
Cordelia and its tragic consequences for them both show the misfortune that flows from anger brought about by hasty judgment. Lear
wants to divide his kingdom among his three daughters. Two flatter
him with false declarations of filial love. But Cordelia, the only one
who loved him deeply, speaks honestly:

> I love your majesty according to my bond; nor more nor
> less . . .
> Good, my lord,
> You have begot me, bred me, lov'd me: I
> Return those duties back as are right fit,
> Obey you, love you, and most honour you.
> Why have my sisters husbands if they say
> They love you all? Haply, when I shall wed,
> That lord whose hand must take my plight shall carry
> Half my love with him, half my care and duty:
> Sure I shall never marry like my sisters,
> To love my father all.
> (King Lear, act I, sc. 1)

But Lear does not appreciate candor, recognize Cordelia's true love, or see beneath the veneer of his other daughters' lies. Angrily he disinherits her. Not long thereafter Lear is expelled from his home by the daughters he trusted and goes mad, but is lucid enough to realize the horrible mistake he made in his anger and poor judgment. In one of Shakespeare's most moving passages he talks to Cordelia as both are taken prisoner:

> No, no, no, no! Come, let's away to prison:
>   We two alone will sing like birds i' the cage:
>   When thou dost ask me blessing I'll kneel down
>   And ask of thee forgiveness: so we'll live,
>   And pray, and sing, and tell old tales, and laugh
>   At gilded butterflies, and hear poor rogues
>   Talk of court news; and we'll talk with them too,—
>   Who loses and who wins; who's in, who's out;—
>   And take upon's the mystery of things
>   As if we were God's spies: and we'll wear out
>   In a wall'd prison packs and sects of great ones
>   That ebb and flow by the moon.
>   (*King Lear*, act V, sc. 3)

Lear begs forgiveness, and Cordelia was forgiving. Her love for her father remains steadfast. Most parents, however, who are easily angered at their children without just cause and are hasty in punishment are not so lucky. They eventually lose their children's respect and incur their resentment.

Frank but tactful criticism of the individual who has offended us is an important instrument for preventing anger. By approaching the person who has injured you and asking him why he did such and such, he may be induced to apologize. The refusal of an injured party to openly confront his offender results in a concealed hatred of him, which, say the Jewish moralists, is an explicit violation of the biblical injunction "You shall not hate your kinsman in your heart. Reprove your neighbor, but incur no guilt because of him" (Leviticus 19:17). As we have already indicated, many instances of anger and festering resentment result from our misperceptions of the motives of others.

Were we more open about communicating our feelings of hurt, many such misperceptions could be corrected and our anger alleviated. Our culture, however, does not encourage us to be open about our feeling hurt or slighted, because such an admission is considered to be a sign of weakness and vulnerability which we prefer to conceal. In truth, though, it is courageous to be able to do so rather than cowardly, if our purpose in approaching the presumed offender with candor is to establish peace and harmony and avoid animosity. However, since the objective of our rebuke is to prevent our hostility from festering and to provide the offender with an opportunity to explain or excuse himself, we must be extremely cautious in the manner in which we rebuke and criticize. When confrontation of the alleged offender is performed improperly, it may be ineffective in inducing apology and in dissipating wrath. Even worse, it may, on the contrary, incite further anger and generate a vicious cycle of attack and counterattack.

Another important method of anger control is to become aware of our arousal in its earliest stage by recognizing its internal and external cues. This will enhance our ability to control our anger. It is easier to invoke anger-incompatible thoughts, feelings, and behaviors before a high level of arousal has been reached than afterward. Plutarch formulates this idea by making an analogy between anger and the spread of fire:

> So the man who at the beginning gives heed to his temper and observes it while it is still smoking and catching flame little by little from some gossip or rubbishy scurrility need have no great concern about it; on the contrary, he has often succeeded in extinguishing it merely by keeping silent and ignoring it. For he who gives no fuel to fire puts it out, and likewise he who does not in the beginning nurse his wrath and does not puff himself up with anger takes precautions against it and destroys it. ("On the Control of Anger," p. 103)

In this passage Plutarch mentions silence as one way of coping with anger before it gets out of hand. Plutarch realizes that some may invoke the catharsis argument in objecting to the idea of containing anger—is it not preferable to allow anger to be expressed and in so doing lower the level of arousal? He admits that for some passions, such as intense love or grief, expressing emotion helps alleviate the unpleasant feelings. Plutarch maintains, however, that in the case of anger the opposite usually occurs, "temper is the more readily fanned into flame by what people in that state do and say."[37] In corroboration of Plutarch's view, Carol Tavris[38] presents considerable research evidence challenging the notion that catharsis or "ventilation" of anger serves a therapeutic function and reduces anger in the long run.

An additional argument in favor of silence and containment in the face of provocation is that angry words will engender anger in the opponent, producing an intensifying spiral of anger, recrimination, and aggression. I don't think that the advocacy of silence contradicts the notion that the offender should be rebuked. Silence is often the best policy in the immediate anger-provoking situation. Rebuke should be given later and only when the rebuker and the rebuked are calm. Silence and containment, moreover, are only first-line defenses against anger, to be followed by the various cognitive reappraisals that will lessen or remove it.

Another technique for coping with anger is to practice the opposite behavior, on the principle that "gradually the inner man conforms to the outer." Plutarch tells us that when Socrates perceived himself becoming angry he would "lower his voice, cause a smile to spread over his face, and make the impression of his eyes more gentle, preserving himself from fault and defeat by setting up within himself an influence to counteract his passion."[39]

This notion that gradually the inner man conforms to the outer, although not intuitively convincing, has been experimentally supported. As Albert Bandura, a social psychologist and author of many works on aggression, states: "If people behave in new ways, eventually their attitudes change in the direction of their actions. Indeed, numerous studies have shown that one of the most effective methods for altering attitudes and values is by producing a change in behavior."[40]

It is important to realize that the fundamental approach of the moralists is not that we ought to *suppress* anger but rather *dissipate* it by employing the various cognitive, affective, and behavioral strategies that we have described. Forgiveness, compassion, the recognition of human frailty, the cultivation of emotions incompatible with anger such as love or humility, and avoidance of provocation are all meant to preserve us from becoming angry or enable us to substitute some neutral, benevolent emotion. The moralists advocate suppression only where attempts at prevention and dissipation are unsuccessful. Whereas long-term suppression of anger might result in explosive outbursts of rage or in more subtle expressions of it, dissipation means that the anger no longer exists, at either the subconscious or conscious levels. The moralists know that their approach is far from easy—it requires commitment and arduous effort. Nor do they maintain that we should be so indifferent to insult and injury that we never try to rectify injustices. But they believe, as I do, that it is within our power as rational beings to reduce the role of anger in our lives and thereby make ourselves happier and better, and the familial, social, and political worlds in which we live more gentle, just, and compassionate.

Lust

But virtue, as it never will be moved
Though lewdness court it in a shape of heaven;
So lust, though to a radiant angel linked
Will sate itself in a celestial bed
And prey on garbage.
                            —SHAKESPEARE, *Hamlet*

Teenage promiscuity, rape, incest, pornography, prostitution, adultery, sexually transmitted disease, unhappy marriages, and divorce are rampant in our society. In our daily news fare we read of twelve-year-old children with multiple sex partners, of college athletes who gang rape a mentally retarded woman, of men who refuse to wear a condom because it will decrease the pleasure of the sexual act even though they may transmit the AIDS virus to their partners. Jealous lovers, their lust frustrated by a competitor, commit murder, while in embittered relationships sexual desire is manipulated and used as a tool of vengeance rather than as an ancillary of love. Lust, the unrestrained and unethical expression of the sexual impulse, is a major cause of such problem behavior.

A government study on violence against women released in March 1991 indicates that the rate of rape in America is the world's highest, estimated between 1.3 and 2 million per year, the vast majority of which go unreported. In one woman's impassioned appeal to all women to boycott books, movies, and records which depict the violent sexual humiliation of females, we are reminded that "we tolerate a staggering amount of sexual assault on our daughters. Some social psychologists think that as many as 40 percent of our little girls are assaulted by their fathers or other men in their lives. No one puts the number at less than 25 percent. . . . Sexual assault, or the fear of it, controls vast parts of women's lives."[1]

Traditional religious teachings about sexuality are deficient in many ways.[2] But secular society has not yet formulated an alternative sexual ethic that is morally and psychologically satisfying. Rather than ignoring all that religion has to say about sexuality, marriage, and family because we object to some of its views, we would do better to listen to the plausible values it espouses. These can help us restrain destructive lust and nurture healthy sexuality and love, which produce emotional well-being.

Let us briefly consider the three moral traditions, turning first to the classical. Aristotle contrasts the vice of licentiousness with the virtue of temperance with respect to the pleasures that arise from the sense of touch, of which sexual pleasure is the strongest. Unlike the temperate person, the licentious one enjoys the wrong sexual objects or enjoys sexual pleasure with abnormal intensity, in the wrong way, or violently. The licentious person becomes distressed by the absence of sexual pleasure or by abstention from it and can be so carried away by desire that he chooses sexual pleasure over anything else. For Aristotle, licentiousness is particularly reprehensible because it is more voluntary than such other vices as cowardice. It is within our power to habituate ourselves to resist pleasures, and unlike cowardice, which is based on fear of death or injury, we need not subject ourselves to danger in order to train ourselves to overcome lust. Aristotle compares the licentious person to a spoiled child in that both need to submit their appetites for pleasure to authority—the licentious to reason and the child to his teacher.[3]

Greek myths abound in conflicts between men and gods that were provoked by sexual jealousy. The most notable was the Trojan War, which resulted from the rivalry between Menelaus and Paris for the beautiful Helen.

L u s t

Cicero, the first-century B.C.E. Roman philosopher, taking note of the role of lust in Greek myth and tragedy, was wary of obsessive love. For him, love with its underlying coveting of and delight in sexual pleasure, when taken to the extreme of lust, was a form of madness. He expresses disdain for its idealization by the poets, one of whom felt that love deserves a place among the gods. For a proper evaluation of this passion and how best to treat it, we must turn, says Cicero, to the teachers of virtue, the philosophers. Of particular interest is Cicero's claim that though a sickness and a madness, lust is, as Aristotle said, essentially voluntary: "There is no instance where it is not due to belief, due to an act of judgment, due to voluntary choice. For were love a matter of nature all men would love, as well as always love and love the same object, nor should we find one discouraged by shame, another by reflection, another by satiety."[4]

Thus both Aristotle and Cicero, as well as Plato before them, though acknowledging the great power of the sexual impulse, believed that it can be tamed by reason.

In the Judaic tradition, the Hebrew Bible does not consider heterosexual intercourse inherently sinful. Most of its sexual prohibitions are meant to protect sexual or property rights, preserve ritual purity, and prevent sexual practices associated with Canaanite paganism.[5] Sexual intercourse between husband and wife is obligatory and should be enjoyed by both. The Song of Solomon, a collection of love poems, celebrates sensual attraction blended with yearning for the caresses of the beloved, in anticipation of the culmination of passion in marriage:

> I slept, but my heart was awake.
> Hark! my beloved is knocking.
> "Open to me, my sister, my love,
> My dove, my perfect one;
> For my head is wet with dew,
> My locks with the drops of the night."
>
> My beloved is all radiant and ruddy . . .
> His head is the finest gold;
> His locks are wavy,
> Black as a raven.

. . . .

You are stately as a palm tree,
And your breasts are like its clusters.
I say I will climb the palm tree
And lay hold of its branches.

Set me as a seal upon your heart,
As a seal upon your arm;
For love is strong as death,
Jealousy is cruel as the grave.
Its flashes are flashes of fire,
A most vehement flame.
Many waters cannot quench love,
Neither can floods drown it.
If a man offered for love
All the wealth of his house,
It would be utterly scorned.
(Song of Solomon,
        5:2, 10–11; 7:7–8; 8:6–7, RSV)

The description of the lovers in the Song of Solomon, though candid, is not obscene.[6] Biblical candor about sexuality does not come at the expense of modesty and reserve. Likewise, after their sin in Eden, Adam and Eve, ashamed of their nudity, cover their private parts. This is not because sexual organs or desire are in themselves defiling but because when man disobeys God he opens the door to all kinds of sins. Lust is one of them, and since the genitals are the primary instruments of lust, they need to be controlled by reasonable modesty, symbolized by the fig leaf. Immediately after they leave the Garden, Adam and Eve have intercourse and Eve conceives. Their sexual union is not a sin, but a fulfillment of their divinely willed roles of mutually supportive mates and parents of humanity. It also signals reestablished bonds of affection that had been severed when Adam blamed Eve for giving him the forbidden fruit.

In contrast to the love celebrated in the Song of Solomon, the biblical accounts of King David's adultery and of the rape of his daughter Tamar by her half-brother Amnon exemplify vicious lust.

David was strolling on the roof of his palace from where he saw

L u s t

a woman bathing, and she was very beautiful. He sent to inquire who she was, and the answer came, . . . Bathsheba . . . the wife of Uriah . . . [who was a soldier away at the front]. So he sent messengers to fetch her, and when she came to him, he had intercourse with her . . . and then she went home. She conceived, and sent word to David that she was pregnant. David ordered Joab [his chief of staff] to send Uriah . . . to him. David . . . said to him . . . "Go down to your house and wash your feet after your journey" [David assumed Uriah would sleep with Bathsheba thus enabling him to conceal his adultery and ascribe the paternity of the child to Uriah]. . . . But Uriah did not return to his house . . . "Your majesty's officers are camping in the open; how can I go home to eat and drink and to sleep with my wife?" [Did Uriah suspect something?] The following morning David wrote a letter to Joab and sent Uriah with it. He wrote in the letter, "Put Uriah opposite the enemy where the fighting is fiercest and then fall back, and leave him to meet his death." Uriah . . . was killed.

When Uriah's wife heard that her husband was dead, she mourned for him; and when the period of mourning was over, David sent for her and brought her into his house. She became his wife and bore him a son. But what David had done was wrong in the eyes of the Lord.

Nathan the prophet tells David of a cruel rich man who stole the only ewe lamb of a poor man.

David was very angry, and burst out, "As the Lord lives, the man who did this deserves to die! He shall pay for the lamb four times over, because he has done this and shown no pity."

Nathan tells David that he is the cruel rich man. As punishment Bathsheba's child conceived in sin dies and David's family is rent by internecine strife that includes fratricide, rape, incest, and adultery. David acknowledges his guilt and repents.[7]

This story is instructive about lust and the evils that it breeds. David was a religious man who understood the gravity of adultery. When not overcome by sexual passion he had a passion for justice. Did he feel no guilt as he lay with Bathsheba while her husband Uriah was jeopardizing his life to defend his kingdom? David, a brilliant and courageous leader, acted foolishly and cowardly, risking power and prestige, in order to satisfy his sexual urge. Lust is more powerful than shame, guilt, fear, prudence, and gratitude. When we succumb to lust we can be blinded to our most blatant crimes, as David is when he condemns the evil of the rich man in Nathan's parable but remains oblivious to worse evil in himself. He doesn't grasp the analogy of the parable to his own transparent behavior. Unrestrained sexual desire can corrupt even the best of men and lead to irrational, unethical behavior. To acquiesce to lust can cause pain and suffering for the parties involved, including their families. Although sexual passion is a powerful force, we are not absolved of responsibility for the evils we commit when we fail to control it.

❧

If we consider now the subject of adultery in the tradition of modern psychology, one psychologist who specializes in couples' therapy and infidelity has prepared a list of fifteen questions for individuals to think about before they enter into an affair, such as: Why do you want to have an affair, will it achieve your aims, how will you feel afterwards, and is it practical, safe, and worthwhile? Only one or two of the questions address ethical issues, such as, how will it affect your children if they find out? None directly asks the individual to consider whether infidelity is unethical, as if that were a tangential issue, not worthy of a patient's or therapist's time.[8]

A case history of mine involving adultery exemplifies how ethical considerations should be considered in therapy. My client was in his mid-twenties and seeing me for general anxiety. He was suffering from gastritis and had recently lost his job and terminated a long-term relationship with a woman. At the time of therapy he was having a passionate, clandestine affair with a married woman in her mid-thirties who was a mother of three children whom he liked and saw often. The woman, unhappy and frustrated in her marriage, had initiated the affair by sexually seducing my client who was a longtime family friend. The man had genuine and deep affection for the woman and sympathized with her marital plight. She was considerably more aggressive in pursuing the relationship than he was, calling him frequently to arrange for secret rendezvous. The intensity of their physical pleasure in foreplay and sexual relations was very high. However, the situation was stressful and fraught with danger since the relationship had to be concealed. If the husband were to find out about it he might take violent action against his wife and her paramour. Moreover, the woman's incessant psychological demands for affection and pity from my client added to his stress.

One of the issues that I raised early in therapy was whether my client was experiencing any guilt about committing adultery. He acknowledged that the affair was satisfying his sexual desires and filling the vacuum left by the termination of his former relationship. But he did not feel guilty because he thought that the woman was entitled to a more meaningful relationship, emotionally and sexually, than she had with her husband. My client was a sensitive and compassionate person who would not deliberately injure anyone. In my opinion though, the frequent and intense carnal pleasure which the affair provided, and his satisfaction at being needed, prevented him from examining objectively its probable adverse consequences. Some of these would not only affect him but could be emotionally (and perhaps physically and financially) injurious to the woman and to her three innocent children. Although my client was not morally concerned about the adultery per se, he agreed that it was immoral to hurt the children. We prepared a chart for him to fill in after due reflection.

			EFFECTS ON		
	Client	Woman	Husband	Each Child	Parents
OPTIONS					
Continue relationship clandestinely					
Terminate relationship					
Encourage divorce and marry woman					

	Client	Woman	Husband	Each Child	Parents
			EFFECTS ON (CONT.)		
Transform relationship to friendship (nonphysical)					
Go public with the affair					

Considering each option and its probable consequences sharpened my client's ethical sensitivities. He realized that the satisfaction of his own sexual and emotional desires, and those of the woman, were insufficient grounds to justify his behavior. Too many people might be seriously hurt by his failure to decide responsibly what was the right thing to do in the circumstances and then proceed to do it. He also began to question his lover's emotional stability, maturity, and character. Should a mother place her own children in such jeopardy in order to satisfy her emotional needs and sexual appetite? We discussed how sexual pleasure and its anticipation often blind us to the voice of reason and suppress our inclinations to do what we know to be right. Unrestrained sexual passion will induce us to act in ways that to an objective observer are irrational, immoral, and self-destructive. By my shifting the focus of therapy from my client's and his lover's desires and needs to their moral obligations to others, he was able to end the affair. This alleviated some of the stress that had brought on his gastritis. I am not claiming, as perhaps Socrates would, that by getting a patient to realize that what he is doing is unethical suffices to establish self-control. However, the failure to confront a patient or ourselves with the full ethical implications of giving in to lust is a subtle collusion in its malevolent effects. It denies a person who is responsive to ethical claims, but is severely tempted by passion, one means of coping with it.

L u s t

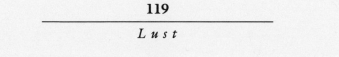

Another story about lust in the Hebrew Bible describes the rape of Tamar by her paternal half-brother Amnon. It follows immediately after the account of their father David's sin, as if to say that a father's sinful lust will soon lead to his son's. Not only does a sinful father lose his moral authority over his children, but they also learn to imitate him.

Amnon became infatuated with his beautiful half-sister Tamar and distressed at not being able to have her. So he feigned illness and requested David to send Tamar to serve him his meals:

> Tamar came to her brother and found him lying down. . . . When she offered [the cakes] to him, he caught hold of her hand and said, "Come to bed with me, sister." But she answered "No, brother, do not dishonour me, we do not do such things in Israel; do not behave like a beast. Where could I go and hide my disgrace?—and you would sink as low as any beast in Israel. . . . He would not listen, but overpowered her, dishonoured her and raped her.
>
> Then Amnon was filled with utter hatred for her; his hatred was stronger than the love he had felt, and he said to her, "Get up and go." She answered, "No. It is wicked to send me away. This is harder to bear than all you have done to me.[9] He would not listen to her, but summoned the boy who attended him and said, "Get rid of this woman, put her out and bolt the door after her." . . . The boy turned her out and bolted the door. Tamar threw ashes over her head, rent the long-sleeved robe that she was wearing [a special garment worn by virgin princesses], put her hands on her head and went away, sobbing as she went. . . . So Tamar remained in her brother Absalom's house, desolate. . . . Absalom did not speak a single word to Amnon, friendly or unfriendly; he hated him for having dishonoured his sister Tamar. (II Samuel 13, NEB)

Two years later Absalom avenged his sister's dishonor by arranging to have Amnon murdered while drunk at a feast.

Rabbinic commentators cite Amnon's lust as an example of contingent and ephemeral love. His alleged love for Tamar is revealed to be nothing more than a desire for her body—not her person. Perhaps before Amnon rapes Tamar he believes that he loves her—lust, we have said, blinds us to our true motives. But after enjoying her body he treats her with contempt and cruelty. Amnon's rape and subsequent degradation of Tamar is all the more heinous because she was his sister, for whom he should have had special concern, and she had come in innocence to nurse him back to health. But lust knows no boundaries—neither sibling affection nor gratitude deters Amnon. The fascinating comment that after the rape Amnon's hatred for Tamar exceeded his previous love for her has several possible explanations. Many instances of rape are motivated by a powerful underlying resentment, directed against women in general. The rapist commits the act of violence as a means of sexually expressing his hatred of women. Sometimes the resentment is more diffuse—not necessarily a hatred of women per se but of oneself, or one's parents, or of society. In the act of rape it is displaced onto the woman who is available when the hatred seethes. Amnon's hatred may have been the underlying motive in the first place, though masked by protestations of love that were eventually unveiled after the copulation. In other instances rape is not motivated by hatred but by the desire for sexual gratification, which the rapist fails to control. Hatred would not necessarily accompany or follow the act, but might do so in certain circumstances. If Amnon's rape was motivated by lust rather than hate, after the consummation of the act he might have hated Tamar because she had initially spurned his overtures or frustrated his pleasure in resisting him during intercourse. Moreover, since lust often exaggerates the attractiveness of the object of sexual desire, gratification of the urge is followed by disappointment. After her rape, Tamar was no longer as attractive to Amnon as when he was aroused by her, and his contempt reflects his disillusion. Furthermore, he might have felt himself a reckless fool for indulging in such behavior for so brief and less than satisfying a pleasure, so he blames Tamar as if she seduced him. True love between persons is enhanced and reinforced by the sexual act. But lust, interested in the other as an object rather than as a person, finds no use for the object once the gratification it afforded has been attained. One of the best tests of authentic love is how affectionate one feels towards one's partner after intercourse but before sexual arousal has recurred. An even better test is whether the love remains strong even when sexual intercourse is impossible for an extended period of time, as when one's spouse is ill.

In two sonnets Shakespeare delineates the psychological characteristics of lust and of love. Reading them together highlights the difference between lust and love:

> Th' expense of spirit in a waste of shame
> Is lust in action; and, till action, lust
> Is perjured, murd'rous, bloody, full of blame,
> Savage, extreme, rude, cruel, not to trust;
> Enjoyed no sooner, but despisèd straight;
> Past reason hunted; and no sooner had,
> Past reason hated, as a swallowed bait,
> On purpose laid to make the taker mad.
> Mad in pursuit, and in possession so;
> Had, having, and in quest to have, extreme;
> A bliss in proof, and proved, a very woe;
> Before, a joy proposed; behind, a dream.
> > All this the world well knows; yet none knows well
> > To shun the heaven that leads men to this hell.
> > > (Sonnet 129)

Like David, lust will commit the most savage crimes to satisfy itself. Like Amnon, lust despises after it enjoys, luring us with illusory promises of heavenly bliss. The imaginations of the lustful titillate them with sexual fantasies that spur them on to a maddening quest for ever new permutations of pleasure.

In contrast to lust is love:

> Let me not to the marriage of true minds
> Admit impediments; love is not love
> Which alters when it alteration finds
> Or bends with the remover to remove.
> O, no, it is an ever-fixèd mark,
> That looks on tempests and is never shaken;

It is the star to every wand'ring bark,
Whose worth's unknown, although his height be taken.
Love's not Time's fool, though rosy lips and cheeks
Within his bending sickle's compass come;
Love alters not with his brief hours and weeks,
But bears it out even to the edge of doom.
    If this be error, and upon me proved,
    I never writ, nor no man ever loved.

(Sonnet 116)

Like the North Star, upon whose constancy the navigator can always rely, love is firm in the face of obstacles. This is because it is a
joining of personalities, not bodies. Aging, loss of exterior beauty,
illness, or misfortune do not diminish love when the emotional bonds
upon which it is based remain intact. Lust is transient, fickle, and
egocentric. Love is permanent, steady, and altruistic. Lust uses another's body to satisfy its appetite for pleasure. Love gives of oneself,
soul and all, to make another happy.

Although rape is most appalling when committed by a stranger, the
story of Amnon and Tamar reminds us that it is often committed
against women well known to the rapist, sometimes even intimately.
Date rape, acquaintance rape, wife rape, incest rape, and statutory
rape of minors are much more common, though less reported, than
the stalking rape of the stranger lurking in the darkness or the serial
rapist/killer. Lust is present whenever anyone coerces him- or herself
sexually on someone else. [10]

Although rape, as an act of violence, is more sinful than seduction,
there are unique vicious elements in the latter. In order to seduce, lust
contrives an elaborate strategy of deception. Even when the actual
sexual act is not a violation of secular or religious law, it is of human
trust. To deceive a man or a woman into believing that you love them
only in order to bed them is a form of theft, no less pernicious than
stealing money. Don Juan, the libertine nobleman of Spanish legend,
seduces women to satisfy his lust. But he also does so to "conquer" by

seduction and to prove (to himself and to others) how virile and attractive he is. His female counterpart is similarly egocentric, seducing in order to establish control over men, to flaunt her beauty, or to be paid for her services. Male and female seducers take but do not give, insensitive to the feelings of their victims.

In the biblical Book of Proverbs, personified Wisdom describes how she observes a seductress at work:

> . . . lo, a woman meets him,
> Dressed as a harlot, wily of heart . . .
> And at every corner she lies in wait.
> She seizes him and kisses him,
> And with impudent face she says to him: . . .
> . . . I have come out to meet you,
> To seek you eagerly, and I have found you.
> I have decked my couch with coverings, . . .
> I have perfumed my head with myrrh . . .
> Come, let us take our fill of life till morning;
> Let us delight ourselves with love.
> For my husband is not at home;
> He has gone on a long journey; . . .
> With much seductive speech she persaudes him; . . .
> All at once he follows her, . . .
> As a bird rushes into a snare;
> He does not know that it will cost him his life.
> And now, O sons, listen to me, . . .
> Let not your heart turn aside to her ways, . . .
> For many a victim she has laid low; . . .
> Her house is the way to Sheol,
> Going down to the chambers of death.
> (Book of Proverbs 7:10–27, RSV)

Several of my female clients have been deeply hurt by men who misled them to believe that they really cared for them just in order to have sex with them. One female client was appalled to learn that her lover was seeing someone else while having an affair with her. She perceived this as betrayal. He felt that, in the absence of an explicit understanding that their relationship would be monogamous, there was nothing wrong in sleeping with different women on different nights. The feeling of being used, of being nothing more than a vehicle to satisfy male lust, is very demeaning and a common complaint of women about their husbands or companions. Although men and women seduce, women are more frequently victims of seduction involving deception. Women's sexual arousal and satisfaction depend more than men's on how they feel about their partner and what they believe he feels about them.[11] So to induce a woman to have sex, it may be necessary for a man who does not feel affection to feign it. Since men don't need to feel loved by women in order to enjoy sex with them, women seducers can be more straightforward.

In sum, the message of the Hebrew Bible, worth reiterating today, is that sexual intercourse when morally appropriate is good—a gift to be appreciated and enjoyed. It serves several functions (not all of them always at the same time). Heterosexual intercourse satisfies legitimate biological and psychological needs of men and women, and propagates the species. It enhances bonds of affection between husband and wife and in so doing stabilizes the family which is responsible for socializing the young into the values of the community.

Some current views about the permissible range of moral sexual behavior differ on good grounds from the Bible's. Where, however, the sexual act is unethical it should not be performed. If we are unfaithful, dishonest, violent, exploitative, or in some other way harm others or ourselves, we are morally guilty of lust. Since most of us can control our sexual appetite, if we fail to do so when required, we should feel guilty. Feelings of guilt and shame are appropriate, however, only insofar as they act to make us aware of our failures and prevent us from repeating our offenses. They are not useful if all they do is emotionally debilitate.

જ⁀

Turning now to the Christian tradition, in Catholic moral theology the virtue opposed to lust is chastity, which is a species of temperance. St. Thomas was unlike many other Catholic thinkers in his attitude to the sexual impulse and coitus. These influential theologians viewed even heterosexual intercourse between spouses as impure. It was tolerated in marriage only as a necessary concession to human sinfulness. Not so St. Thomas. In his analysis of Aquinas's views on sexuality, Joseph Pieper condemns the antisensual, Manichean elements in much Christian thought about sex. For Aquinas, chaste sex, which he defines as neither intemperate nor unjust, is morally good. For sexual behavior to be morally good it must follow the "order of reason," which for Aquinas means that it serve the marital functions of procreation, proper child rearing, and loving companionship between husband and wife. Chastity disciplines sexuality in these directions, whereas unchastity destroys the inner structure of the person. The destructiveness of unchasity lies in the way it constricts an individual, making him incapable of seeing objective reality:

> An unchaste man['s] . . . constantly strained will-to-pleasure prevents him from confronting reality with that selfless detachment which alone makes genuine knowledge possible. . . . The destructive power of intemperance manifests itself: in place of deliberation guided by the truth of things, we find complete recklessness and inconsideration; a hasty judgment that will not wait until reason has weighed the pros and cons; and even if a correct decision were reached, it would always be endangered by the fickleness of a heart that abandons itself indiscriminately to the surging mass of sensual impressions.[12]

We might disagree with mainstream Catholic theology's limited notion of what constitutes ordered, rational, and hence moral expressions of sexuality. At the same time we can appreciate Aquinas's insight into the power of lust to distort reality and injure the self and others.

ৰ্৯

This can be illustrated by an example from modern psychotherapeutic practice. In treating a female patient I understood "just and ethical" sexual relations to include her having sex outside of marriage. She was a single Catholic woman in her mid-thirties, seeking help for anxiety about not having found a man to marry. She was still a virgin and was obsessively worried that any man with whom she might establish a relationship would consider her psychologically unbalanced and reject her when he discovered this "secret" of hers. She had never masturbated and did not know what an orgasm was (except from reading about it). She feared that she was incapable of a sexual relationship. Compounding these anxieties was her awareness of the ticking of her biological clock. She very much wanted to marry and assume the responsibilities and satisfactions of being a mother and housewife. Her distress at not being a wife and mother was so great that when she visited married friends or relatives with young children she would become very depressed. This woman had been raised by a domineering aunt who had constantly warned her to be careful about the men she dated. Men, the aunt believed, are primarily interested in satisfying their lust with women they date and any sexual activity outside of marriage was improper and dirty.

I addressed several issues relating to sexuality in therapy. First, I told her that there was no reason for her to be ashamed of still being a virgin, if she felt it was right for her. Rather than being psychopathological she had been moral—and the kind of man she would want to marry would respect rather than deride her for that. However, she now felt that maintaining virginity until marriage was no longer morally important to her. For the sake of her psychological well-being and her sexual experience, she would be willing to have intercourse with a man as long as she felt emotionally attracted to him, even in the absence of a definite commitment on his or her part to marriage. Such intercourse would be advisable, she felt, as long as it was based upon mutual consent in a context of affection if not passionate love. This woman was not motivated by sexual lust—on the contrary, she was troubled by her absence of sexual arousal.

In the course of our discussions, she indicated that although at the intellectual level she saw nothing ethically or logically wrong with her present views about sexuality, at the emotional level the years of conditioning made her uncomfortable even talking about it in explicit terms. She found it difficult to mention the genital organs without considerable anxiety. Among her dreaded nightmares was that her aunt would discover her in bed with a man (all in theory, of course, since she hadn't yet met one), point a finger at her, and shout in contempt and disdain, "You slut! Is that how a good Catholic girl behaves!?." These nightmares, as well as daytime fears about what her aunt would think of her if she ever did what she now wanted to, made her extremely anxiety-ridden. She suffered from another conflict between the competing emotions themselves, the fear of her aunt if she were to lose her virginity and the fear of humiliating rejection if she were to retain it. These conflicts made her very insecure in her relationships with men she dated, hampering her from establishing a bond with one of them.

I was convinced that my client was comfortable with engaging in premarital sex, and I had no qualms about helping her prepare emotionally for it. We drew up a list of statements about sexuality that articulated her positive beliefs about it. She was to study these until she could readily call them to mind. I then assigned her readings on how to explore her body, give herself sensual pleasure, and masturbate. If, while doing these exercises at home, she felt shame, guilt, or anxiety, she was to immediately reflect upon the statements that she had rehearsed to help her overcome such feelings about sexual behavior and pleasure. Here are some of them:

1. God created my body with the capacity to enjoy sex, and as long as I do so in a moral way, it is good.
2. Sexuality is an interesting aspect of life, and it is natural and appropriate that I experience it.
3. My ultimate objective is to get married and have children. If I am capable of enjoying sexual experiences my relationship with my eventual husband will be better and so will our family life.
4. Sexual pleasure is only one element of a relationship with a man. Companionship and love are what is really important. But mutual sexual satisfaction can enhance companionship and love.
5. There is nothing dirty about sex when it is engaged in properly and with due restraint. It is the creative force in life. It is only through intercourse that children are born and life continues. In my life sex will be clean and a force for good.

6. My aunt instilled in me some erroneous ideas and feelings about sex. Just because she wasn't comfortable with sex doesn't mean that I shouldn't be.

Not long after these sessions my client met a man with whom she established a deeply affectionate, intimate relationship. She found herself capable of enjoying the sexual side of it, as both a recipient and a provider of gratification. She was capable of frequent orgasms. Though she didn't feel any intense guilt or anxiety about her sexual activity, she was still afraid of what her aunt's (and other relatives') reactions would be if they found out that she was living with a man on weekends. Eventually she overcame this apprehension as well, when she had to inform her aunt that she was going to be spending a week in Hawaii with her male companion.

What were the effects of therapy? My client overcame unpleasant feelings about premarital sex with an affectionate companion who was also a marriage prospect. She enjoyed its sensual pleasures. However, the sexual dimension of her relationship with him was much less important to her than the mutual love that evolved. After an eighteen-month courtship they were married. Therapy made her much happier. It improved her chances of having a satisfying marriage because it alleviated her anxieties about her sexuality. This was not done at the expense of her engaging in what she (or I) considered to be immoral behavior.

Was she guilty of the sin of lust? Did I help her commit it? Probably so from the official Catholic, conservative Protestant, and Orthodox Jewish points of view. But if lust is the unrestrained, irrational expression of the sexual drive, did that happen here? Her sexual behavior was never promiscuous or indiscrete, nor was it primarily hedonistically motivated. It was embedded in a context of genuine affection and served the ends of marriage and family. It was entered into after due deliberation and consideration of its consequences. The only people it hurt were her aunt and some religiously conservative relatives, but it did so because they hold values which she no longer shared. We did not think that at the age of thirty-seven her responsibility to avoid hurting her aunt was more important than her right to overcome the emotional pain she was experiencing and to prepare herself for a smoother marital future.

L u s t

A characteristic of lust, and of our sexually provocative popular culture, is to exaggerate the importance of sex in life. To a certain extent
this is a reaction against earlier puritanical attitudes. But more is at
play in our mass culture than just a legitimate attempt to arrive at a
balanced attitude towards sex. Many thoughtful individuals, religious
and secular, favor candid discussion of sex, encourage some masturbation and sexual fantasizing, and recommend variety in sexual foreplay and technique for married couples or committed partners in
nonpromiscuous relationships. These may be reasonable correctives to
overly restrictive religious or Victorian sex ethics. But to give the
impression, in advertising and the mass media, that happiness depends
upon being forever sexually attractive and fulfilled, is to propagate a
grand lie. To produce pornographic films and books which create
distorted feelings about sex and incite some people to crimes of lust, is
sinful if not criminal. To use sexual suggestion to induce people to buy
alcohol, tobacco, or other products makes sex a tool for exploitation
and frequently degrades women. All of these are psychologically and
morally destructive. What often lurk behind impassioned advocacy of
sexual liberation are lust and greed. Interestingly, feminist critiques of
the advertising and media industries' depiction of women as primarily
sexual objects converge with the objections of conservative religious
groups to the sexual suggestiveness of advertising and films.

The truth is that sex is far less important than many in our culture
would have us believe. The amount of time most of us spend directly
or indirectly on sexual activity is small compared to the time we spend
working, eating, raising children, studying, caring for our health, and
engaging in leisure activities. Some people do spend a lot of time
thinking, talking, worrying, and joking about sex, or pursuing it. They
do so not because of a natural biological or psychological need but
because our sexually obsessed public culture bombards us with sexual
stimuli, to which they respond. Were we not exposed to these stimuli
we wouldn't be paying much attention to sex as long as we were
leading reasonably satisfactory sex lives. This would not be because we
would repress our libidinal impulses or be ashamed of them. Rather,
we would be realistic about our sexual needs, accord them their due,

and turn to other satisfying pursuits, whether social, intellectual, spiritual, or physical. Naturally there will be times when we would be preoccupied with sex, since our sexual needs fluctuate. There will also be lust to tempt us beyond our needs. But these periods of preoccupation with sex would be relatively insignificant if we lived in a healthy sexual environment. When not taken to an extreme, modesty in dress, demeanor, behavior, thought, and word, as demanded by Judaism and Christianity, confine sexual stimuli to appropriate settings. They prevent them from absorbing too much of our time and energy.[13]

How can we control our lust? The moralists suggest several approaches. We must first understand why it is wrong and how it is harmful. We should avoid situations which will tempt us and direct our energies to nonsexual activities. A Jewish legend, modeled on the story of Job, tells of the saintly rabbi, Matya ben Heresh, who studied Torah all day long and never set his eyes upon a woman. This irritated Satan who cannot tolerate piety, so he appeared before the Lord to request permission to tempt Matya. The Lord, confident in Matya, granted it. Satan appeared before Matya in the guise of a beautiful woman. Upon seeing her, Matya turned away. But she reappeared whichever way Matya faced. Afraid that he would not be able to overcome his lust, he thrust red-hot nails into his eyes. This act of piety so overwhelmed Satan that he withdrew, and the Lord sent the angel Raphael to heal Matya's wounds and restore his sight. There are several messages in this story. Even the most pious can be tempted by lust. When that happens, first reject Satan. If that fails, be willing to make radical sacrifices rather than give in to sin. If you are willing to do so you will eventually overcome temptation. Similar legends abound in Christian accounts of their saints. It is hard for us to imagine plucking out our eyes in order to avoid sin, because we don't take sin so seriously. But if one felt an uncontrollable urge to commit some heinous crime of lust like rape, perhaps it would be better to inflict a wound on himself rather than on an innocent victim. Some people argue that castration is an appropriate way of treating the incorrigible sex offender. Whether or not it is, the principle of removing the stimulus to sin can be applied in less dramatic ways, such as avoiding obscenity or taking medication that inhibits sexual desire.

Tradition teaches that to avoid sins of lust we should seek legitimate means of satisfying our sexual needs, which traditionally meant marriage. Today, more options are acceptable to many, such as living together in a monogamous but nonmarital relationship or self-stimulation through masturbation and fantasy. Although these latter are traditional sins of lust, unlike rape, adultery, or incest they are ethically neutral and psychologically benign. If done in moderation they are often beneficial, since they alleviate sexual tension when no partner is available.

Psychoanalytic theory assumes that our libidinal impulses are the most powerful forces in our lives. According to this theory, they are generally repressed or sublimated into other spheres of human activity, such as art and literature. But repression and sublimation are not successful in satisfying our sexual drive for long. It emerges as neurotic conflicts, circumvention of social norms in clandestine sin, eruptions of sexual passion, or episodes of cultural licentiousness. There is little that can be done to significantly improve the situation since there is an inherent conflict of interest between the individual's sexual instinct and civilization's interest in repressing it.[14] Although Judaism and Christianity agree that lust is a powerful force which must be controlled, they do not share Freud's pessimism about arriving at a healthy balance between the sex drive, happiness, and morality. Many secular psychologists too believe that Freud exaggerated the significance of sexuality.

A better sexual culture than our own would be more permissive than traditional religion in its tolerance of private, nonpromiscuous sexual behavior. But it would be more critical of widespread misrepresentation and exploitation of sex, the severing of sex from love, and the encouragement of selfish sexual indulgence.

In what other ways is lust manifested in popular culture? Lust, we have said, falsifies. Once in a while, when in a public area, I have taken a few minutes to look closely at the hundreds of people within sight. Invariably most of them are neither beautiful nor handsome. A few are attractive, some very much so. Many are downright ugly. Few real people look like media stars, models, or mannequins. Yet millions of us real, run-of-the-mill people, old and young, short and tall, fat and skinny, ugly and the few beautiful, have loved, or are in love, or are capable of giving and receiving love. We enjoy sex, intimacy, and commitment. Deep, life-long attachments are forged between every combination of physical types, from the ugly to the beautiful. But the media, and the advertising, cosmetic, and diet industries, would have us believe that love and sexuality are the sole prerogatives of the physically beautiful. If you want to be loved and to choose the right person to love, focus on the externals, the body, the erotic qualities of people. It is not what is in hearts and minds that counts, but only how much sexual appetite you and your prospective partner can arouse and satisfy for one another.[15] This should be the basis for choosing and maintaining relationships. This false message, when not explicit, is always implicit. And it causes us much grief and self-doubt. The less thoughtful among us actually believe it, at least for a while—until we learn that surface beauty will not sustain affection and companionship. (How happy and stable are the marriages or relationships of those handsome movie stars?) Shared interests, values, and goals, companionship and support, and for the especially lucky, an admiring mutual love, are the essential components of enduring and satisfying relationships. Nevertheless, even the more thoughtful among us, who already know this, can hardly be immune to the cult of physical beauty and the glorification of sexual pleasure.

Nor is sex necessarily the most meaningful way of communicating love and affection. No doubt, sexual play and intercourse can be powerful ways of expressing love and tenderness. But many couples are very happily married even though they have relatively infrequent intercourse. Their sexual drives may be low, or there may be some impediment to coitus. As long as they understand and accept the reasons for their low level of sexual activity, without resentment, recrimination, or feelings of inadequacy, and express their love for one another in nonsexual ways, the bonds between them can be strong and stable. Lust falsely asserts that love in the absence of sex is not possible and that sex satisfies in the absence of love. It accords the sexual urge more than its fair share in promoting happiness. In fact, lust can rarely be satisfied, for as Aristotle observes, "in an irrational being the appetite for pleasure is insatiable and indiscriminate, and the exercise of the desire increases its innate tendency." The Talmud put it this way— there is a small organ which when constantly fed is hungry but when deprived is full. The profligate is more often frustrated than content.

L u s t

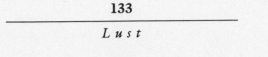

Traditional religious literature on sex discusses the ideal frequency and quality of sexual relations between husband and wife. Nearly all of the moralists were men, and their views reflect male assumptions about female sexuality. These were based upon cultural and religious pre-conceptions, observation, and reports by women they knew. From the perspective of modern psychology, the traditional views of female sexuality need to be revised. For example, some Jewish moralists believed that women are less rational and more emotionally labile than men, and so are more easily seduced into sexual sin. Therefore they must be kept under close watch and cannot be trusted with male strangers. Even so, rabbinic Judaism's norms for sexual relations in marriage reflect an appreciation of women's sexual needs that is psychologically and morally sounder than either radical feminist or Victorian ideas about female sexuality. Rachel Biale summarizes the views of Jewish law on how male sexuality should be adapted to that of the female:[16]

> The Halakhah [Jewish law] confines the sexual drive of a man by harnessing it to the sexual rhythms and needs of his wife. Sexual abstention is mandated by the cycle of menstruation. Sexual activity is directed to fulfilling the mitzvah [obligation] of onah: meeting and responding to the sexual needs of the woman. The "quiet" introverted sexuality of the woman circumscribes the active, extroverted sexuality of the man. It becomes the center and the regulating mechanism of the intimate marital relationship. (p. 146)

The primary concern of the moralists was to restrain lust. However, religious law and moral theology also addressed problems that arise between husband and wife because of a weakened or absent libidinal drive in either one. Jewish law, for instance, recognizes the right of a wife to a divorce on the grounds that her husband disgusts her so much that she is unable to have intercourse with him. It prohibits a man from physically or psychologically coercing his wife to engage in sex and affirms the woman's right to enjoy intercourse with a husband who does not disgust her. Therefore, if attempts at reconciliation are unsuccessful, she is entitled to her freedom. However, little of the traditional literature on the sexual appetite deals with how to stimulate sexual interest where it is lacking. This contrasts sharply with contemporary psychology. Psychologists, psychiatrists, sex therapists, and marriage counselors devote much attention to advising their clients on how to enhance sexual experience. There are several reasons for this. For patients and therapists who are sexual hedonists, maximizing pleasure is good. Some consider it abnormal to abstain from sex or to enjoy it less than one might. The religious moralists, however, who maintain that sexual experience is moral and even desirable, preach moderation. Just as one should not be a glutton in food, one should not be lecherous in sex.

Another reason for the modern emphasis on methods of enhancing sexual experience is that some people suffer from a "lack of lust," which causes marital problems. Traditional religious thinkers were aware of impotence and frigidity, and discussed them in terms of their consequences for marital rights and obligations. But they were probably unaware of the extent of weak sexual desire in the general population and only considered them problematic if they affected a marriage. They did not consider them psychological problems which warrant therapeutic intervention. From a Catholic perspective, for example, it might be a blessing to have a weak libido—one need be less concerned about the temptations of lust. The modern psychologist and his secular client tend to view chronic low levels of sexual desire or responsiveness as a condition to be treated. This is especially so when discrepancies between partners result in friction, as they often do. Sometimes, though, psychologists and marriage counselors assume that a lack of sexual interest is often a symptom of another problem in the relationship. Where two intimates are unhappy with each other for reasons unrelated to their sexual compatibility, this unhappiness inevitably affects their sexual interest in one another. Where this is so, proper marital and sex therapy tries to improve the quality of their emotional and psychological relationship, which should enhance the sexual one.

❧

The nymphomaniac provides an interesting contrast between how traditional religion and modern psychology might analyze a pattern of sexual behavior. The nymphomaniac is the woman who is extremely promiscuous, seeking frequent and indiscriminate sexual encounters with all available males. Unlike the prostitute, the nymphomaniac has no expectation of payment for engaging in sex.[17] Traditional religious thinkers would see this behavior as an example par excellence of female lust. The woman's passion for sexual pleasure is intense and she has either chosen to succumb to temptation, or else her lust has so overwhelmed her that she has lost all rational control over it. In the former case she is a sinner; in the latter, perhaps a victim. In both cases the assumption is that she intensely enjoys sex. Nymphomania was studied by Stephen Levine[18] who found that many nymphomaniacs are unable to derive emotional satisfaction from sex. The disruptive increase in their sexual desire may often result from a brain disorder, psychosis, substance abuse, or the acting out of some emotional problem. Although they may enjoy the physical aspects of the sexual experience, they do not pursue sexual pleasure for its own sake alone but because of serious personality or biological deficiencies. These nonsexual factors contributing to the nymphomaniacs' promiscuity do not exonerate them completely from moral responsibility for their behavior. But to focus on lust alone as the explanation is too simplistic and therapeutically inadequate an approach. Contemporary religious moralists are trying to integrate their concept of lust as a sin and the remedies for it with the findings of modern psychology that suggest powerful environmental or genetic determinants of sexual excess or deviance. The challenge to religion and psychology is to arrive at a proper balance between a free-will/moral responsibility perspective and a determinist causal one in accounting for inappropriate sexual behavior.

える

Some of the apprehensions about lust and sexuality of traditional Jewish and Christian moralists are not shared by contemporary liberal representatives of these two faiths. Eugene Borowitz, a Reform Jewish rabbi and theologian, wrote a guide for Jewish college students to help them make ethical decisions about sexual intercourse before marriage.[19] He analyzes four "sexual ethics." The first is the "ethics of healthy orgasm," which maintains that the desire to satisfy one's own sexual needs by engaging in premarital intercourse is sufficient ethical justification for doing so, provided one uses a reliable method of birth control to prevent an unwanted pregnancy. According to this "ethic" it is psychologically healthy to engage in intercourse and if one does not look out for one's own needs no one else will. Indeed all of us, claim the proponents of this view, are motivated by selfishness. Egotism is a rational grounds for justifying frequent sexual intercourse with whoever is available to satisfy one's biological urges. It would follow from this view that it is appropriate to engage in frequent, casual sexual encounters with prostitutes or transitory acquaintances. There isn't much of a difference ethically speaking, between tasting from a variety of foods which happen to be available when one is hungry, and enjoying different men or women whenever one's sexual appetite is aroused. Borowitz rejects this ethics of healthy orgasm because it misconstrues human nature and its unrestrained egotism will eventually hurt others.

The remaining three options, the "ethics of mutual consent," the "ethics of love," and the "ethics of marriage," each merit serious consideration. The ethics of mutual consent sees nothing wrong in premarital sexual intercourse between two single individuals, who though not in love, agree to satisfy each other's sexual needs through regular sexual intercourse, entered into without coercion or deceit. The ethics of love maintains that sexual relations are too significant an aspect of our emotional lives to be divorced from love. Mutual consent is not a sufficient justification—a sincere relationship of love between the partners is also required. Love includes intense passion, deep affection, and caring and concern for the other. However, the legalism of a marriage ceremony adds nothing to love and therefore is not necessary in order to ethically justify the intercourse. The proponents of the ethics of marriage maintain that love should be a prerequisite to marriage but that without the personal commitment to establishing an enduring relationship, which is done formally and in public view via the institution of marriage, love alone is not enough. Moreover, it is unrealistic to assume that passionate love is so sustainable that it can be made the necessary criterion for justifying intercourse. The companionship, shared goals, mutual support, and joint responsibility for raising children, which are all part of marriage, justify sexual intercourse between spouses even when the passion of love has subsided. Therefore love is not enough, when it refuses to undertake formal commitment. On the other hand, the ethics of love is too restrictive and too idealistic to be practicable. Borowitz favors the ethics of marriage, which has been the dominant view of Jewish tradition for at least a millennium. However, he accepts that each of these three positions has ethical and psychological strengths and weaknesses. Every individual should carefully consider and then decide upon the relative importance of sex, love, and marriage in his hierarchy of values. Borowitz's sophisticated analysis of the ethical and psychological issues that one should consider in arriving at a mature and honest personal sexual ethic is a model that psychologists might adopt when working with clients who have to decide on their sexual life-styles, as did my Catholic woman client. Decisions about one's sexual behavior should not be made in the heat of passion, or on psychological grounds alone, but must include ethical analysis.

Roland Gittelson, a Reform rabbi and author of a guide to love, sex, and marriage for teenagers, adopts the generally accepted view of the psychological and medical community that masturbation, when not compulsive or obsessive, is a healthy and desirable outlet for the sexual impulse.[20] Similarly, the widely read Protestant theologian, Richard J. Foster, writes:[21]

> Frankly, sex in marriage should be a voluptuous experience. It is a gift to celebrate, excellent in every way. . . . Gladly we respond to the counsel of Proverbs: "May her breasts satisfy you always" (Proverbs 5:19).
> Frequency of sex and variations of sexual technique simply are not moral issues, except in the sense of consideration for one another. In other words, married couples are free in the Lord to do whatever is mutually satisfying and contributes to the relationship. There is nothing inherently wrong with oral sex or mutual masturbation or many other ways to give pleasure to each other if they are mutually agreed upon. (pp. 138–139)

Although religious liberals view lust differently from conservative traditionalists, they agree that love and justice are of central importance in the sexual relationship between a man and a woman.[22] To divorce sex from ethics and charity is the sin of lust—and lust, thus understood, is the source of much vice and emotional unhappiness today.

Gluttony

Their kitchen is
their shrine, the
cook their priest,
the table their
altar, and their
belly their God.
—CHARLES BUCK

The amount and variety of food on display in the average American supermarket would put to shame the lavish Roman banquet hosted by Trimalchio, Petronius's satiric symbol of hedonistic decadence.[1] We are a society inundated with food and drink. New immigrants to the United States, from less economically fortunate countries, are awestruck by this abundance, although it doesn't take them long to accept it as natural, and if they can afford it, to indulge in the offerings. No less abundant than food itself are the stimuli that induce us to partake of it. Everywhere we turn we are bombarded with information (and misinformation) about food. Newspapers have their gourmet food sections and television saturates us with delectable commercials that arouse our lust in hopes that we will sublimate it by eating.[2] Hundreds of cookbooks and magazines and thousands of hours of broadcasting are devoted to whetting and satisfying our appetites for food and drink. Our gluttony and the greed of the food industry and its advertisers are responsible for this saturation of our consciousness with eating and drinking. Our preoccupation with food has many undesirable physical and emotional effects. We eat too much and much of what we eat isn't good for us. Millions of us, but women in particular, are obsessed with dieting,[3] either because we are overweight, which is unhealthy, or because we want to be sexually attractive. We binge and starve and binge again, swinging between food-related anxiety, depression, and guilt and the pursuit of sensory pleasure in food "addiction." This is because we do not have a well-reasoned philosophy about the role that food and its pleasures should play in our lives. We need moral guidelines for the consumption of food and strategies for implementing them if we are to assert control over this important area of our lives. Otherwise we succumb to our hedonistic impulses and to their manipulation by those interested only in marketing their wares but not in our physical, emotional, and spiritual welfare.

❧

We must become aware of our gluttony in order to learn to overcome it. Patients of mine who have a problem with excessive eating are usually surprised, and often shocked, when they calculate the time they invest each week in food-related activities. It has ranged from 40 to 85 percent of their waking hours.

To help make a patient aware of the centrality of food in her* life global activities are analyzed into their components. Thus, for example, she is asked to record the time spent on travel to and from food stores; purchasing food; planning, preparing, and eating meals; and cleaning up afterwards. Other questions relate to elimination, indigestion, or food-related illness and to mental activity associated with food, such as reading, thinking, and fantasizing about it. She is also asked to estimate the time devoted to commenting about meals and to ruminating about the impaired self-esteem she experiences because she is upset about her weight. Finally the patient is to figure the percentage of her work time that is spent earning income to provide for food and related expenses. We then discuss whether she really wants to spend so much of her life on her digestive system. Most patients agree that there

---

* I refer to the patient here as "she," since most patients who seek help for eating disorders are women.

are more meaningful things they would prefer to do in lieu of time spent on food.

Preoccupation with food involves more than time. No less important is the mental energy invested in eating and drinking. Patients are asked to consider the following:

How are your emotions affected by the importance of food in your life? Are you annoyed or angered when a dish doesn't live up to expectations? Are you ever unable to concentrate on tasks because you are thinking about a forthcoming or delayed snack or meal? Do you ever quarrel with your spouse, children, or companion about where, what, how much, and how to eat, or who should prepare the food or clean up after the meal? After such self-examination the patient usually concludes that she is allocating too much psychic energy to food. She realizes that she has become its slave rather than its master.

Weight-control and eating-disorder treatments abound in self-help books, support groups such as Overeaters Anonymous, commercial ventures such as Weight Watchers, and medical and psychological clinics. Some treatments are fraudulent, others passing fads. Several are moderately effective in helping the participants strengthen their control over what they eat. What nearly all lack, even the moderately successful treatments, is a moral philosophy about food. One institute at a symposium sponsored by the International Association of Eating Disorders Professionals describes people with eating disorders as "alienated from their own self, creativity and autonomy" and uses experiential and play therapy to help them overcome their alienation. Another makes the superficial comparison that "relationships with food parallel all other relationships."[4]

૨�

To provide us with a philosophy to guide our relationship to food we turn instead to the moralists who analyze gluttony. They also suggest many strategies to help us control our eating, some of which have their counterparts in modern treatment programs though many do not.

In popular usage gluttony means eating to excess. In devotional and theological thought, the sin or vice of gluttony encompasses more. The moralists are especially interested in our motives for eating and our attitude towards the physical pleasure that our digestive system can provide. When they are improper we are guilty of gluttony. The vice includes many behaviors associated with food in addition to the sheer quantity we consume. The resources we invest in procuring, preparing, and consuming food, the way we serve it, how selective we are in what we will eat, the timing of our meals and our table manners, are all part of gluttony when they are morally inappropriate.[5]

St. Thomas[6] defines gluttony as "an immoderate appetite in eating and drinking. . . . We regard an appetite as immoderate when it departs from the reasonable order of life in which moral good is found." Its opposing virtue, abstinence or temperance, is "doing without food under the regulation of reason."

What constitutes an immoderate appetite for food? Religious teachers realized that there is an element of subjectivity in this, since people's natural appetites, needs, and situations vary. The moralists also disagree about what is the proper attitude to food.[7] Nevertheless, they agree on many criteria we can use to evaluate whether we are guilty of gluttony.[8]

Immoderate eating is considered sinful for several reasons. Medieval religious writers plausibly assume that most of us who eat more than is necessary to sustain health do so because we want to enjoy the pleasures of the palate, gullet and stomach. This hedonistic eating is a sin, and to do so regularly is to be a glutton.

Many of the negative features of the glutton as described in medieval literature are depicted vividly by Spenser in his pageant of the Seven Deadly Sins in *The Faerie Queene*:

> And by his side rode loathsome Gluttony,
> Deformed creature, on a filthie swyne.
> His belly was upblowne with luxury,
> And eke with fatness swollen were his eyne;
> And like a Crane his necke was long and fyne
> With which he swallowed up excessive feast,
> for what whereof poor people often did pyne:
> And all the way, most like a brutish beast,
> He spued up his gorge, that all did him deteast.

> Still as he rode he somewhat still did eat,
> And in his hand did beare a bouzing can,

Of which he supt so oft, that on his seat
His drunken corse he scarse upholden can:
In shape and life more like a monster than a man.

Full of disease was his carcas blew,
And a dry dropsie through his flesh did flow,
Which by misdiet daily greater grew.
Such one was Gluttony, the second of that crew.
(Book I, Canto IV, Stanzas 21–23)

The contrast between the moralists and modern psychologists who write about the control of eating is most pronounced in their attitudes towards bodily pleasure. At one extreme are the religious ascetics who feel guilty about experiencing pleasure even when eating and drinking only to satisfy their natural hunger and thirst. For example, St. Augustine composed this prayer:

> Thou, O lord, hast taught me that I should take my meat as I take my physic [medicine]; but while I pass from the trouble of hunger to the quietness of satisfaction, in the very passage I am ensnared by the cords of my own concupiscence. Necessity bids me pass, but I have no way to pass from hunger to fulness, but over the bridge of pleasure; and although health and life be the cause of eating and drinking, yet pleasure, a dangerous pleasure, thrusts herself into attendance, and sometimes endeavours to be the principal . . . and the worst of the evil is this . . . that an excuse is ready, that under the pretence of health . . . the design of pleasure may be advance and protected. (*Confessions*, Book 10, Section 31)[9]

At the other extreme stands the epicure or hedonist, who sees nothing wrong with the pleasures of food. On the contrary, for him, carnal pleasure is the greatest good, to be cultivated and pursued in infinite variety. Secular psychology, though not considering physical pleasure to be man's greatest good, is closer to the hedonistic than to the ascetic view.

Jeremy Taylor's view is more moderate than Augustine's. In his discussions of gluttony Taylor provides guidelines for the right measure of eating and the place of pleasure in it.[10]

We should not eat until we are full but only until we no longer experience hunger or thirst, and the hunger we satisfy should be natural, not induced by artificial means. Too often we deliberately expose ourselves to the sights and aromas of foods that whet our appetites and make us feel "hungry" even though these foods will not satisfy any nutritional need.

Taylor recognizes that at times of depression it might be useful to consume more than the minimum necessary for physical health, since the pleasure of the food or wine may function as an antidote to dejection. We must, however, do so with caution, lest this antidote become a habit or addiction.

For Taylor, the pleasure that goes with eating cannot be avoided—it is as natural as the shadow that follows an object. Therefore, when the end is proper, such as physical or psychological health, it is permissible to enjoy the pleasure without any guilt. In this he disagrees with Augustine.

If we can satisfy our health needs equally with either of two foods, one bland, the other tasty, is it permissible to choose the one that provides more pleasure over the other? Whereas Augustine would say no, Taylor says yes, and in *Sermons. The House of Feasting* (henceforth cited as S) justifies his position with an antiascetic argument:

> It is lawful when a man needs meat to choose the pleasanter, even merely for their pleasures; that is, because they are pleasant, besides that they are useful; this is as lawful as the smell of a rose, or to lie in feathers, or change the posture of our body in bed for ease, or to hear music, or to walk in gardens rather than the highways; and God has given us leave to be delighted in those things, which he made to that purpose, that we may also be delighted in him that gives them . . . provided that [the pleasure] be in its degree moderate, and we temperate in our desires. (S, p. 122)

Although the pleasures derived from moral eating are proper, we should not dwell on them or try to extend their duration, whether by physical or psychological means as did the Greek hedonist Philoxenus:

> Philoxenus was a beast; he wished his throat as long as a crane's, that he might be long in swallowing his pleasant morsels; he mourned because

the pleasure of his eating was not spread over all his body. . . . Do not
run to it beforehand, nor chew the cud when the meal is over; delight
not in fancies, and expectations, the remembrances of a pleasant meal.
(S, pp. 122–123)

Finally, Taylor cautions us to be masters of our food rather than its
servants. When we pay too much attention to maximizing the pleasures of eating by the elaborate use of sauces, spices, and flavorings, we
allow ourselves to become worshipers of food rather than its sovereign.

࿔

It is interesting to compare the attitudes of the four different traditions
to the pleasure of eating. Today, the need to justify our pleasure strikes
us as strange. We take it for granted that physical pleasure, insofar as
it does not impair our health, is desirable. One way the food industry
encourages us to eat a lot is to make us believe food makes us happy.
The industry constantly conjures up new ways for us to consume and
enjoy food. Since for some people food is a substitute for sexual pleasures or maternal love, advertisers take advantage of these associations
to sell their products.

The contrast between religious and secular attitudes towards the
pleasure of food is evident when we compare Taylor's guidelines with
Wollersheim's behavioral program of weight control.[11] Both strive to
teach people to reduce their total intake of food and eat fewer rich
kinds. As Wollersheim observes:

The therapist explains [to the group enrolled in the weight-control
program] that the purpose of this program is . . . [not] to take away their
eating pleasures. On the contrary, the program is designed to add to
their pleasure of eating by teaching them to eat properly and to eat
intentionally like a gourmet, one who really enjoys her food to the
fullest with all of her senses (visual, olfactory, tactile, gustatory). One
who eats indiscriminately just stuffs food hastily into her mouth without
really enjoying the eating experience. By changing one's eating habits,
one can "eat less but enjoy it more." One can learn to enjoy food by
looking at it, appreciating the coloring of the food and its arrangement

and enjoying its aroma. Most importantly, one can learn to eat slowly
and enjoy each small mouthful with her lips and teeth. . . . By changing eating patterns to consume fewer calories, one can at the same time
learn to enjoy eating more. (p. 64)

A variety of techniques is recommended to achieve the weight loss
goal of the behavioral program, including the cultivation of new physical pleasures to replace those of overindulgence. The goal of religious
admonitions against gluttony is not weight loss per se but temperance
in matters of food. Though the teachings often include mockery of
the obese and, if followed, result in loss of weight, this is incidental
to their moral aim. Many of the techniques recommended by both
religious and secular therapists are quite similar, or can be adapted to
each other's ends. This should not blind us, however, to the value
differences between them. Taylor, for example, develops the thesis
that temperance brings greater happiness than gluttony, and that we
can be happy with simple fare. This resembles Wollersheim's thesis
only superficially. For Taylor it is not by the deliberate cultivation
of alternative sensory pleasures that one learns to control excessive eating, but by coming to appreciate that abstinence is conducive to spiritual progress and long-term happiness whereas gluttony leads to their
opposites.

Why are the moralists wary of the pleasures of eating?

Some authors identify the desire for physical pleasure with the bestial, and we should try to be as little like the beasts as possible. Having
been created in the image of God, who has implanted in us a soul that
shares elements of the divine, we should free ourselves from a preoccupation with the bodily. This attitude has its pre-Christian roots in
Platonic dualism and to a lesser extent in Aristotle's denigration of the
senses of taste and touch.

Moreover, the pursuit of pleasure reflects a weakness of reason and
the will. The failure to use one's reason and will is contrary to God's
intent for man and is therefore a sin.

For some writers, such as Maimonides and Taylor, the fact that the
intemperate pursuit of the pleasures of eating and drinking is often
detrimental to one's health makes it sinful. One has a religious obligation to preserve one's health so as to be better able to worship God.

A sick body interferes with our ability to concentrate on the godly and to engage in acts of charity.

A related idea is that immoderate eating diverts us from things we should be doing of a spiritual or intellectual nature. I cannot pray or perform certain mitzvot and eat at the same time. The time I spend in acquiring and preparing food could be better spent on studying the sacred Scriptures or on helping the poor and the unfortunate.

Finally, the inordinate pursuit of the pleasures of eating and drinking can lead to other sinful acts. Thus I might steal, lie, or cheat in order to get the food I crave. Gluttony often leads to lust, since both result from the sense of touch and because the glutton's moral inhibitions are weakened by alcohol.[12] If I eat excessively there might be less food available for those who need it.[13] Overeating will make me less mentally alert and so I may make errors of judgment, lose my temper, behave indiscretely, or talk excessively or foolishly. The glutton may be so involved with satisfying his appetite that he will neglect his responsibilities to his family and shame them and himself by his immoderate behavior.[14] A particularly grave effect of filling oneself with food and drink is to make the person less aware of his mortality and dependence on God for his life, health, and prosperity. Therefore, the glutton will be inclined to abandon God. The biblical paradigm for this is the gluttonous, disobedient son who refused to accept parental authority. Since it is the parents who are responsible for socializing the child to accept divine authority, the glutton who rebels against them will rebel against God as well:

> If a man has a wayward and defiant son, who does not heed his father or mother and does not obey them even after they discipline him, his father and mother shall take hold of him and bring him out to the elders of his town at the public place of his community. They shall say to the elders of the town, "This son of ours is disloyal and defiant; he does not heed us. He is a glutton and a drunkard." Thereupon the men of his town shall stone him to death, thus you will sweep out evil from your midst: all Israel will hear and be afraid.[15, 16] (Deuteronomy 21: 18–21, JPS)

The moralists want us to revise our ideas of pleasure and happiness and the relationship between them, and thus reorder the hierarchy of values in our lives. Most secular people do not share the religious moralists' anxiety, sometimes even disdain, about bodily pleasure. Our culture goes to the other extreme, extolling sensuality and seeking happiness by stimulating and then satisfying our sense of touch and taste. There is, however, a middle ground, in the teachings of the Hebrew Bible, Aristotle, the Talmud, Aquinas, and Taylor, which makes sense for us today whether or not we are religious. The detrimental moral, psychological, and physical effects of excessive eating and of a preoccupation with food, to which these works points, are relevant today as are their suggestions about how we can control our eating.

Turning now to the Judaic tradition, the views of many Jewish moralists are similar to moderate Christian approaches. One should eat to satisfy one's physical and psychological needs. Judaism proscribes eating certain foods (the laws of kashrut). However, it is not a sin to eat permitted foods in moderation. Maimonides, for example, adopts Aristotle's view that virtue is the mean between two extremes, and he applies that to eating. He synthesizes biblical and rabbinic teachings about food with Aristotle's when he says that a primary purpose for the food taboos is to cultivate the virtue of moderation in eating. The Jew will learn to control his desire for food and acquire the moral disposition of temperance by adhering to the kashrut laws. Maimonides condemns extreme ascetic behavior as being counter to the divine will. If God had wanted us to fast frequently and deprive ourselves of all food-related pleasures, he would have commanded us to do so.

Judaism even goes so far as to mandate pleasurable eating on many occasions. On the weekly Sabbath, on festivals, and at religious ceremonies such as a wedding, a circumcision, or the completion of the study of a tractate from the Talmud, there is a religious obligation under Jewish law to delight or rejoice, partly through partaking of tasty food. Moreover, the Talmud and later codes of Jewish law formulated many blessings to be recited before and after eating. The blessing before eating is to acknowledge God's munificence in providing food and request permission to enjoy His gift to man. The grace after a meal is to thank Him for food that has just been consumed. Food, then, is perceived primarily as a good, even though at times it can lead to evil.[17,18]

Although the devotional writers sometimes use the slave metaphor, ensnarement by the devil, or the "evil inclination" to describe the glutton's apparent loss of control over his eating, they still maintain that it is within his power to overcome temptation by the exercise of his will. If they didn't believe that, they wouldn't be exhorting him to do so. Modern weight-control programs developed by psychologists also assume that with proper training and practice the overeater can acquire self-control skills. There are, however, many in the medical community who have little faith in the cultivation of such skills and see the glutton's ultimate salvation in appetite-reducing drugs. But appetite reduction through medication and the learning of cognitive and behavioral skills to control one's food intake aren't logically incompatible.[19] Even if overeating is "caused" by some chemical substance or physiological process, this does not mean that the disposition to overeat can only be changed by direct chemical means. All eating, normal as well as deviant, has physiological components, which is why gluttony is a "carnal" vice. Yet we usually regulate our normal eating without imbibing any drugs, for example, by the timing and quantity of the food we eat. Both moralists and behavioral and cognitive therapists believe that we can regulate much of our overeating without recourse to medication. Therefore, though we may claim to be helpless victims of our cravings or of the devil, neither priest, nor rabbi, nor behavioral psychologist will exonerate us from the responsibility for much of our gluttony.

Bishop Taylor structures his discourse on gluttony around the passage "Let us eat and drink; for tomorrow we die."[20] This proverb is an apt motto for the hedonist philosophy advocated by sinful pagans and it expresses the values of the glutton, whether or not he is aware of it. It is understandable, says Taylor, that pagans would adopt such an outlook, because their view of man (to which the modern secular view corresponds in many ways) can logically lead to hedonism. Christians, however, have no such justification:

> They [pagans] placed themselves in the order of beasts and birds, and esteemed their bodies nothing but receptacles of flesh and wine, larders and pantries; and their soul the fine instrument of pleasure. . . ; and therefore they treated themselves accordingly. But then, why [should] we do the same things, who are led by other principles . . . who know what shall happen to a soul hereafter, and know that this time is but a passage to eternity, this body but a servant to the soul, this soul a minister to the Spirit, and the whole man in order to God and to felicity. (S, p. 11)

The gluttonous attitude mocked by Isaiah is advocated by Trimalchio, Petronius's symbol of hedonistic decadence. Trimalchio is a nouveau riche multimillionaire who sponsors an elaborate banquet for his friends with countless exotic dishes, each served with unique flair by a retinue of slaves, to the accompaniment of entertainments. A guest describes one grotesque scene:

> As we drank and admired each luxury in detail, a slave brought in a silver skeleton, made so that its limbs and spine could be moved and bent in every direction. He put it down once or twice on the table so that the supple joints showed several attitudes, and Trimalchio said appropriately: "Alas for us poor mortals, all that poor man is is nothing. So we shall all be, after the world below takes us away. Let us live then while it goes well with us."(*Satyricon*, p. 53)

The guests then resumed gorging themselves on the vast array of delicacies that followed.[21]

By preaching against gluttony, Taylor wants to help cure mankind of their folly and redirect their behavior to true happiness. To accomplish this he demonstrates that the pleasures of the world, specifically with respect to food and drink, do not produce happiness. On the contrary, intemperance in eating is actually an enemy of true happiness. He also formulates concrete rules for temperate eating which if followed will produce felicity.

G l u t t o n y

Taylor ingeniously attacks the epicure/glutton on his own ground. Since gluttony will make us unhappy it doesn't pay for a hedonist to be a glutton. But how does gluttony lead to unhappiness?

It is obvious, says Taylor, that to satisfy our basic needs, a minimum of food and drink is adequate. However, to guarantee a constant supply of food to satisfy our appetites beyond our needs, we engage in undesirable activities which bring harm to ourselves and to others. We work longer and harder than we should in order to earn enough money to indulge our excessive appetites. We are envious of others who can afford more, tastier, or exotic food. Once we allow our appetite for food to get out of hand, it is difficult to set limits on it. We end up never being content with whatever food we have but always searching for some novel or unique gustatory pleasure. When food becomes a status symbol for us, we need to ostentatiously display our "superiority" by conspicuously consuming costly gourmet dishes served on expensive dinnerware. In other words, the more we desire food, the more anxious and driven we make our life. We sacrifice the psychological serenity that comes with moderation and simplicity.

Intemperance, Taylor continues, is an enemy to health, without which it is impossible to experience pleasure or happiness. Furthermore, and paradoxically, the more we eat the less we enjoy our food, whereas by eating sparingly we enjoy our food all the more. Excessive eating and drinking cause us to sin, to think and act like fools, and to thereby impugn our reputations.

Taylor evokes powerful images of the glutton as a diseased fool for neglecting his health:[22]

For this is the glutton's pleasure, "To breathe short and difficultly, scarce to be able to speak, and when he does, he cries out, I die and rot with pleasure." But the folly is as much to be derided as the men to be pitied, that we daily see men afraid of death with a most intolerable apprehension, and yet increase the evil of it, the pain, and the trouble, and the suddenness of its coming. (S, p. 115)

The glutton who prays for health in church is a hypocrite:

For why do men go to temples and churches, and make vows to God and daily prayers, that God would give them a healthful body, and take

away their gout and their palsies, their fevers and apoplexies, the pains
of the head and the gripings of the belly, and arise from their prayers,
and pour in loads of flesh and seas of wine, lest there should not be
matter enough for a lusty disease? (S, p. 115)

Anyone who has gone to church or to synagogue and prayed for
good health, only to emerge at the end of the service to partake of a
sumptuous reception replete with food detrimental to health, can appreciate the contemporary relevance of Taylor's remarks.

In this vein I encourage my clients who are struggling with their
impulse to overeat to think along the following lines: Is it really worth
your while to enjoy the immediate pleasures of ice cream, pastries,
chocolates, and steaks if, as a consequence of your indulgence, you
will end up in the intensive care unit of your local hospital or become
chronically ill with high blood pressure or a heart condition? If you eat
moderately, in the long run you will actually get more pleasure from
food since you will live longer to enjoy it. Gluttons tend to suppress
anxiety-evoking thoughts and deny unpleasant facts about the harmful
effects of excessive eating. The moralists try to counter this tendency by
repeatedly reminding us of what we would rather ignore.

Wollersheim uses a similar technique which she calls UACs—
Ultimate Aversive Consequences:

> Each participant should develop and write out a rather long list (at least
> ten) of the Ultimate Aversive Consequences (UAC's) of overeating and
> being fat. The trouble with overeating is that its undesirable conse-
> quences are far removed in time from the act of overeating. When a
> person is in a stimulus situation which tempts her to eat, she usually is
> not seriously contemplating the undesirable consequences that will be-
> fall her because of her indiscriminate eating. However, if an individual
> can seriously contemplate and mentally rehearse these UAC's at the
> time a stimulus to eat inappropriately presents itself, these UAC's will
> serve to punish thoughts about overeating and the actual behavior of
> overeating in such situations will be less likely to occur. ("Behavioral
> Techniques for Weight Control," pp. 72–73)

What the moralists and preachers such as Taylor do, in effect, is
compose an inventory of the ultimate negative consequences of glut-

tony. If, as they expect, we read their works regularly, the constant reminder of these consequences will eventually help us rein in our passion for food. Such harmful effects are not confined to impairment of health, but to any undesirable outcome of excessive eating. For Taylor, these include the spiritual and moral consequences of gluttony. Wollersheim does not include moral or ethical considerations in her examples, all of which are egocentric—how overeating hurts me, not how it might impact on others:

> Statements of actual or imagined social rejection, sarcastic treatment, critical references to bodily contours or proportions, extreme personal sensitivity over excess weight, demeaning inferences concerning professional incompetence or carelessness can all be effective, e.g. "When I wear shorts my legs look like hams"; "That blind date never asked fat me out again." (p. 73)

One could add to these effects of gluttony another, that by imparing your health those dear to you and for whom you are responsible as parent, child, or spouse can suffer.

In a recent court decision, a woman who took drugs during pregnancy was found criminally liable for the injuries they caused to her unborn child. The legal merit and social wisdom of this controversial ruling, which is being appealed, is heatedly debated. Proponents maintain that it will deter drug use during pregnancy. Opponents argue that it will deter addicted pregnant women from seeking counseling. Whatever the ultimate resolution of legal responsibility, the case for moral accountability is strong. Why shouldn't we be held accountable for the damage we cause to others as a result of our intemperance in pursuit of pleasure?

Consider the following situation. A doctor has warned you that excessive eating, consumption of alcohol, or smoking is detrimental to your health and will make you ill enough to require hospitalization or be incapacitated. You ignore the doctor's warnings. Can your child, whom you are legally responsible to care for and support, obtain a court order restraining you from overeating, drinking, or smoking on the grounds that your failure to control yourself jeopardizes the parental care and support to which he is entitled? Even if a court would not grant such an order, from a moral perspective your child has a valid claim against you. Such moral considerations should be incorporated into treatment programs for overeating.

One of the moral arguments against gluttony made by Taylor is that it often results in the neglect of the spiritual and material needs of others in society:

> Strange therefore it is, that for the stomach, which is scarce a span long, there would be provided so many furnaces and ovens, huge fires, and an army of cooks, cellars swimming with wine, and granaries sweating with corn; and that into one belly should enter the vintage of many nations, the spoils of distant provinces, and the shell-fishes of several seas. . . . It is so little we spend in religion, and so very much on ourselves, so little to the poor, and so without measure to make ourselves sick, that we seem to be in love with our own mischief . . . that we strive all the ways we can to make ourselves need more than nature intended. (S, p. 116)

Here Taylor is criticizing the gluttonous society, not only the individual glutton. He refers to the collective stomach of the upper classes of a socially stratified society in which the wealthy ate lavishly while the poor barely eked out a living. The glutton, indulging in his meats and reveling in his wines, is too busy to think about the poor and their needs. The money he spends on superfluous food and drink could be better used to help the poor, whom he oppresses in order to acquire the wealth to indulge his voracious appetite. Taylor wants us, individually and collectively, to reflect upon the social and ethical context in which we live our vice. If he can convince us of these evils of gluttony and awaken our sense of its moral injustice, there is hope that we will exercise greater self-control and de-emphasize the role of food in our lives.

Moral and ethical considerations should be integrated into contemporary weight-control therapies. Organizations dedicated to famine relief have successfully encouraged people to fast on certain days and to donate to the hungry the money they would have spent on food. Clients in therapy for overeating might be receptive to such agreements as well.

Taylor elaborates on the hypocrisy of gluttony in a Christian society, since it breeds injustice, indifference, and cruelty:

The above mixed media painting by Otto Dix is a modern rendition of an ancient theme: the procession of the seven deadly sins, adapted here to express the artist's view of German morality in 1933. Sloth, an old woman, carries a caricature of an envious Hitler on her back. Behind Hitler are anger, and pride, depicted as Death. Gluttony appears as a bloated head with a diseased mouth and cheek. Lust sports a syphilitic scab and lewdly displays her breast. Greed, with the head of a human victim filling his voracious mouth, completes the procession. *(Reproduced with permission of Staatlichen Karlsruhe)*

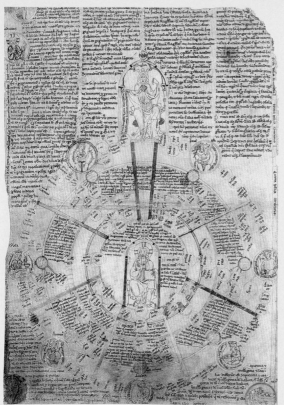

This early thirteenth-century illuminated manuscript page (left) from either France or Germany was used for didactic purposes. Five concentric circles depict (from outer to inner) the seven Vices, Petitions, Gifts, Virtues, and Beatitudes. Pride, the Queen of the Vices, sits on her throne above the outer circle. All seven sins are shown as female figures. *(Courtesy the Houghton Library, Harvard University)*

The woodcut at right is from a set depicting the eternal punishments of sin, printed in Troyes in 1496. This picture shows the torments of the gluttonous in Hell; those who ate compulsively in life are force fed toads, rats, and snakes. *(From* Devils, Demons, Death and Damnation *by Ernst and Joanna Lehner, Dover Publications, 1971)*

Pigritia.

Inuidia.

Auaritia.

These three drawings are from a seventeenth-century set by Jacques Callot. Each sin is depicted with a demon hovering overhead and a symbolic animal companion: sloth (top left) a donkey; envy (top right) a dog and a snake; and avarice (left) a giant toad. *(Courtesy of the Fogg Art Museum, Harvard University; a gift of William Gray from the collection of Francis Calley Gray, by exchange)*

NEMO SVPERBVS AMAT SVPEROS, NEC AMATVR AB ILLIS

Above and on the following three pages are Bruegel's splendid depictions of the seven deadly sins: *Pride* (above), *Envy* and *Anger* (opposite, top and bottom), *Avarice* and *Sloth* (succeeding page, top and bottom), *Gluttony* and *Lust* (facing page, top and bottom). Each engraving contains many illustrations of its sin, and bears a Latin motto at the bottom with a moral. *(Pieter Bruegel, the Elder, 1558; National Gallery of Art, Washington, Rosenwald Collection)*

INVIDIA HORRENDVM MONSTRVM, SÆVISSIMA PESTIS.
Een onsterfelycke doot es nijt / en wreede peste Een boost .li. L..... .p

INVLDIA.

ORA TVMENT IRA, NIGRESCVNT SANGVINE VENÆ.
Gramscap doet den mont swillen / en verbittert den moet Sij beroert den gheest / en maeckt swert dat bloet

IRA

P. brueghel Inuentor .   H. Cock excude Cum gratia et priuilegio 1558

QVIS METVS, AVT PVDOR EST VNQVAM PROPERANTIS AVARI?
Eere / beleeftheyt / fchaemte / noch godlyck vermaen En fiet die fchrapende ghiericheyt niet aen

AVARITIA

P. brueghel · Inuentor · Cock · excud · cum priuileg · 1558

SEGNITIES ROBVR FRANGIT, LONGA OCIA NERVOS.
Traecheyt maeckt machteloos / en verdrooght Die fenuwen dat de menfch niewers toe en dooght

DESIDIA

brueghel · Inuentor · H · Cock · excud · cum priuileg · 1558

GVLA

.M.

H·Cock excud· cum gratia et priuilegie ·1558

EBRIETAS EST VITANDA INGLVVIESQVE CIBORVM·
Schout dronckenschap / en gulsichlick eten Want ouerdaet doet godt en hem seluen verghten·

Bruegel· Inuentor
Cock· cum· cū· priui·

LVXVRIA

.M.

LVXVRIA ENERVAT VIRES, EFFOEMINAT ARTVS·
Luxurje stinckt / sy is vol onsuuerheden Sy breeckt die Crachten en sy swackt die leden

This decorative tabletop by Hieronymous Bosch depicts the eye of God at the center of the world surveying humans in all their sinfulness. Vanity admires herself, angry men engage in quarrels, gluttons gorge themselves, the avaricious pervert justice by accepting bribes, the lustful cavort amidst feasts, the envious slander and eye one another suspiciously, and the slothful sleep instead of praying. The circle of the sins and human existence is framed by Death, the Last Judgment, Heaven, and Hell. (*Courtesy Museo del Prado, Madrid*)

Intemperance is the nurse of vice . . . by faring deliciously every day, men become senseless of the evils of mankind, inapprehensive of the troubles of their brethren, unconcerned in the changes of the world, and the cries of the poor, the hunger of the fatherless, and the thirst of widows. . . . For, to maintain plenty and luxury, sometimes wars are necessary, and oppressions and violence: but no landlord did ever grind the face of his tenants, no prince ever sucked blood from his subjects for the maintenance of a sober and moderate proportion of things. (S, p. 118)

Taylor's association of gluttony with social apathy and cruelty is somewhat hyperbolic. There are, after all, many compassionate and charitable gluttons. However, there is some correlation between a preoccupation with food and neglect of other responsibilities. A patient of mine obsessed with food nearly ruined her family life. As a child she had learned, as most of us do, to associate food with psychological security. For her, however, the psychological need for food became pathological. She spent so much time thinking and talking about food, and preparing and consuming it, that her affectionate and caring relationships with her husband and children were deteriorating. She couldn't find the time to assist her learning-disabled son with his homework. Her older daughter, who was going through an adolescent crisis and desperately needed a mother's understanding was shunted aside because "mother is too busy now" preparing large-scale dinner parties. The guests were ostensibly being invited over so frequently because "mother likes to maintain friendships" but really as a rationalization for indulging in food. Her husband found her a less attractive companion because she had so narrowed her interests and had also put on considerable weight. She had become so food- and ego-centered that she was ignoring the legitimate needs of those she deeply loved. In therapy we examined the reasons for the development of her gluttony in childhood and why she persisted in her habit in adulthood. Therapy, however, also focused on the moral implications of her behaviors. The patient was made aware of the values implied by her food obsession. She had to come to understand that she was, in effect, placing food on a higher level in her hierarchy of values than love and concern for husband and children. She had to be confronted with the kind of person her gluttony had transformed her into, and to ask herself if that was really the kind of person she wanted to be. When she came to realize that her excessive preoccupation with food had grave moral implications, she had taken an important step towards recovery.[23]

The glutton assumes that the more and more varied the food he eats the greater will his pleasure be. Taylor teaches that this isn't necessarily so. The pleasure of eating depends on how hungry or full we are. The practical application of this principle can help us control gluttony:

> A constant full table is less pleasant than the temperate provisions of the virtuous . . . for necessity and want makes the appetite, and the appetite makes the pleasure; and men are infinitely mistaken when they despise the poor man's table and wonder how he can endure that life, that is maintained without the exercise of pleasure, and that he can suffer his day's labor, and recompense it with unsavoury herbs, and potent garlic, with water-cresses, and bread coloured like the ashes that gave it hardness: he hath a hunger that gives it deliciousness. (S, p. 117)

To reeducate my patients about the relationship between pleasure and food I ask them to reflect on an example such as this. Which do you think you would enjoy more—a cool glass of water that would quench your extreme thirst on a hot day, or a third milkshake on a satiated stomach? The reforming glutton can use this principle to help him overcome temptation and allow himself pleasure by carefully regulating his food intake. To strengthen my patients' self-control I tell them that when they are tempted by food that they know they should not eat, they should think about the treat that is in store for them when in a few hours they will eat permitted food on an emptier stomach. As you longingly eye the lemon meringue pie, imagine instead the pleasure you will derive from your coffee and yogurt in an hour from now, when you will actually be hungry. Although coffee and yogurt are less tasty than lemon meringue pie, they are quite pleasurable when we haven't eaten for many hours.

Of course, some gluttons may have no interest in curbing their appetite. They may be like those Romans who were so hedonistic that, after partaking of a sumptuous feast to the point of satiation, they would retire to a special "vomitarium" where they would induce themselves to disgorge their food so that they could resume a second or third round of gluttony. They weren't bulimic, just idolatrous worshipers of their bellies. However, most overeaters are not so extreme in their idolatry. They realize that their eating habits are wrong but they can't seem to control them. Moralists and psychologists, in pointing the way to self-control, must reject the hedonist's linkage of happiness with physical pleasure above all else.

We should weigh the fleeting, transient nature of the pleasure experienced in eating against the extended pain it causes. A few minutes of pleasure produce many days of illness and remorse. Isn't this too costly a price to pay for the ephemeral benefits of inordinate eating? As Taylor observes:

> Pleasure . . . passes away at the present, and leaves nothing at all behind it, but sorrow and sour remembrances . . . for though the sorrow dwells with a man pertinaciously, yet the pleasure is swift as lightning, and more pernicious; let [the glutton] turn his hour-glass, he will find his head aches longer than his throat was pleased; . . . if these be the pleasures of an epicure's table, I shall pray that my friends never feel them. (S, pp. 117–118)

The Romans who used the vomitarium were not disgusted by what they did. For most people, however, to even think of ejecting food is abhorrent. Another way the moralists join battle against gluttony is by vividly associating it with aversive images, such as puking, passing wind, belching, and eliminating. We saw some of these images in Spenser's personification of Gluttony. In Chaucer's *Pardoner's Tale*, the Pardoner mocks the glutton:

> Alas, the filth of it! If we contemn
> The name, how much more filthy is the act!
> A man who swills down vintages in fact
> Makes a mere privy of his throat, a sink
> For cursed superfluities of drink!
> . . . O thou belly! stinking pod

Of dung and foul corruption, that canst send
Thy filthy music forth at either end,
What labor and expense it is to find
Thy sustenance!

(p. 264)

The glutton is reminded that the flesh he accumulates will eventually rot and be consumed by maggots. By establishing associations between gluttony and unpleasantness, the moralists hope to discourage it. Some therapists use a similar method, covert aversive conditioning. The patient is instructed to imagine and rehearse a "scene" which associates inappropriate eating with a disgusting consequence, and then to recall the scene when he is tempted by food he is not supposed to consume.[24]

A frequent image of the glutton in medieval devotional and popular literature is a person whose slovenly public behavior is despicable, wasteful, and foolish. He behaves like a sow and a dolt and is not respected by others. He is a sinner who has succumbed to the power of the devil, an outcast from the good society who keeps disreputable companions. Although many elements of this portrait are particularly appropriate for the drunkard, they are used to describe the food glutton as well. Spenser has him riding on a filthy swine (as befits him), deformed, fat and swollen, sweaty, bereft of reason, monstrous, sick, and detested by all. *Jacob's Well*, a popular fifteenth-century work, tell us how selfish the glutton is:

> The glutton is like a bear . . . the bear delighteth much in honey, and therefore he goeth to an hive, to a swarm of bees, and licketh away their honey that they travailed for; so the glutton delighteth in delicacies, that he is not ashamed to devour and waste that [which] many others have sore travailed for. (p. 142)

He interprets the gospel story about demons exorcized by Jesus who enter into a herd of pigs who then rush into a lake and drown, as an exhortation against gluttony. Adam and Eve also get into the picture, because gluttony motivated them to eat the forbidden fruit:

The fiends [demons] have power to dwell in them [that are like hogs in gluttony] and to drenchen [drown] them in the sea of hell. For when a strong man hath down another and holdeth him by the throat, it is hard for him to recover again. Right so it is of a man that the fiend holdeth in the sin of gluttony in his throat; for the fiend seeketh the throat of man by gluttony [gluttony being a sin of the throat], as the wolf seeketh the throat of the sheep. For so he [the Devil] took Adam and Eve, when they eaten of the apple. (p. 141)

In other medieval passages the glutton is often compared to a dog that eats greedily or to a kite that swoops rapidly and mercilessly upon its prey.

These vivid descriptions are meant to arouse feelings of unease in use if we behave like gluttons. They are also calculated to make us aware of how we look to others, of which we are often quite oblivious. Since we want to be respected, calling our attention to the negative impression our behavior makes on others can function as a deterrent. If we learn to evoke these images when we are tempted by food, we will have strengthened our "will" or self-control.

In conducting weight-control therapy, I employ the same principle. Clients are asked to reflect upon the following:

Have you given thought to how you appear to others when they observe your gluttonous behavior? Do you realize how you lose their respect when they see you rushing to be first on line for food, filling your plate to the brim, gobbling your food as though you hadn't eaten for days and won't be eating for several more, returning for seconds and thirds? You are so engrossed in your food that you aren't aware that others are staring at you with contempt. Don't deceive yourself that no one pays attention to how you act when you see and eat food. How do you react when you see someone else behaving like a pig? Wouldn't you have reservations about befriending or employing him? Would you like your spouse or children to be so crass and animal-like at the table? Yet, your passion for food so overwhelms you that you don't realize the dishonor you are causing yourself by your gross eating habits. You are also dishonoring your family, who are ashamed to see you behaving like a glutton in the presence of their friends, teachers, or colleagues.

Taylor lifts us to heaven for a moment to show us how we appear from afar as we chase after food:

> when thy Soul dwells above, and looks down upon the pleasures of the World, they seem like things at a distance, little and contemptible, and men running after the satisfaction of their sottish appetites seem foolish as fishes, thousands of them running after a rotten worm that covers a deadly hook. (*Rule and Exercises of Holy Living*, p. 70)

He suggests more rules to follow which will help us become temperate in eating. We should suppress our desire for food in its early stage before it overwhelms our ability to exercise self-control; our eating habits should be regular and deliberate, not hasty or haphazard; we should avoid tempting feasts and eat only when necessary, and never to the point of satiety. His advice about how to raise children with restrained eating habits has a surprisingly progressive ring:

> I have known some wise persons . . . to cure the passions and longings of their children by letting them taste of everything they passionately fancied; for they should be sure to find less in it than they looked for, and the impatience of their being denied would be loosened and made slack: and when our wishings are no bigger than the thing deserves . . . we shall find all pleasures so little entertainment. (RE, p. 69)

Taylor recommends that we

> Divert [our sensual desires] with some laudable employment. . . . For since the faculties of a man cannot at the same time with any sharpness attend to two objects, if you employ your spirit upon a book or a bodily labor, or any innocent and indifferent employment, you have no room left for the present trouble of a sensual temptation. (RE, p. 68)

For some overeaters consumption of food is their main source of satisfaction because they lack interests and skills that can provide alternative enjoyment. One of my clients in an eating-control program found that as she was spending less time on eating she was experiencing increased boredom. She did not know how to spend her newly available free time productively. I had to educate her, therefore, about activities she could substitute for food preparation and eating. I told her to think of several inexpensive, enjoyable, readily accessible, and easy-to-do activities which could function as food substitutes. For example, did she like to read, listen to music, watch television, play solitaire, reminisce over a family photo album, write a letter, or look at reproductions of paintings? Perhaps she would enjoy learning a new hobby like knitting, weaving, wood carving, drawing, or stamp collecting. These activities require no major investment of money or energy, range from the gently relaxing to the intensely pleasurable, and have no undesirable side effects. The client prepared a list of her preferences which she attached to the cupboards and refrigerator. Written in bold letters at the top were "NO CALORIE FOOD SUBSTITUTES," and "INDULGE YOUR SENSE OF SOUND AND SIGHT." As she learned to occupy herself with these pleasurable activities, it became easier for her to control her eating.

Although the pleasures provided by the senses of sound and sight aren't always as intense as are those of taste, they can produce many enjoyable experiences that cannot be matched by any amount of food. Reading or listening to an interesting story afford more pleasure, for many people, than munching potato chips. For a person trying to break out of a cycle of gluttony, it will be easier to give up chips if she consciously decides to read a book, watch a movie, or listen to a record instead.[25]

To discourage gluttony the moralists praise its opposing virtue, temperance (or abstinence). They dwell upon its considerable benefits, whether in this world or in the soul's afterlife. The rewards of temperance in this world will be health, tranquility of the soul, social approval and respect, divine love and approval, and the knowledge that one is good. Because these rewards are often delayed whereas the pleasures of gluttony are immediate, it is important that we remind ourselves of these future benefits to help us cope with the temptations of the present. Secular therapists use the same principle. They tell the patient to associate smaller portions of food, slow eating, low calorie foods, and exercise with images of future bodily attractiveness and "sexiness," greater ease of movement, higher levels of energy, and increased social activity. Although the principle is the same for the moralists and the therapists, they differ in some of the rewards they promise. Unlike certain therapists, the moralists do not want us to acquire the virtue of temperance so that it can serve the vice of lust.

An important reward for abstinence is the feeling of heightened willpower it confers. Gluttony for the moralists is a weakness of the will. As we establish control over our eating we subject our senses to the rule of reason, which is what is expected of man. Realizing that we are rulers over food rather than its subject we feel good and our determination to continue along the journey from gluttony to temperance is strengthened.

The moralists observe that, once we get used to resisting the temptation to eat foods that we like very much, these foods lose much of their attractiveness. I tell my patients that although they will find it difficult to resist an ice cream sundae early in their struggle against gluttony, if they persist, it won't be as enticing several weeks later. This may seem counterintuitive, since deprivation often increases craving. But frequently the opposite happens, particularly when the patient has acquired alternative eating habits. After a few weeks of successful resistance they will be able to ignore the food that was so alluring before. The inner turmoil, the vacillation between approach and avoidance that characterize early stages of abstinence, give way to indifference. Knowing this in advance makes it easier for the patient to make the initial commitment to self-control and then to follow through. There are physiological and psychological reasons for this phenomenon. Some foods for which we have a strong craving might be moderately "addictive." As we withdraw them from our system, the addiction is weakened. Moreover, the less we eat of a food, the weaker the association between it and our memory of its pleasant taste. As we learn to consider excessive eating and inappropriate foods toxic and enslaving, their attractiveness diminishes. Finally, having replaced them with other satisfying food and activities, they lose some of their former allure.

In Dante's Purgatory the gluttonous are subjected to a torment similar to that imposed by Zeus upon Tantalus for stealing the food of the gods. Famished and thirsty, the gluttons long for delicious fruit-laden trees and cool springs of water which they can see but never reach. However, the purpose of this penalty in Christian purgatory differs from that in the afterlife of Greek mythology. Tantalus is tortured with eternal starvation and frustration as vengeance for his crime. The starved gluttons are tantalized by food and drink to purge their souls of the sin of gluttony and train them in the virtue of temperance. As they experience forced deprivation in the presence of food they will learn to control their appetites and to refocus their love, which has been misdirected to the sensual, back to its proper object, God.[26] Those of us who cannot wait for or rely on God to forcefully purge us of our gluttony must do so on our own. Let us hunger after righteousness rather than after food.

Greed

If money be not thy servant, it will be thy master. The covetous man cannot so properly be said to possess wealth, as that may be said to possess him.

—FRANCIS BACON

In 1990 Congress passed a law that provided for life imprisonment for certain financial crimes in recognition of the social damage and danger of greed gone amok. This law was a reaction to public anger at the Savings and Loan scandal of the 1980s in which avaricious bankers, lawyers, and accountants, seeking easy riches, fraudulently deprived thousands of Americans of their savings, causing immeasurable suffering. The greed of the 1980s brought with it a surge in criminal and unethical schemes, such as insider trading on the stock market, company takeovers that resulted in massive layoffs followed by bankruptcies, and scientific fraud. Greed inflicted catastrophe on many innocent victims, and its adverse social consequences will be felt for many years.

This should come as no surprise, since the pursuit of wealth is a dominant value in our society. The media feature adulatory stories about thirty-year-old multimillionaires who have achieved their college goal of amassing a fortune within a decade of graduation. Rarely do journalists who revel in the rich ask whether such a goal is commendable, at what psychological or spiritual cost it was achieved, if ruthless or immoral means were used, and what "good" will be done with all of this wealth. Our constitution guarantees the freedom to pursue happiness and our capitalist ethos simplistically equates freedom with lack of restraint and happiness with wealth. The premise is that unrestrained pursuit of wealth will eventually makes us happier, because the more money we accrue the happier we will be. But in so worshiping money, placing our hope and trust in it—a form of idolatry—we blind ourselves to the social and personal costs of greed. The assumption that greed is good and that riches guarantee satisfying lives is false, and the teachings of the moralists about the sin of avarice illuminate why.

Greed (also known as avarice and covetousness) manifests itself in many ways. The cutthroat competitor, the workaholic, the swindler, the miser, and the gambler are all greedy. Sometimes even the spendthrift is guilty of greed. Basically, greed is the inordinate love of money and of material possessions, and the dedication of oneself to their pursuit. This love of money is fed by other vices and leads to many evils.[1] In trying to satisfy greed we can injure ourselves and others, psychologically and physically. This is the paradox of greed—though its aim is to increase our pleasure through the purchase of goods and services, it often does so at the expense of pleasure and happiness.

A patient of mine provides an example of this. He hadn't taken a much-needed vacation for years although he could easily have afforded to do so. He could never get himself to spend a substantial sum of money on either himself or his wife. He was always complaining that airlines and hotels overcharge, and maintained that he enjoyed staying at home. It was quite obvious, though, that for his emotional health and for his wife's sake they needed to get away from the monotonous routine and pressures of their regular environment. The truth was that he found it extremely difficult to part with money, particularly for a nontangible asset. Things that were touchable could be assigned some money-equivalent value, so he was able to exchange money for them and buy a VCR or a new car. But the scenic beauty of nature, the enhanced intimacy and love that a tranquil getaway with his wife would facilitate, were, to him, ephemeral intangibles that were no substitute for money. This man's stinginess nearly cost him his marriage.

Another of my clients had been successfully immersed in the frenzied greed of the financial markets' subculture of the 1980s. By day he was a workaholic, by night a hedonist. He came to see me because he was unhappy with what he was doing with his life and with what his life was doing to him. He was wise and sensitive enough to realize that his money wasn't making him happy, and that the moral and spiritual values he once cherished were being eroded by his pursuit of wealth and pleasure. Yet he found it difficult to rectify the situation as long as he remained in the environment which supported it. After a period of sustained honest reflection about what he felt he would want to be remembered for if he were to die suddenly, he concluded that it wasn't his financial success or the gratifications of his body that his money bought. He decided to make a dramatic rupture with his present. He moved to a farm in rural Vermont where he now lives a life of material simplicity. He uses his business and organizational skills to consult with local government on projects to improve the lot of the rural poor. Although he earns only a small fraction of what he once did and lives more modestly, he is a much happier person than he ever was in the heyday of his high-flying life-style. Nor does he miss the wealth of earlier times, now that he has adapted to the less that is really more. As Epicurus put it, wealth consists not in having great possessions but in having few wants.

Although greed is a cause of much unhappiness, there are few contemporary therapies for it since it is rarely perceived as undesirable. Only when it results in criminal behavior or in extreme disruption of personal or family life is some intervention deemed necessary. The courts will punish crimes that result from greed and therapists will treat an inveterate gambler or a high-powered executive whose drive for financial success produces intolerable stress or physical illness. For the most part, though, society encourages greed, although euphemisms are usually used when doing so, such as "financial success," "economic security," "the good life," or "having it all." This avoidance of the word *greed* reflects our ambivalence about greed because we know that it is essentially selfish and that when practiced to an extreme it can be very dangerous, leading even to murder.

Turning now to the moralists, they do not consider every instance of the pursuit of wealth as sinful. In judging whether we are guilty of avarice they take into account why we want to acquire wealth and how we do so. They consider, too, the uses to which we put our wealth and our attitude towards worldly possessions.

Why do people pursue wealth? There are many reasons. Foremost among them is the desire to satisfy hedonistic impulses. We may want gourmet food, luxurious residences, exotic vacations, or sexually attractive partners, all of which are expensive. Some of us seek money not so much for the physical pleasures which it can buy, but for the prestige that it confers or the heightened sense of self-esteem that it creates. Another motive is to use money as an instrument of power and control. When these desires drive us to devote our lives to garnering riches we are caught in the vice of greed.

For some greedy people, the challenge of the chase after money itself is the incentive. Just as many sportsmen don't need or want their catch but enjoy the process of bagging it, so too there are money hunters who are driven to acquire wealth because it involves skill, risk taking, and the exhilaration of victory when they succeed. Such a person is Larry the Liquidator, an extremely wealthy and ruthless specialist in corporate takeovers, in the hit play about avarice, *Other People's Money*. The actor who plays Larry in the film version explains the motive for Larry's incessant drive to surpass his previous business successes. "He's a man who has a passion for making money. He enjoys it. It's kind of a game that everybody plays. To talk about greed is like saying that Joe Montana is a very greedy quarterback because he throws a lot of touchdown passes or Willie Mays was a very greedy centerfielder because he caught a lot of fly balls."[2] While the comparison to great athletes might explain why Larry wants to excel in business, it ignores the harm done by the greedy and the rules that they flout in order to achieve their goal.

There are people whose avarice is a result of envy. They pursue wealth and the things that money buys in order to assuage their feeling that they are less "successful" than others to whom they compare themselves. Much of their assets are squandered on conspicuous consumption and ostentatious displays of wealth rather than on truly enjoying what they own.

Sometimes a person pursues wealth because of pressure from a spouse. Different attitudes and expectations of a husband and wife towards money and material things can be a serious source of tension. Many marriages have disintegrated because of the inability of spouses to arrive at a mutually acceptable understanding of how much income is adequate for them and how that income should be allocated. An individual may work at an unsatisfying and frustrating but lucrative job in order to satisfy not his own but his spouse's financial aspirations. Long hours away from home and unhappiness at work often result in the inability to satisfy the emotional needs of children and mate. The entire family become victims of the greedy partner in the relationship.

Another common motive for the pursuit of wealth is to alleviate anxiety about future security. If I suffer a financial setback or become gravely sick, disabled, or old and feeble, who will provide for my needs? These reasonable concerns become obsessions for some people. The person is so anxious about the future that he mortgages his present to it. He is driven to accumulate as much money as he can to insure against the disaster that always looms ahead. Such obsession with economic security becomes exacerbated when the person wants to guarantee not only his own future but that of his family as well. This too is greed.[3]

For devout Calvinist Protestants religious belief is a motive for pursuing worldly goods and even wealth. Success in this world is considered proof that one is among the elect few preordained by God to be saved. Insofar as worldly success signifies salvation rather than damnation, it serves to alleviate the intense anxiety of a devout Calvinist about where he stands in God's scheme of things. Unlike Catholicism, Calvinism does not look upon the poor as being uniquely loved and blessed by God.

Altruism is another motive for the pursuit of wealth. Some people strive to acquire wealth so that they can use it to help others. This is often, though not always, grounded in religious values. Jewish and Christian devotional writers typically consider possessions to be deposits entrusted by God to man to be used for the furtherance of godly objectives. In Judaism one is to use wealth "for the sake of heaven"; Christians speak of stewardship; both religions expect us to use our wealth to enhance the "glory of God" through acts of charity and benevolence.

We see, then, that there are many motives for pursuing money and wealth. Usually several of these combine to influence the behavior of any single individual. The moralists consider inordinate efforts to accumulate possessions as avaricious when our motives are selfish or hedonistic, our means unjust, and we put our trust in riches.

∂℮

The vice of avarice is depicted with great insight in biblical story, prophecy, and proverb, Greek myth, and medieval moral allegory. The authors of these works expected that reflecting on their messages would help us avoid greed.

The biblical prophets Elijah, Isaiah, Jeremiah, Amos, and Micah were passionate critics of greed and the injustices to which it led. They had the courage and conviction to confront kings and priests when they abused their power and stole from the weak. One biblical story tells of Ahab, king of Israel and his Canaanite wife Jezebel, a nefarious and domineering queen. Adjoining the king's palace was a vineyard owned by Naboth, which Ahab coveted. Ahab offered to pay Naboth for his vineyard or give him a better one in its stead. Naboth rejected the king's offer. The vineyard, which he had inherited from his father, was more precious to Naboth than money. Ahab, frustrated by Naboth's refusal, returned to his palace dejected. When Jezebel heard the story she mocked her husband and told him that she would arrange to get Naboth's vineyard for him. Jezebel hired two men to falsely accuse Naboth of having reviled God and the king, and had him tried and executed. Thereupon she told Ahab to go and take possession of the vineyard, which he set out to do. The word of the Lord came to the prophet Elijah instructing him to meet Ahab in the vineyard and confront him with his crime. There Elijah harshly berated the king with words that have ever since become a powerful condemnation of greed that leads to murder—"Thus said the Lord: Have you murdered and also taken possession?" And Elijah continued, "Thus said the Lord: In the very place where the dogs lapped up Naboth's blood, the dogs will lap up your blood too."[4]

G r e e d

This episode reminds us that some people will stoop to murder in order to satisfy their greed. It teaches that although we may be initially reluctant, as Ahab was, to directly engage in grossly unjust actions in order to satisfy our desire for something, we are easily swayed to let others do the dirty work for us and to reap the benefits of their acting on our behalf. By being able to shift blame and responsibility to others we can rationalize our evil behavior and assuage whatever guilty conscience we might have. We see from the story how our greed often corrupts others, such as the perjurers, whose collusion we need in order to satisfy our desire for someone else's property. We learn how influential a spouse can be in nurturing our greed. Rather than praising King Ahab's initial reluctance to deprive Naboth, his subject, of his vineyard against his will, Jezebel mocks her husband for his allegedly "unkingly" behavior. This mockery probably contributed to Ahab's ultimate acquiescence in the horrible crimes of perjury, murder, and theft. These are the very crimes which a king of Israel was to prevent and punish since it was his responsibility as God's annointed to guarantee justice and righteousness in ancient Israel. The story also presents Elijah, on whom we are to model our behavior, as fearless enough to challenge the most powerful authority of the land when he sees the injustices that greed has spawned. Jezebel and Ahab had earlier put to death many prophets of the Lord and would have been only too ready to do the same to Elijah. Yet he is willing to expose himself to their wrath for the sake of justice. Finally, the biblical message is that greed and its daughters, injustice and murder, will not go unpunished.

Another prophet, Amos, has harsh words for the wives of wealthy oppressors of the poor, who urge their husbands to fraudulently deprive the indigent of their meager possessions in order to satisfy their own desire for pleasure:

> Hear this word, you cows of Bashan . . .
> Who defraud the poor,
> Who rob the needy;
> Who say to your husbands,
> "Bring, and let's carouse!"
> My Lord God swears by his holiness:
> Behold, days are coming upon you

THE SEVEN DEADLY SINS

When you will be carried off in baskets . . .
And flung on the refuse heap.

(4:1–3, JPS)

Isaiah condemns Jerusalem, the faithful city that had once been filled with justice and righteousness but whose rulers are now rogues, thieves, and murderers, "every one avid for presents and greedy for gifts; they do not judge the case of the orphan and the widow's cause never reaches them."[5]

The focus in all three of these biblical passages is on greed as evil insofar as it leads to social injustice, oppression, and crime. Another biblical book, Ecclesiastes, criticizes the avaricious person on psychological and pragmatic grounds. This passage, which contains a series of reflections on the folly of avarice, is frequently cited by medieval devotional authors, Jewish and Christian:

> The man who loves money can never have enough. . . . Sweet is the sleep of the laborer whether he eats little or much; but the rich man owns too much and cannot sleep. . . . A man hoards wealth. . . . And then that wealth is lost through an unlucky venture, and the owner's son left with nothing. . . . As he came from the womb of mother earth, so must he return, naked as he came; all his toil produces nothing which he can take away with him. . . . Exactly as he came, so shall he go, and what profit does he get when his labor is all for the wind"? (5:10–16, NEB)

In other words, you will never be satisfied with the wealth that you accrue so don't deceive yourself into thinking that after acquiring riches you will be able to turn off your greed. The more you own the more you have to worry about, since you are always afraid that someone will steal your riches from you. Don't convince yourself that your motive for pursuing wealth is to assure an inheritance for your children—the vagaries of fickle fortune are too unpredictable to make that a reasonable motive for loving money and dedicating one's energies to getting it. Moreover, when you die your riches will not accompany you—so the time and energy you spend accumulating them could be spent in activities that are more useful and beneficial.

In Greek myth the vice of avarice is represented by Midas, a king in

G r e e d

Macedonia who was known for his love of pleasure and his great wealth—wealth which did not satisfy him. Midas had done a favor for the god Dionysus and when in return he asked Midas what reward he would like, Midas responded immediately, without reflection, that he wished that all he touched would turn into gold. Dionysus granted Midas his wish. All that he touched turned into beautiful solid gold, including his wife and children. Midas had more gold than could be imagined. But all he had was gold. Depressed at the deprivations which his greed had brought upon him, Midas begged Dionysus to release him from his golden touch.

There is profound wisdom in this myth about the dangers of greed. Money has no inherent value. An abundance of gold in and of itself provides no satisfactions or happiness. However, the avaricious individual too often forgets this truth. The repeated association of money with pleasure, power, and prestige confers an intrinsic worth on it for him, which makes it attractive even when it is no longer used to acquire these things. Just as dogs can be conditioned to salivate at the sound of a bell which had once signaled food but no longer does, the avaricious person is aroused by money even as it accumulates unused. This is what characterizes the avaricious miser who will sacrifice almost anything in order to fill his coffers and who hoards rather than uses his wealth. Midas, being foolishly greedy, had to suffer deprivation of love and companionship before he learnt that gold has no intrinsic worth.

In the story of Midas we see also how greed dehumanizes us. As we become preoccupied with evaluating all things, ourselves included, in terms of monetary worth, we lose the ability to see things for what they really are. Beauty, friendship, love, and life experience are assigned economic value. If they cannot be translated into a monetary yardstick they are considered unworthy of our attention. I know an eight-year-old boy who, growing up in a society which venerates wealth, but sensing that it is an inadequate criterion for assessing deeper human values and commitments, tested his father's love for him by asking whether he would give him up for adoption for a million dollars. When the father said that he would not, the boy upped the ante. How about ten million? The father finally succeeded in reassuring his son by telling him that he would not give him up for all the money in the world. "My love for you," he said, "is more important than money and anything that it can buy, even a thousand trips to Disneyworld" (using an example of something the child valued and knew was costly).

J. Philip Wogaman, a Christian ethicist, discusses the distinction which philosophers make between intrinsic and instrumental values.[6] Some things are valued because they are instrumental in acquiring something else. Others are valued in and of themselves. We love our children not as a means to acquiring something other than the experience of love, but because the love itself is important to us, giving meaning and satisfaction to our lives. In the sphere of aesthetics, we enjoy music or art for their intrinsic worth, not as instruments for acquiring some external benefit. In contrast, money, compact disc players, or cameras are valued because of the uses to which they can be put. We value the pictures that the camera takes, the music that the CD player allows us to hear, and the objects or privileges that money enables us to acquire. In our society there is a tendency to treat human relationships and other intrinsic values as if they were instrumental ones, measurable in economic terms. Is this friendship worth cultivating in order for me to advance my career? Perhaps it "pays" to marry this person because of his high income. Religious values are defiled, when, for example, one attends religious services at the Episcopalian rather than the Baptist church only because at the former he will be able to meet members of the business aristocracy who might become his clients or customers. When individuals and institutions become dominated by the motive of wealth accumulation to the point that they ignore, distort, or destroy intrinsic values that inhere in human relationships, they are guilty of the sin of greed. Like Midas, they have transformed spiritual, aesthetic, and humane values into gold, instead of using gold to nurture those intrinsic values.

Avarice is vividly portrayed by Edmund Spenser, the Elizabethan poet. This personified portrait of avarice is a caricature, using well-known images and descriptions of the greedy that had been part of popular medieval religious culture. In it the poet calls our attention to features of this vice which correspond to many greedy people's attitudes and behaviors. The picture is composite and exaggerated, but many of its elements ring true:

> And greedy Avarice by him did ride,
> Upon a camel loaden all with gold:

G r e e d

Two iron coffers hung on either side,
With precious metal full as they might hold;
And in his lap an heap of coin he told;
For of his wicked pelfe his God he made,
And unto hell him self for money sold:
Accursed usury was all his trade,
And right and wrong alike in equal balance weighed.

His life was nigh unto deaths door ypaste;
And thred-bare coat, and cobbled shoes he ware;
Ne scarse good morsel all his life did taste,
But both from back and belly still did spare,
To fill his bags, and riches to compare:
Yet child ne kinsman living had he none
To leave them to; but thorough daily care
To get, and nightly fear to lose his own,
He led a wretched life, unto himself unknown.

Most wretched wight, whom nothing might suffice;
Whose greedy lust did lack in greatest store;
Whose need had end, but no end covetise;
Whose wealth was want, whose plenty made him poor;
Who had enough, yet wished ever more;
A vile disease: and eke in foot and hand
A grievous gout tormented him full sore,
That well he could not touch, nor go nor stand.
Such one was Avarice, the fourth of this fair band.
(*The Faerie Queen*, Book I, Canto IV, Stanzas 27–29)

In this portrait not only does the greedy person accumulate as much gold as he can, but he is constantly counting it. He has made gold his God and has committed all sorts of sins to satisfy his greed, such as the taking of exorbitant interest. The avaricious individual deprives himself of clothing and food, not out of any spiritually motivated ascetic renunciation, but in order to preserve his wealth and compare it favorably with that of others. By day he works himself to exhaustion in order to earn more and more and by night he suffers the anxiety of losing what he has garnered. He does this even though he has neither family nor children to support or to whom he can bequeath his wealth. All in all he leads a miserable life, but is blind to his own wretched state and unaware of the irrationality of his ways. This miserable victim of his own greed is never satisfied, for the more he accumulates the less he feels he has. Although objectively his needs are limited, his lust for money is infinite. He is never psychologically or emotionally fulfilled. Finally, he is sick with the sores of gout which incapacitate him, an ironic and appropriate punishment for his sin, since he cannot enjoy his money even if he would want to.

Spenser's depiction of the greedy sinner emphasizes his miserliness. As we indicated earlier though, pursuit of wealth, and the use of unjust means to acquire it, are often motivated by the desire to spend rather than to save. The hedonist and the spendthrift are greedy not because they want to hoard money but because they want to use it to pursue pleasure. They never seem to have enough to satisfy their pride, lust, or gluttony. Their greed is not love of money for money's sake but rather stems from their inordinate love of the things money can buy.

In the Middle Ages the avaricious person is often equated with the idolater. He is like the Israelites in the wilderness who longed for a god and enthusiastically worshiped a golden calf. So too do the greedy suffer from a misdirected and exaggerated love, directed to gods of this world rather than to the true God. In our age of weakened faith we are especially prone to seeking substitutes for God, and money and what it can buy become foremost among them.

The irrational behavior and the insatiable appetite for harmful worldly goods of the avaricious are captured in a fourteenth-century moralist's vision of five greedy men. One eats sand, another inhales sulphurous fumes, a third consumes fiery sparks, a fourth tries to swallow the entire atmosphere, and the fifth eats his own flesh. Self-destruction is the ultimate consequence of greed.[7]

An interesting behavior related to greed is pathological gambling. Psychologists are still debating the causes of this aberrant, self-destructive behavior. The range of explanations runs from gambling as addiction/illness and hence morally excusable to gambling as an extreme manifestation of sinful greed, subject to the gambler's will and hence morally culpable. In traditional moral literature gambling was a bough of the tree of avarice and the gambler was a grievous sinner. Not only was he totally preoccupied with making money, the money earned in gambling was sometimes considered stolen because the loser didn't

G r e e d

expect to lose and hence hadn't given his full consent to the transaction. The gambler wants to make an easy buck and needs money to support his high level of expenditures on pleasure-producing goods and services. Unlike the greedy miser, the pathological gambler cannot hold on to his money. Either he is spending it on pleasure or on further gambling. It is often difficult to believe how much harm such gamblers will do to their careers, and more tragically to their families, as they sell assets, steal, and gamble away monies that are needed to provide their children's basic necessities. Because the pattern of behavior seems so self-injurious and compulsive, as do some types of drug addiction, some psychiatrists see gambling in a similar light, and are even searching for a physiological "cause" that will account for the syndrome. It is doubtful, however, whether the gambler would continue to gamble compulsively if he were to change his attitude towards the pleasures that he seeks to satisfy with the money that he hopes to win. There might be some gamblers motivated by the thrill of the risk in gambling rather than the actual use to which money can be put. They aren't greedy per se but use gambling to satisfy some other psychological need which could perhaps be satisfied by other high-risk adventures instead. But most gamblers want money in order to spend it, for the prestige it confers, or are too slothful to work hard to earn it. They need a moral remedy to overcome their gambling, which would require a fundamental transformation of their values.

The corrupting effects of greed and gambling are ironically portrayed by Chaucer in *The Pardoner's Tale*. The Pardoner tells of three gamblers who had sworn bonds of eternal friendship to each other in God's name. A messenger of Death tells them of a treasure of golden florins hidden under an oak tree. Afraid to remove the gold by day they decide to wait until nightfall, and in the meantime send the youngest to town to fetch bread and wine so that they can revel in their good fortune:

> As soon as he had gone the first sat down
> And thus began a parley with the other:
> "You know that you can trust me as a brother;
> Now let me tell you where your profit lies;
> You know our friend has gone to get supplies
> And here's a lot of gold that is to be
> Divided equally amongst us three.

THE SEVEN DEADLY SINS

Nevertheless, if I could shape things thus
So that we shared it out—the two of us—
Wouldn't you take it as a friendly act?"
"But how?" the other said. "He knows the fact
That all the gold was left with me and you;
What can we tell him? What are we to do?" . . .
"Well," said his friend, "you see that we are two,
And two are twice as powerful as one.
And look; when he comes back, get up in fun
To have a wrestle; then as you attack,
I'll up and put my dagger through his back
While you and he are struggling, as in game;
Then draw your dagger too and do the same.
Then all the money will be ours to spend,
Divided equally of course, dear friend.
Then we can gratify our lusts and fill
The day with dicing at our own sweet will."
Thus these two miscreants agreed to slay
The third and youngest, as you heard me say.
(p. 272)

No less corrupt than his greedy "brothers," the gambler who went to town decided that he wanted all the gold for himself. So he bought poison, poured it into two of three bottles of wine, and returned to his friends:

Why make a sermon of it? Why waste breathe?
Exactly in the way they'd planned his death
They fell on him and slew him, two to one.
Then said the first of them when this was done,
"Now for a drink. Sit down and let's be merry,
For later on there'll be the corpse to bury."
And, as it happened, reaching for a sup,
He took a bottle full of poison up
and drank, and his companion, nothing loth,
Drank from it also, and they perished both . . .
(p. 272)

G r e e d

The irony of *The Pardoner's Tale* is that the Pardoner who exhorts against avarice is himself guilty of it. He is the prototype of Jim Bakker and other greedy TV evangelists who fraudulently market religion in order to satisfy their own lust for money. The Pardoner appeals to the religious anxieties of his audience:

> Dearly beloved, God forgive your sin
> And keep you from the vice of avarice!
> My holy pardon frees you all of this,
> Provided that you make the right approaches,
> That is with sterling, rings, or silver brooches.
> Bow down your heads under this holy bull!
> Come on, you women, offer up your wool!
> I'll write your name into my ledger; so!
> Into the bliss of heaven you shall go.
> For I'll absolve you by my holy power,
> You that make offering, clean as at the hour
> When you were born . . . That, sirs, is how I preach.
>
> (pp. 274–275)

The sin of greed and what constitutes immoderate pursuit of wealth are closely related to general attitudes towards wealth and poverty. If wealth is morally good then so will be the pursuit of it. If wealth is evil, the pursuit of it will also be evil. There are striking differences in attitude towards wealth between Greek and Roman philosophers, the Hebrew Scriptures, Rabbinic Judaism, the New Testament, Catholicism, and Protestantism.

In his *Nicomachean Ethics*[8] Aristotle discusses the moral virtue that constitutes the right attitude towards money, which he calls "liberality." According to his scheme, virtues are the mean between vices which are extremes of excess and deficiency. Liberality is the intermediate disposition between the vices of prodigality and illiberality. The liberal man uses money wisely. He gives it to the right people, in the right amounts, on the appropriate occasions, and for the right ends. Moreover, he enjoys giving, since, according to Aristotle, virtue is usually pleasant and never painful. The appropriate amount to give is not absolute but relative to the person's resources. Liberal people do not easily become rich because they are not interested in retaining money. They value it not for itself, or the things it can buy, but for uses to which it can be put, particularly through giving it to others. They are indifferent to it in the sense that they do not wish to retain it just in order to possess it. On the receiving end, the liberal man will not accept money from a wrong source or through unjust means.

The vice of prodigality consists of an excess in liberality. The prodigal squanders his money on self-indulgence or gives too much to the wrong people, at the wrong times, and for the wrong ends. He wastes his property in a sort of self-destruction, and because of his need to spend money is always seeking new sources of income, without paying particular attention to whether he is really entitled to the money he receives.

At the opposite extreme is the miser, who suffers from a deficiency in liberality. Aristotle describes various subtypes characterized by this vice, all of whom share the trait of stinginess or niggardliness. They will not part with their money, and some particularly avaricious ones will use any means to acquire money, even if they are unethical or illegal. They do not care about the bad reputation they acquire along with their ill-gotten gains. Zeno the Stoic compared them to "the barren sandy ground of the desert which sucks in all the rain and dew with greediness, but yields no fruitful herbs or plants for the benefit of others." It is mainly these who are referred to in medieval popular devotional literature as the greedy and avaricious sinners.

According to Aristotle, man's natural inclination is towards the vice of illiberality more so than towards the vice of prodigality. He is more sanguine about the possibility of the prodigal's acquiring the virtue of liberality through proper training than of the illiberal or sordidly avaricious person's ability to correct his moral deficiencies.

Thomas Aquinas, too, analyzes the virtue of liberality or generosity and the sins of avarice and prodigality. He distinguishes two ways in which avarice may mean a failure in moderation with regard to material things. The first is that kind of avarice which directly harms one's fellow man, as when one person's accumulation of wealth causes another person to suffer extreme want "since the resources of this world cannot be possessed by many at one time."[9] The second type of avarice refers to man's inner attitude towards wealth. If one has an immoderate love of wealth or inordinately enjoys its possession, he is sinning against himself. Even though this is not a sin against his body, his desires are defiled by his love for money.

Neither Aristotle nor Aquinas condemns the desire for material things per se. It is only the failure of moderation in this desire which is a vice or a sin. It is natural and faultless to desire material things insofar as they are conducive to a proper human objective. In fact, both consider prodigality a vice because the prodigal fails to be properly attached to his possessions—he is irresponsible with respect to money. Aquinas, for whom reason and moderation were elements of moral virtue, does not condemn the pursuit and use of worldly possessions as long as they are in accordance with natural law and for the love of God.

Seneca, the Roman Stoic philosopher, was immensely wealthy and defends the right of a Stoic to enjoy wealth.[10] Wealthy Stoics such as Seneca were criticized as being hypocrites who do not practice what they preach. If, as they taught, happiness and virtue do not depend on externals, and one should be indifferent to the vagaries of fortune, then why should a Stoic acquire and enjoy wealth? By doing so is he not belying his professed indifference? Seneca's elaborate response to these criticisms is strikingly similar to later Jewish and Christian religious teachings enjoining love of mankind, generosity, and a sense of stewardship over money.

Seneca says that he does not consider riches to be a good in themselves and will indeed be indifferent to them:

> being neither cast down if they lie elsewhere, nor puffed up if they shall glitter around me. . . . I shall always live as if I had been born for service to others . . . nothing shall seem to me so truly my possessions as the gifts I have wisely bestowed . . . the wise man does not love riches, but he would rather have them; he does not admit them to his heart, but to his house, and he does not reject the riches he has, but he keeps them and wishes them to supply ampler material for exercising his virtue. . . . In poverty there is room for only one kind

of virtue—not to be bowed down and crushed by it. . . . No one has condemned wisdom to poverty. . . . The philosopher [the lover of wisdom] shall own ample wealth, but it will have been wrested from no man, nor will it be stained with another's blood. . . . Place me in a house that is most sumptuous, . . . I shall not look up to myself on account of these things which, even though they belong to me, are nevertheless no part of me . . . cast me among the beggars; nevertheless I shall not find reason to look down upon myself . . . In the eyes of the wise man riches are a slave, in the eyes of the fool a master . . . the wise man—whoever steals his riches will still leave to him all that is his own; for he ever lives happy in the present and unconcerned about the future. (pp. 151–171)

Lowered self-esteem, depression, and even suicide are frequent responses to loss of employment or reversals of financial fortune. One reason for these responses is that people define their worth in terms of their possessions, and so are unable to put their new situation into proper perspective. Furthermore, having become so attached to their money, property, and standard of living, they suffer intense separation anxiety and grief at their loss. How much better would they be able to cope with their reversals were they to adopt Seneca's attitude towards money! Unfortunately, our society does not cultivate Seneca's values and so we are emotionally devastated by material losses.

In our culture financial success is what confers status and enhances our self-esteem, and many assume that the best motives for success are greed, competition, and hedonism. So our culture nurtures avarice, economic warfare, and a gospel of pleasure. In so socializing our citizens we make them slaves to money. But is this really necessary in order to encourage people to work hard and accrue wealth or to engage in entrepreneurial initiatives? Is it not possible to encourage the generation of economic wealth for the sake of the broad social benefits that can accrue from business and industry? Max Weber points out that initially, at least, greed was not the motive for the highly successful Calvinist capitalistic enterprise, but rather working for salvation and the glory of God through stewardship. Yet for the most part our society relies on vices rather than virtues to fuel the engine of wealth production. I am not discussing here the relative moral value of capitalist versus socialist economic systems, but rather, within the framework of our capitalist economic culture, the role that can be played by altruistic as against selfish motives. Even if the selfish motives of greed and hedonism might be more effective than virtuous ones, and will produce greater economic good for more people, the negative effects of socializing our youth to be avaricious and materialistic will make them less compassionate human beings. Is this not too great an ethical and moral price to pay for the greater socioeconomic benefits that might result from a greed-motivated business culture?

Unlike Seneca, his contemporary Jesus had a much more negative view about wealth and a much more positive one about poverty. The Gospels are replete with celebrations of the poor and condemnations of the wealthy. Jesus says: "I tell you this: a rich man will find it hard to enter the kingdom of Heaven. I repeat, it is easier for a camel to pass through the eye of a needle than for a rich man to enter the kingdom of God" (Matthew 19:24); "No servant can be the slave of two masters; for either he will hate the first and love the second, or he will be devoted to the first and think nothing of the second. You cannot serve God and Money" (Luke 16:13); "How blest are you who are in need; the kingdom of God is yours. . . . But alas for you who are rich; you have had your time of happiness" (Luke 6:20, 24). A somewhat different and ambivalent attitude towards money is expressed in two passages in I Timothy, a pastoral epistle attributed to Paul (though probably not authored by him). The first tells us:

> Those who want to be rich fall into temptations and snares and many foolish harmful desires which plunge men to ruin and perdition. The love of money is the root of all evil things, and there are some who in reaching for it have wandered from the faith and spiked themselves on many thorny griefs. (6:9–10, NEB)

This negative assessment of the love of money and the pursuit of wealth, although not of wealth per se, is balanced by the later passage in which Timothy is told:

> instruct those who are rich in this world's goods not to be proud, and not to fix their hopes on so uncertain a thing as money, but upon God, who endows us richly with all things to enjoy. Tell them to do good and to grow rich in noble actions, to be ready to give away and to share, and

so acquire a treasure which will form a good foundation for the future. Thus they will grasp the life which is life indeed. (6:17–19, NEB)

Whereas Jesus had demanded that his followers give away all their riches and serve God alone, the early Church had a more realistic attitude. Not every convert to Christianity was willing to make such a radical break with his past. Moreover, the Church needed money in order to support itself and its charitable institutions. It was now possible for the rich to enter the kingdom of heaven together with the poor, as long as they had the proper religious attitude towards their wealth. They were to realize that the only true riches are spiritual treasures, and to use their wealth to support their needy co-religionists. It is greed for money that is evil in Timothy rather than lucre being filthy in itself.

Jesus' condemnation of wealth and exaltation of poverty goes against the attitude of the Hebrew Bible and of its Jewish heirs, rabbinic Judaism. The rabbinic contemporaries of Jesus and the early Church inveighed against putting one's trust in money, the social injustice of the avaricious, and the pride and arrogance that wealth too often produces. However, they did not assume that piety goes best with poverty or that wealth inevitably leads to sinfulness. There are many verses in the Torah which declare economic prosperity to be a mark of God's favor. The rabbis' teachings about money focus on the obligation to engage in *tzedakah*—providing liberal support for the poor, with sensitivity not only to their material needs but to their emotional ones as well.[11]

The different attitudes towards money and wealth in the Gospels each found its expression in later Christianity. The ideal of poverty was upheld in the call to the monastic life. But since the Church realized that this was not feasible for all Christians, those who would continue to pursue worldly things were to avoid avarice and practice the virtues of *caritas* (charity) and generosity. Everyone, from rich to poor, was to be guided by the same virtues and vices, each in accordance with his life situation and his means. However, since Jesus had explicitly condemned wealth and embraced poverty, even devotional literature written for the majority who were not expected to be monastics incorporated some of the radical Gospel teachings on the merits of poverty and simplicity. William Langland's popular devotional allegory, *Piers the Plowman,* for example, advocates poverty as the best road to virtue and to God. It provides an interesting contrast to Seneca's opinions about the relationship between wealth, poverty, and virtue. Langland links his praise of poverty with the seven deadly sins. He claims that the rich are more prone to fall into these sins than are the poor. The seven deadly sins cannot dwell for long where poverty is borne with patience. For example, pride reigns among riches, but since the poor man is always eager to please the rich he will be obedient, which is incompatible with boastful pride. With respect to lechery, the poor are not welcome at whorehouses since they have little silver with which to pay the prostitutes and wine and dine them. Langland makes a virtue of necessity and adversity, not without a note of humor in his argument. However, he seriously affirms that voluntary poverty, entered into by someone who could have been rich and influential, leads to bliss. This is because in forgoing property, power, and pleasure for the love of God, man enters into a unique passionate relationship with Him. He who marries poverty and learns patience for the sake of God experiences the deepest, most authentic relationship with the Divine. For Langland involuntary poverty has its benefits in that it makes sin less probable whereas voluntary poverty—casting away one's possessions in order to serve God and not Mammon—confers a spiritual pleasure that far outweighs any material ones. Both kinds inhibit avarice.[12]

Defenses of poverty by religious writers have been seen by some critics of religion as justifications of a stratified social and economic structure in which the rich few lord it over the numerous poor. Here, they say, is the crassest example of religion as an opiate for the masses. However, such a cynical assessment of the religious perspective is unwarranted, although religious teachings about the blessedness of poverty may have reinforced an inequitable distribution of wealth by discouraging initiatives to economic self-improvement. Many religious teachers were themselves not men of wealth nor did they refrain from bitter criticism of the rich and their sins. They emphasized the spiritual benefits of poverty because they believed that God determined who would be rich or poor and that wealth and its pursuit can corrupt. They knew that wealth can desensitize us to the sufferings of the poor. As Jonathan Swift observed, "Nothing is so hard for those who abound in riches as to conceive how others can be in want." They also sought to assuage the pain of the poor. A nonbeliever will not accept the notion that wealth and poverty result from divine will rather than individual effort and social, political, and economic institutions. Even so, many of the religious teachings on the corrupting influence of wealth, the sinfulness of avarice, and the advantages of contentedness and generosity are reasonable, independently of a belief in God. Jeremy Taylor is one of the religious moralists who offers us a useful guide to understanding and overcoming greed.

In his discussion of the Christian virtue of Mercy, Jeremy Taylor includes "Remedies against Covetousness, the third enemy of Mercy."[13] He introduces his remedies by noting that insofar as covetousness is reflected in refusal to give alms it can be corrected by cultivating motives for charity. Insofar as covetousness is reflected in dishonesty it can be corrected by understanding and cultivating the virtue of justice. In addition to these general considerations, he presents more remedies for greed which are ideas that, if reflected upon and internalized, will assist us in our struggle to overcome our avaricious impulses.

Covetousness, says Taylor, in the sense of the selfish pursuit and accumulation of wealth without expending that money on noble enterprises, makes a man miserable rather than happy, as the Midas myth taught. Although Seneca's defense of wealth as making life easier and more pleasant is more plausible than denying any contribution of wealth to happiness, Taylor's point is true in many cases. A common syndrome seen by therapists is the greed-driven executive who is so preoccupied with amassing wealth that in the process he destroys his health, relationships, and values. In the therapist's office he seeks the inner peace, tranquility, and affection that elude him in his race for riches.

Thus, avarice, as we noted earlier, is a paradox. The incessant, selfish search for happiness through wealth often produces misery instead. Taylor's assertion is validated in a psychological study of the relationship between selfishness and happiness in which it was found that the happiest people are those who help others rather than those who focus on helping themselves.[14] Since avaricious people desire riches not in order to help others but to satisfy themselves, they will be less rather than more happy.

Riches can deceive us into thinking that having them we have all.

But riches, says Taylor, do not in and of themselves confer knowledge, skill, courage, chastity, or any other virtue or meaningful personal achievement. Nor do they protect one from vice. Moreover, "no wealth can satisfy the covetous desire for wealth."[15] Riches, therefore, are in a certain sense, the opposite of what they are construed by the avaricious to be—they are useless and unprofitable. In charting our lives we should not lose sight of the difference between means and ends, as the vice of greed has us do. Money may be a useful means to certain desirable ends—but it cannot function as a substitute for those ends. Whether our ends be the cultivation of our personal talents, the enhancement of our knowledge, the nurturing of a warm and loving family, or the improvement of our moral and spiritual state, we must beware lest the apparent attractions of money deflect us from our higher goals. In a study of the psychological and emotional problems experienced by those born into great wealth, many heirs to fortunes said that rather than being happy in their riches they were emotionally hampered by them. Those that were spoiled in their childhoods had no motivation to develop themselves, to accept challenges, to cultivate identities as capable, independent human beings. Their wealth disabled rather than enabled them. Wealth does not inevitably have these adverse effects but we should not assume that it is always desirable. When wealth is not used wisely, which is one definition of avarice, it can generate psychological losses as well as profits.

Riches, says Taylor, can be troublesome. Because we have wealth we seek means to spend it in ways that have little instrinsic value and take up time and energy that could be put to better use. Whereas in Taylor's day it was only the rich who could afford to waste time and energy on conspicuous and unnecessary consumption, nowadays most of us can and do. Our gluttony, lust, greed, pride, and envy are stimulated and serviced by the greed of certain businesses and advertising agencies. These do all they can to create new "needs" and to saturate our environment with products that we could well do without. They tell us that unless we live as lavishly as our neighbors we are inferior to them. Certainly business and advertising perform useful social functions, creating and informing us about useful goods and services. In the process they stimulate economic growth which benefits society. But there are aspects of their activity that have harmful psychological, moral, and social effects. They tempt us to indulge our time, money, and effort on acquiring goods which do little to enhance us morally or spiritually. Studies of advertising reveal that among advertising's profound and inescapable effects are reinforced material-ism, irrationality, selfishness, social competitiveness, and sexual pre-occupation.[16] We are continually exposed to an abundance of consumer goods and made to feel that we need them in order to be sexually attractive, successful, and happy. We get caught in a cycle of greed. Since a product exists we have to earn money to acquire it. Then a new or improved product appears on the market and we have to get that one too. We must read newspapers and magazines for their ads and for their reviews of the merits and costs of each product so that we get the best value for our money. Entire Sunday afternoons can be spent doing this, with many hours during the week devoted to com-parison shopping—all to save a few dollars when buying something we can well do without. We cannot, of course, blame greedy businessmen or advertisers when we succumb to greed and the feverish, foolish hunt for pleasure and material things. They may provide us with the temp-tations, as the devil does in traditional Christian theology, but it is we who engage in the vice and bear responsibility.

Covetousness, says Taylor, is like an illness—to be cured as anal-ogous physical illnesses are cured. From classical times through the Middle Ages, and even today, medical metaphors have been used to describe the vices. Greed was not only a deadly sin but also a deadly disease, most commonly being considered a sort of spiritual dropsy.[17] It is characterized by an insatiable thirst for riches even though one is already filled with them, just as physical dropsy is characterized by an insatiable thirst for water even though the body is already filled with fluid. Physical and spiritual dropsy are similar also in that the more the afflicted person tries to satisfy his thirst, the more his thirst is stimu-lated. The covetous man, who in the midst of plenty pines for more, has also been compared to Tantalus, who though up to his chin in water is forever thirsty. The illness of insatiability cannot be healed by trying to satisfy the avaricious person's appetite. On the contrary, he is to practice simplicity and scarcity. Allowing him to indulge his desire will only exacerbate his illness. Therefore he who wishes to disentangle himself from greed should practice living modestly. This was the les-son learnt by my client who broke away from his avaricious life-style for the simplicity of rural Vermont.

Covetousness of the miserly type, says Taylor, is foolish because the miser isn't willing to benefit from the wealth which he labors so hard to acquire. Moreover, he loves money even more than he loves God and religion, and places his trust in it rather than in God. I suppose that the motto "In God We Trust" was originally engraved on our coins not to deify money, as our society presently does, but for the opposite purpose, to remind us that although we need to use money we should not place our trust in it but rather in God. And like idolatry, greed is a root of evil. "It teaches men to be cruel and crafty, industrious in evil, full of . . . malice; it inquires into our parents' age . . . makes friendship an art of rapine and changes a partner into a vulture and a companion into a thief."[18]

In various contexts we have spoken of the harmful social consequences of greed that go beyond its impact on the personal happiness and morality of the greedy person himself. Yet the social desirability or undesirability of greed is still a subject of intense debate among social scientists, philosophers, and theologians. Some consider greed to be a major source of evil in our capitalist society, as we have illustrated. They argue that socialist cultures and economic systems discourage and control greed and envy and produce more humane and just societies. On the other hand, proponents of capitalism maintain that greed and envy are engines of social and economic progress. They encourage people to work hard in order to produce greater wealth for the society as a whole. In the long run this raises the standard of living for all and results in the greater good for the greatest number of people. Many centuries ago an analogous debate raged within Christianity between the Catholic church and Protestant reformers about entrepreneurship, moneylending, and capitalist enterprise. The former considered these to be manifestations of the deadly sin of avarice, the latter saw them as socially useful and religiously justifiable. Aleksandr Yakovlev, a member of the Soviet Communist party Politburo and a leading architect of the ideological and economic revolution that took place in the Soviet Union in the late 1980s, saw the analogy between the seventeenth-century and the twentieth-century debates. Addressing his critics from within the Communist party who were opposed to radical reform of the Soviet economy from a socialist to a free-market one on the grounds that capitalism breeds and feeds upon avarice, and results in the unfair distribution of wealth, he stated:

> Christ drove out the . . . merchants, intending his religion for the poor. This took place more than two thousands years ago, and only a year and a half ago, several centuries after the reformation, did the Vatican publicly admit that only earned wealth helps to purify the soul and leads to heaven, that entrepreneurship should be encouraged, for it allays the condition of man in this world, provides him with a means for rising up.
>
> Comrades, can it really be that with our scholastic arguments over the market we will repeat this record of being late? (*New York Times*, July 4, 1990)

For the foreseeable future we will continue to live in a capitalist environment in which greed will play a major role. It is incumbent upon us, then, for our own sakes and for the benefit of society at large, that we be ever aware of the dangers posed by greed so that we can at least curb its excesses. If we fail to do so we might be blessed with material wealth but at the expense of poverty of the spirit.

CHAPTER EIGHT

Sloth

Where there is hatred let me sow love,
Where there is despair, hope
Where there is sadness, joy
—FRANCIS OF ASSISI

A recurring anguish patients express to psychotherapists is that they feel no meaning or purpose in life. The loss of meaning can manifest itself in diverse ways. Some experience a general lethargy or lack of interest in formulating and pursuing long-term goals, or in severe cases, even short-term ones. The afflicted individual may neglect his responsibilities, whether to himself, his family, his community or, in the case of religious persons, to God. Feelings frequently associated with this syndrome are guilt and a sense of worthlessness, hopelessness, and sadness. When these feelings reach unbearable levels of intensity the individual may commit suicide.

Some therapists go so far as to consider the loss of a sense of meaning, often associated with a weakening of religious commitments, to be the main cause of much of modern man's unhappiness. Carl Jung tells us:

Among all my patients in the second half of life—that is to say, over thirty-five—there has not been one whose problem in the last resort was not that of finding a religious outlook on life. It is safe to say that every one of them fell ill because he had lost what the living religions of every age have given to their followers, and none of them has been really healed who did not regain his religious outlook.[1]

For Viktor Frankl, the founder of logotherapy, the primary motivational force in our lives is our striving to find meaning.[2] The neurotic is someone who has failed at this task, whether for want of trying or for lack of success. Until he senses that his life experiences, including suffering, or his active endeavors, such as work, satisfy a self-transcending goal, he will be unhappy. Loving and being loved, and alleviating the pain and suffering of others, are especially effective in endowing our lives with meaning and direction.

The melancholy of modernity and the centrality of love and mutual caring as the antidote to pain and despair, are expressed by Matthew Arnold in the poem "Dover Beach":

> The Sea of Faith
> Was once, too, at the full, and round earth's shore
> Lay like the folds of a bright girdle furled.
> But now I only hear
> Its melancholy, long, withdrawing roar,
> Retreating, to the breath
> Of the night wind, down the vast edges drear
> And naked shingles of the world.
>
> Ah, love, let us be true
> To one another! for the world, which seems
> To lie before us like a land of dreams
> So various, so beautiful, so new,
> Hath really neither joy, nor love, nor light,
> Nor certitude, nor peace, nor help for pain;
> And we are here as on a darkling plain
> Swept with confused alarms of struggle and flight,
> Where ignorant armies clash by night.

Sociologists call this widespread anguish of modern life anomie, alienation, or despair. Added to the effect of the weakening of religious convictions is the breakdown of the deep emotional bonds that link the individual to his family and community. The nuclear family has undergone such dramatic stress and change that in many instances ties between parents and children, brothers and sisters, husbands and wives are ruptured. Lacking a sense of concern for anyone else, and without recourse to a loved relative in times of doubt or crisis, life is felt to be a journey no longer worth traveling.

&

It would be a mistake, however, to assume that depression, anomie, or despair are unique to modern man. Loss of meaning, purpose, and hope, coupled with indifference to the welfare of others, have been known for centuries in religious communities as the deadly sin of sloth. In contemporary usage sloth means physical laziness. But physical laziness is a small part of what sloth referred to in the past. The sin of sloth has two components: *acedia*, which means a lack of caring, an aimless indifference to one's responsibilities to God and to man, and *tristitia*, meaning sadness and sorrow. In its final stages sloth becomes despair at the possibility of salvation.[3] It can culminate in suicide. Christian moralists considered the suicide of Judas Iscariot to be a graver sin than his betrayal of Jesus because it signaled his despair at repenting and returning to God and the good.

Sloth, then, is the loss of one's spiritual moorings in life and the ensuing spiritual vacuum manifests itself in despondency, and flight from the worship of God and service to man. St. Thomas emphasized the inner, spiritual state of the slothful, his unhappiness with the divine call to pursue religious and moral virtue.[4] Dante considered sloth to be misdirected love, a preference for the flesh over the spirit. In popular devotional literature, such as *Piers the Plowman*, the emphasis is on the neglect of one's religious obligations, for example, failing to rise early to attend church, to confess one's sins, or to support the needy. Sadness and apathy lead to shirking of responsibility but also result from it.

A related feeling is spiritual aridity or "dryness," a condition of particular concern to mystics. When experiencing aridity the individual has difficulty praying with proper devotion, performing rituals with enthusiasm, and feels painfully distant from God. This state, like sloth, also results in despondency and despair. However, whereas the slothful are not overly troubled by their disinterest in spiritual matters, those who suffer from spiritual aridity yearn for spiritual reinvigoration.

The opposite of sloth is zeal and joy in service to God and in the performance of religious and moral duties. It is not only doing the right thing, but doing it out of love. In the Jewish tradition, Abraham exemplifies this virtue to perfection. In Genesis God tested Abraham's faith by demanding his beloved son Isaac as a sacrifice. Abraham was compassionate and just, and would never willingly sacrifice an innocent child. Isaac was especially precious because he was born after many years of childlessness. Compounding Abraham's pain and perplexity was the fact that God had promised him that through Isaac he would become the father of a great nation. Considering the qualms that Abraham must have experienced, one would expect him to procrastinate. But the Bible tells us that on the appointed day Abraham "arose early in the morning" (Genesis 22:3), setting out with Isaac for the sacred mountain to perform the ultimate act of obedience. This teaches us that the zealous perform God's will with alacrity. Abraham was of course profoundly saddened by the prospect of losing his son, but at the same time he was able to feel joy in doing God's bidding— joy rooted in faith that whatever God has willed for man is best.

A person whose life is not directed by some self-transcending religious or ideological commitment might find little reason to go on in the face of pain, bereavement, loss of wealth or status, or the inability to pursue and experience pleasure. A religious person who had conceived of God as always compassionate, benevolent, and just might react to such misfortune with a loss of faith. Highly distressing in itself, the loss of faith also deprives the sufferer of sustaining consolations. Bereft of psychological support, the sufferer becomes depressed, apathetic, and indifferent. Job's initial cry of anguish after suffering the loss of his family, possessions, health, and, most importantly, his faith in God, is one of the most powerful accounts of this response:[5]

> Perish the day on which I was born,
> And the night it was announced,
> "A male has been conceived!"

S l o t h

May that day be darkness; . . .
May that night be desolate . . .
Why did I not die at birth,
Expire as I came forth from the womb? . . .
For now I would be lying in repose, asleep and
at rest . . .
Why does He give light to the sufferer
And life to the bitter in spirit;
To those who wait for death but it does not
come
Who search for it more than for treasure,
who rejoice to exultation,
And are glad to reach the grave;
To the man who has lost his way,
Whom God has hedged about?
                    (Job 3:1–4, 11, 13, 20–22, JPS)

Job had previously displayed a great sense of responsibility and obligation to friends, family, and the unfortunate. He cared for the poor,
the sick, the widowed, the orphaned, and the enslaved. Thus not only
has God unjustly punished Job, he has also hurt those others whom he
used to serve. Perhaps this inability to act on his good impulses plays
a role in his dejection.

Some depressions seem related to chemical imbalances in the body
or brain.[6] However, even where chemical imbalances play a role in
precipitating depressions, the specific thoughts and attitudes of depressed people are culturally conditioned. The depressive reactions of
two people suffering from the same chemical or hormonal imbalance
but differing in their religious worldviews will be quite different. A
devout individual will interpret what he feels and experiences within
the framework of religious ideas and values; an agnostic will interpret
his experience within a context of religious skepticism. The first might
view his sadness as a punishment for sin, while the second might
accept it as a natural effect of an abnormal physiological condition.

These differing interpretations will lead to different ways of dealing
with depression, which is why psychotherapy must take into account
the belief and value systems of patients. Religious teachings about sin,
and sloth in particular, could be very effective for the believer as

elements in therapy.[7] The agnostic would be responsive to them if he were convinced that they are valid independent of their origin in an allegedly sacred text or church dogma.

Some people with strong spiritual or moral convictions, whose lives are filled with meaning and purpose, can experience "moral burnout." They may, for example, become frustrated in their aspirations to rectify the evil and injustice in society. Although they still value the ideals that energized them in the past, their disillusionment induces apathy and sadness. They give up hope and retreat into sloth.

For certain individuals sloth may also result from the feeling that they are spiritual and moral weaklings, unable to live up to their own ideals. Such a person often comes to feel that since he can't live up to the highest standards of virtue or spirituality, it is futile to aspire to them at all. One client of mine was a rabbi who regularly preached the religious obligation of assisting the unfortunate. For several months his teenage son had been confronting him with the accusation that he didn't practice what he preached. "Why don't we provide room and board in our large suburban home for some homeless, destitute person? How can I respect you when I see you rise to your pulpit every Saturday morning to talk about 'love thy neighbor' when I know that you yourself are ignoring opportunities to do just that?" The rabbi wasn't prepared to open his home to a stranger but agreed with his disenchanted son that this is what a devout Jew would do. He was torn between his authentic commitment to the biblical message and his pain about his failure to live up to it. He was also deeply hurt by the loss of his son's respect and affection. I was able to encourage him to meet his son's challenge part way, by spending more time personally ministering to the neglected and vulnerable elements of his community, and by organizing synagogue programs for them. We discussed the idea that virtue has gradations—it isn't all or nothing. We explored the fear of the stranger and of the loss of privacy which makes it so difficult for most of us to do what his son challenged him to do. I might add that although my client was hurt by his son's accusations he was proud of him as well, for having taken the ethical teachings of Judaism so seriously.

Many depressed people feel that life is meaningless and say that it is therefore not worth living. It is often difficult to know whether these feelings of existential anxiety are the underlying cause of their despondency, or only symptomatic. To dismiss such feelings as surface symptoms which will pass if antidepressants are prescribed or life stresses are ameliorated implies a disrespect for many patients' intelligence and values. Unfortunately, this approach is characteristic of many secular therapists whose theories and methods are unable to respond to the existential anxieties of their clients.

On the other hand, the search for meaning and the alleviation of apathy and anomie has spawned a multitude of bizarre and faddish "therapies," to which many people flock in search of comfort. For example, the New England Center for the Education of Body, Mind and Spirit sponsors a "Dolphin Facilitated Workshop" on the premise that "we have much to learn from [dolphins] and the mystery of their heightened capacity for communication and community. As we open ourselves to participating in this mystery," the catalog continues, "we extend and enliven our own sense of community as humans. . . . Their abiding presence opens our hearts and minds for are we not, indeed, interconnected?" Another workshop, "Shamanic Womancraft" promises that through shamanism, Goddess mythology, tantric yoga, menstrual mysteries, and other female lore, "you can expect to be inspired and come to realize female sexuality as spiritual praxis— and a way to ultimately transform your relationship to all life." There are a host of such workshops based upon Eastern spiritual wisdom, meditative techniques, or occult practices which promise salvation via the appropriation of the mystical insights of non-Western cultures. There is, of course, much of value in Buddhism, Hinduism, or Confucianism which, if properly adapted to our Western consciousness, could improve the quality of our psychological and spiritual life. But the proliferation of superficial and instant therapies is a symptom of our spiritual malaise rather than a cure for it. As Aristotle long ago argued, virtue and its fruit, happiness, are difficult, lifelong pursuits.

ॐ

In contrast to these fanciful fads, our focus is on how the two religious traditions of Judaism and Christianity understand sloth and its opposite, zeal. Sloth is the most explicitly religious of the seven deadly sins. The others, though imbued with theological assumptions, are nevertheless easily comprehended by the most secular among us as vices or significant defects. We can and do define anger, envy, gluttony, pride, greed, or lust without reference to God. Yet notwithstanding the unique religious qualities of sloth, much of what the devotional authors say about it may be useful to both sufferers and therapists.

The special religious essence of sloth is first of all evidenced by the lack of attention to any such vice in the Graeco-Roman philosophical tradition which dealt extensively with the other six deadly sins. Sadness and depression (or *tristitia*) are ascribed to the "disease" of melancholia rather than the realm of moral vice. Only Judaism and Christianity link these phenomena to man's resistance to divinely imposed obligations.

What are these divine expectations of man? We are to love God and worship Him, through prayer and other means. We should be grateful for the gift of life. We should have compassion for fellow humans and extend our hand to those in need. As individuals we are to be scrupulously honest in our personal relationships and in our occupational endeavors, and as communities it is our duty to establish societies governed by just laws. A major obstacle to doing all of these, according to Judaism and Christianity, is our natural inclination to gratify our physical and psychological desires which often conflict with religious and moral responsibility.

This religious conception of man as primarily responsible to others differs radically from a modern secular view of him as a being whose main and legitimate interest is self-preservation and fulfillment through the acquisition of property and the pursuit of pleasure. In recent studies comparing our culture with others, we were found to have the highest individualistic and least collectivist values. Commenting on this American trait, the sociologist Robert Bellah says:

> The individualism that's on the rise recently in the U.S. is one of "What's in it for me?" with immediate gratification of one's needs coming before all other loyalties. Commitments like marriage only hold while they pay off . . . in earlier days the individualism in America was one that also honored community values. Today we have an ideology of individualism that simply encourages people to maximize personal advantage . . . considerations of the common good are increasingly irrelevant. (*New York Times*, December 25, 1990)

In contrast, in collectivist societies, which are often religious, a person's loyalty to his family or group takes precedence over his personal goals. Such societies have among the lowest rates of crime, dysfunctional families, and alcoholism.

These two perspectives—a religious, collectivist and a secular, individualistic—compete in our society, and many people subscribe to a hybrid set of values containing elements of both. Many who espouse the religious/altruistic view spend considerable energy on the satisfaction of their personal desires. Many secular individualists recognize the needs of the less fortunate and direct some of their resources to altruistic ends. Moreover, selfish hedonists often use the rhetoric of altruism to avoid social disapproval, despite the fact that their self-centered actions belie their words. The movie *Godfather III* parodies these two tendencies, as it depicts rapacious mobsters projecting philanthropic concern by establishing foundations to help the needy and religious leaders motivated by greed colluding with criminals. The tension in such hybrid characters at times erupts when the contradiction between these two views pulls the individual in opposite directions. An intense conflict between selfish and selfless values can result in neurosis.

A person who is primarily concerned with satisfying his own physical desires and in achieving wealth or power will often find that care and concern for others are obstacles in his path. In extreme cases such individuals may commit the most heinous crimes. In a brutal case that shocked the nation, it is widely assumed that Charles Stuart, in a deviously calculated scheme, murdered his pregnant wife and their unborn child in cold blood and tried to deflect suspicion from himself by claiming that the assailant was a black man. Stuart had high hopes of opening a restaurant which would make him rich and respected, and apparently felt that his wife and child-to-be were impediments to his greed and pride. From his evil perspective, marked by total indifference to any obligation to others or concern for them, it was proper for him to remove any obstacle to his grandiose scheme, even his own kin. True to the ultimate consequences of sloth, Stuart committed suicide by jumping off a Boston bridge when he learned that his crime was about to be discovered and his hopes shattered. This final act of desperation was not motivated by "normal" feelings of guilt or moral responsibility. He expressed no remorse in the suicide note he left. In the psychiatric community he was cited as an example of the extreme narcissistic personality who is totally engrossed in his own self-interest and self-image (*New York Times*, January 16, 1990). In religious vocabulary he was guilty of sloth, as Judas was, and as was also, the fratricidal Cain, another medieval symbol of sloth taken to its extreme. Cain is the unrepentant sinner who defiantly responds to God's call "Where is Abel, your brother?" with "Am I my brother's keeper?"[8]

That sloth, in combination with other vices, can lead to heinous crime is offered as an explanation for the savage group rape and near murder of a woman jogger in New York's Central Park several years ago during a "wilding" spree. As one analysis put it, "Fueled by anomie, boredom, lust and anger, packs of teenagers have terrorized the northern fringes of Central Park for the last several years. . . . The attack on the investment banker was the result of a night of wilding that 'just got out of hand,' said . . . a friend of one of the suspects, who said he has joined in wilding in the past" (*Boston Globe*, May 3, 1989). Additional motives that account for this behavior are the low self-esteem and envy of the minority youth who perpetrated it. The absence of a sense of moral responsibility and of spiritual purpose creates a vacuum which is filled by the deadly sins and their offspring. *Jacob's Well*, a medieval moral tract, puts it this way—when the devil finds a slothful person, empty and void of good works, he sends the other deadly sins to dwell within him.

Although most of us who experience conflict between our responsibilities and our desires do not murder or rape, we often do harm others. We may insult them, deceive them, or simply neglect and ignore them. Do I spend the evening watching an entertaining television program or do I help my child, who may be having difficulty at school, with his homework? Do I visit a sick friend in the hospital, do I take the time to listen to my spouse's expressions of frustration or unhappiness, do I donate time or money to charity, when it means that I will not be able to do something else that would give me greater personal gratification? And if I do any of these things, are they done begrudgingly, or do I perform them feeling that these simple acts of kindness are the really meaningful moments in my life? If we truly valued good deeds we would perform them joyously.

The religious traditions of Judaism emphasize zeal in doing *hesed* (acts of charity and loving-kindness). A woman I knew well, of very modest means, who had been raised on the principle of *hesed*, would use the limited clothing allowance which her husband was able to provide her to purchase food for the sick and elderly poor. Although she dressed shabbily, she radiated an inner beauty for having been able to help the less fortunate. On Fridays she would trek, by bus, with bowls of soup, chicken, and other Sabbath foods to the old Jewish neighborhood where these elderly poor resided, in order to personally deliver meals to them for the Sabbath. She was uncomfortable when anyone praised her and did not perceive herself as doing anything remarkable.

The Jewish and Christian traditions are permeated with values such as *hesed, tzedakah* (philanthropy and righteousness), love, and charity. Each tradition records accounts of individuals who realized the highest ideals of self-sacrifice in their lives. Preachers used exhortation and anecdote to encourage the faithful to emulate these models. We have no reason to doubt that these religions successfully socialized many people to be zealous in kindness. Our own society, however, though it cultivates zeal in the pursuit of egotistic satisfactions, slothfully neglects altruism. A paradox of sloth is its ability to mask itself in fervid but misdirected activity. In the absence of higher spiritual or moral aims, many people try to alleviate their underlying despair by the avid pursuit of pleasure. They hope thereby to fill their spiritual vacuum. Medieval writers emphasized that spiritual sloth did not preclude zeal and energy in secular matters. One of them compares the slothful to a ravenous, roaming dog, greedily seeking out sin and folly. His mouth hungers for delicacies, his tongue for idle words, his hands for foul things to touch and do, his heart for worldly things to worship, his ears for gossip and slander, his eyes for vanities.[9] But since it is well-nigh impossible to satisfy our natural impulses for lust, greed, gluttony, and envy, zeal in the pursuit of pleasure can never provide satisfaction. When we eventually realize that our desires are limitless and our Sisyphean struggle to satisfy selfish passions leaves us with a spiritually and morally empty life, we mourn our wasted years and grow disconsolate. Because we are accustomed to view depression from a medical rather than a moral or spiritual perspective, we may not even recognize the spiritual roots of our despair.

My clients in therapy frequently express their frustrations. Yet it is rare to hear an adult ascribe his unhappiness to a frustrated desire to do good. Such feelings are more common in idealistic adolescents. The

teenage daughter of a friend was very upset because she wanted to help
the homeless but was prevented by constraints that her parents imposed
upon her out of concern for her safety in the neighborhood where the
shelter was located. When John Milton went blind after an active life
of civic and religious duty, he composed a sonnet "On His Blindness"
expressing not anger but grief at being unable to serve God:

> When I consider how my light is spent
> Ere half my days in this dark world and wide,
> And that one talent which is death to hide
> Lodged with me useless, though my soul more bent
> To serve therewith my Maker, and present
> My true account, lest He returning chide.
> "Doth God exact day-labor, light denied?"
> I fondly ask. But Patience, to prevent
> That murmur, soon replies, "God doth not need
> Either man's work or his own gifts. Who best
> Bear His mild yoke, they serve Him best . . .
> They also serve who only stand and wait.
>
> (p. 190)

The poet consoles himself with the thought that God will not expect
something of him that he cannot perform and that it is possible to serve
God even when incapacitated. Unlike the slothful sinner who resents
having to labor at doing good, Milton was dejected at not being able
to continue his active life of service. Upon reflection he realized that
service can take different forms, and that once he accepted his blindness as God's will, new ways for him to serve would emerge. Many
people shirk responsibility even when healthy and vigorous. To see
opportunities for doing good even in the face of illness is the response
of zeal to sloth.

The sin of sloth consists in our submission to the natural human
tendency to avoid our obligations when they demand effort and sacrifice. This failure often occurs not because we are evil, but because we
take a narrow view of life. If we could fully appreciate the long-term
positive consequences of benevolent behavior for ourselves and for
society, we would overcome the annoyance we feel when in acting

S l o t h

charitably we forgo immediate pleasures. Unfortunately, our popular culture encourages immediate gratification as an ideal. Our children's heroes are athletes, rock singers, or media celebrities rather than scientific researchers, dedicated teachers, or philanthropists, all of whose contributions to society unfold over time.

Analyses of sloth and zeal, in Jewish and Christian devotional literature, provide us with considerable insight into why we avoid doing what we know to be good. They show us how to cast off our moral torpor and make us more sensitive and responsive people.

Moshe Luzzatto, an eighteenth-century Jewish mystic and moralist, discussed lethargy and zeal in his book *The Path of the Just*.[10] According to Luzzatto, even when we know what we must do to save our soul, inherent laziness induces us to avoid action. We then offer excuses to justify our inertia in the performance of God's will. After a while we come to believe our excuses. A rabbinic midrash mockingly describes the rationalizations of the sluggard when he is told that he has an opportunity to study Torah with a scholar:

> They tell the sluggard "Your teacher is in a nearby city, go and learn Torah from him." He responds "I fear a lion on the highway." "Your teacher is in your own city." "I fear a lion in the streets." "Your teacher is near your home." "I am afraid a lion is outside." "Your teacher is in a room inside your home." "I am afraid that if I rise from bed the door will be locked." "But the door is open." "I need a little more sleep."

It is not fear of the lion that causes the sluggard's inaction, but rather his laziness that induces his fear, feigned or real, and his avoidance of duty.

੨੦

This insight is repeatedly confirmed by modern psychologists. We have a remarkable and sometimes dangerous ability to see, hear, and believe whatever is convenient and attractive, even if it is directly contradicted by experience or logic. Some people blame their problems on "bad luck," on "society," or on other individuals. As psychotherapy patients they stubbornly resist facing reality and acknowledging what is obvious to the therapist—namely that to a considerable extent their own actions (or inactions) lie at the root of their unhappiness. The patient's sloth is so deeply embedded in his personality and so distorts his thinking that he actually believes the slender excuses that "justify" his inertia. He even seems to prefer his unhappy state to assuming the more burdensome responsibilities of a productive life.

A patient of mine sought psychotherapy for his periodic panic and anxiety attacks, which occurred when he was in public places or thinking of going to them. He was chronically unemployed and socially isolated. Whenever he took on a job he would quit or be fired after only a few months, because he would inevitably get into an argument with his employer. He developed a pronounced hatred for successful people, blaming them for his unhappiness, to the point of fantasizing about murdering them. In every session he slid into a bitter diatribe against business and government. The man, who had never been married, acknowledged that he had a strong fear of failure and, though in his forties, was still very dependent on his mother for emotional support. She, in turn, benefited from his being unemployed, because he was available to give her attention at all times. She enjoyed her role as the compassionate, nurturing mother. My client did not realize that his panic attacks and his verbal hostility and aggression, which severely restricted his ability to look for a job or maintain one, were being used by him to assure that he remain attached to his mother and avoid a world which he found threatening to his sense of self-worth. The repeated disparagement of others and the projection of blame for his inadequacies onto "them," enabled him to delude himself into thinking that his life was unsuccessful because he was a good person living in a bad world, where he didn't fit. In therapy his defenses were exposed. Like the sluggard's fear of a lion, his fear of driving on a highway to a job interview was not the cause but the result of his avoidance of mature life obligations. As he came to realize this, his ability to overcome his panic attacks improved. Since my client was essentially a humane and sensitive person, who really wanted to do good with his life, I encouraged him to find employment or to volunteer in a social service sector, where it would be difficult to accuse his employers or co-workers of greed and selfishness as he was wont to do before therapy.

Luzzatto was particularly concerned about intellectual sloth, inasmuch as Judaism places a high value on the study and interpretation of complicated and difficult texts dealing with matters of law, ethics, and ritual. Proper mastery of these texts requires a dedicated investment of time and energy, and is a prerequisite for ordination as a rabbi. Responsibility for guiding ordinary people in their religious and personal lives is vested with the rabbi. Therefore sloth in the study of Torah may lead to error and sin, since a student lacking diligence and zeal may misinterpret and pervert the Torah's meaning.

Luzzatto's example has its modern analogue in the revelations about certain scientists who wished to take a shortcut on the path to scientific eminence. They were negligent in their methods and in some cases even falsified data. Several years ago the scientific community was startled by the "discovery" of cold fusion, which later proved to be spurious. The chemist and physicist who had made the "discovery" were at best irresponsible as scientists, if not deliberately deceitful. Intellectual sloth, compounded by greed, envy, and pride, has led some to the crime of fraud and resulted in instances of irreparable harm. For many years a respected psychologist had fabricated evidence in favor of a particular treatment for mental retardation, which became widely accepted, and more effective treatments were not implemented.

ॐ

We will turn now to a consideration of remedies for sloth. Luzzatto suggests several. One of them is based upon the principle we have seen applied to other sins, that our behavior influences our inner dispositions. To acquire a virtue we should simulate the behavior that typically follows from that virtue. Thus one remedy for sloth is to force oneself to behave zealously. With practice one will acquire the trait of zeal. This principle of medieval devotion goes back to Aristotle, who considered moral habits (acquired in early education) fundamental to the cultivation of virtue.

From the perspective of contemporary psychology this precept seems too general. The mere practice of virtue does not always generate a virtuous disposition. However, there are cases where this process may succeed. Until one practices benevolence one does not experience its rewards—the awareness that one has alleviated another's distress, the donor's good feelings generated by the recipients' expressions of gratitude, or the community's approval. Research on altruism confirms that it is strengthened by seeing pain and sadness transformed to joy and happiness. With repetition these effects may cultivate an inner disposition to benevolence. Furthermore, by practicing benevolence we learn to deal with the forces within us that dissuade us from it. Goodness is as much a habit nurtured by practice as it is an attitude. For example, each time we are called upon to contribute to a charitable cause we have a tendency to resist parting with our money. Each time we overcome this tendency we weaken it. Therefore, Maimonides teaches, it is preferable to give alms to the poor repeatedly, even if in small sums, than to give a large sum once. Although the total amount given is the same in the two cases, we acquire the virtue of generosity by repeating generous acts until they become second nature.

There are, of course, numerous cases where virtue does not produce observable benefits. Indeed, as we have noted, it can deprive us of such benefits. Jewish and Christian moralists could fill this void in reinforcement by invoking the rewards and punishments of an afterlife. Luzzatto, in fact, opens with the assertion that the purpose of life on earth is to prepare the soul for an eternal existence in the hereafter. Few secularists today will accept this assertion. Yet most would agree that it is desirable to be remembered kindly after our death. We also live on in our children, which is why we undertake the often painful and frustrating tasks associated with childbearing and parenthood. Shakespeare, in several sonnets addressed to someone whom he deeply admired, appeals to that person to marry and have children so that his (or her) beauty and grace shall live on after death and decay. We also live on in the consciousness of others. In other sonnets Shakespeare says that the poem itself will memorialize the person to whom it is addressed by the very fact that he or she is recalled whenever the poem is read. One sonnet combines both themes with the lines:

> But were some child of yours alive that time,
> You should live twice;—in it, and in my rhyme.

Of course, not only does the subject of his sonnet live on, but Shakespeare himself overcomes death through his poetry.

S l o t h

More importantly we live on by the effects our lives have on others. Hence another incentive for benevolence is the conviction that if we are good the positive effects of our good works will be enjoyed by those who follow us. They will also remember us fondly. These considerations are strong motives for institution building, scientific research and the writing of non-remunerative books. For many people the knowledge that their influence can extend for years and even beyond death is deeply satisfying. One of the great rewards of a devoted teacher is to learn that after many years his students use and appreciate what he taught them and remember him with affection and gratitude. Jewish mysticism teaches that all our acts have cosmic effects. Perhaps this doctrine alludes to the fact that every worthwhile endeavor of ours can initiate a sequence of events whose positive effects reverberate widely and into the distant future. And as a deterrent to malevolence, we should remember that our evil acts also have wide-ranging and long term consequences that often outlive us. Recognizing our power and potential to affect the future should induce us to zeal in doing good.

Devotional writers also appeal to our sense of gratitude to rouse us from sloth and energize us to action. For Luzzatto, the most important consideration for a person to bear in mind who wants to acquire zeal in service is the gratitude he owes to God. All of us, irrespective of our condition in life, have some good for which to be grateful. The poor man has something to eat and the sick man is still alive. The only way we can repay this good is by acknowledging God's goodness and doing His will. Reflection on this will inspire even the slothful to zeal.

The assumption underlying this advice is that life is a precious gift, even a life replete with suffering. Rather than condemn God for the pain and tragedy that might be your lot, thank Him for your very existence. Some people might question the justness of such a God, as Job did, but such an appreciation of life does sustain many people in the most difficult of adversities.

For the religious person today this reflection is very meaningful. For the secularist it is less compelling, particularly if he views life as a chance evolutionary development rather than the product of a divinely guided process. However, many secular people also affirm that to be alive is a gift, whether endowed by God or by nature, and a privilege to be cherished. It follows that just as life is valuable for me it is equally valuable for others. He who would live his life in accordance with this conviction will engage in activities that are life enhancing for others as well as for himself.

The sentiment of gratitude is directed not only to God or to the creative source of life. It should also be directed towards others who make our lives possible and meaningful. It is humbling to consider how dependent we are on the efforts of others, whether they act out of self-interest or on our behalf. The more complex and technologically sophisticated our society becomes, the more dependent we grow on others. Imagine what havoc would occur if we were deprived of transportation, communication, and energy for but a week. Too often we need to experience a disruption of some service, as during a strike or storm, to remind us of how much we owe to others. This interdependence is grounds for instilling a social conscience. I owe it to others to support their needs in appreciation of their supporting mine. Slothful indifference to the needs of others is ingratitude, whereas appreciation of my debt to others should inspire activity on their behalf. How much more so should gratitude inspire care and concern for those who continuously labor for us, such as parents and dedicated teachers. We often hear of a person whose philanthropy was motivated by the feeling that he owed his achievements in life to some person or institution that befriended him in a time of need. Since he could not reciprocate directly, he did so vicariously, by supporting a cause dear to his benefactor. Unfortunately, gratitude as a moral virtue is not emphasized in our culture.

Turning to another Judaic tradition, sloth was of great interest to hasidic teachers of the eighteenth and nineteenth centuries. Of particular concern were the frustrations of devout disciples, who, hard as they might try, were unable to worship God properly, whether in prayer or in deeds. This frustration bred apathy and sadness. The hasidic masters teach that sadness has no intrinsic value and is justifiable only if it is a stage on the path to joy in the Lord. One may be sad or "bitter of soul" as part of remorse over sin. Such sadness can break the barriers that separate man from God, and spur a repentance that will culminate in the penitent's rejoicing in God's salvation. However, even though such a sadness has spiritual benefits, it must be carefully regulated. The hasid should allow himself to experience it only at self-designated times, and as a result of rational analysis of his sins. Instances of sadness and despair not associated with repentance are inappropriate. If sadness is caused by problems of health, family, or livelihood, the hasid must learn to accept this affliction with joy. He must believe that misfortune is only an apparent evil whose concealed good will eventually be revealed.[12] Sometimes hasidic disciples were deeply troubled by "impure" thoughts and desires. Their masters told them to consider that ideas and impulses are not more than that—the hasid should be happy that his behavior has remained pure.

One need not be a hasid in order to apply similar notions to sadness and despair that result from a dissatisfaction with one's spiritual life. A person who feels spiritually unhappy because he has lost hope of ever achieving his spiritual goals will be comforted if he realizes that it is better to aspire to virtue and fall short than not to aspire at all. The Talmud teaches that a man's merit is measured by his good intentions and efforts. Some idealists become frustrated because they feel their attempts to alleviate suffering or rectify injustice are futile. Regardless of their accomplishments, they see how evil and suffering still abound. In response to such a mood of dejection Rabbi Tarfon, a second-century sage, taught, "the day [life] is short; the task is great; the workmen [human beings] are lazy; the reward is great, and the Master is insistent. . . . You are not called upon to complete the work, yet you are not free to evade it."[13]

Another worthwhile reflection to combat sloth is that, although one's efforts might not have a broad social impact, from the perspective of the individual who has been helped, you have done a world of good. Judaism teaches that whoever saves a single individual is considered as if he saved an entire world, and conversely, whoever destroys a single individual is considered as if he destroyed an entire world. Our democratic tradition, too, affirms that every individual is precious and significant. If so, then my efforts on behalf of even one person who needs me can endow my life with significance. Many parents of a handicapped child devote their lives to the loving care of that child. In so doing they sacrifice their own freedoms and pleasures. Numerous husbands and wives patiently tend to the needs of an incapacitated spouse out of love, gratitude, or a sense of duty, at great physical and psychic cost. For the most part these people will attest that their zealous devotion to the person in need invested their lives with profound meaning.

Devotional writers assume our ability to overcome the emotions of sloth—lethargy, indifference, sorrow, and despair—and our responsibility to do so. Although they understand that events can generate these emotions, they do not absolve us from controlling them. They teach us to ponder religious ideas that will change our feelings. Today's cognitive therapists agree that depressive moods can respond to reflective self-evaluation. For example, Aaron Beck's cognitive theory and treatment of depression focus on teaching a depressed person to change his assumptions about events and himself. By doing so he can often dispel sadness and lethargy.[14]

Another approach to overcoming despair is behavioral. Hasidic masters teach that one can induce joy by dancing and singing. Because one is supposed to approach God joyously, hasidic groups incorporate dances, songs, and melodies into prayer, when communication with God is most direct. These songs and dances, which are performed with fervor, often succeed in overcoming sadness and apathy. Since prayer and celebration are frequent activities in the life of the hasid, they are significant in uplifting his overall mood. The strength of melody, song, and dance in combating sloth is enhanced because it is integrated with a religious and spiritual ideology. The hasid sings and dances to words expressing spiritual messages and aspirations.

Can such a technique be used today as an antidote to sadness? Music is a powerful stimulus for affecting mood, and is used very effectively in film soundtracks and music therapy. I often prescribe music as a relaxant for anxiety and stress. Choral singing is therapeutic for many people, particularly when the qualities and lyrics of the repertoire induce hope, optimism, joy, and a celebration of the good. Although music, which is ephemeral, cannot dispel spiritual apathy or despair for long, it can be a useful adjunct to a value-oriented treatment of depression, if the music reflects the values being addressed in therapy.[15]

The Christian view of sloth as a grave sin originated in Egyptian monastic desert communities of the fourth and fifth centuries. Originally it referred to the fatigue, boredom, and listlessness frequently experienced at midday by monks in their cells. In their torpor they would experience "evil" thoughts that made them want to flee their monastic life. In later centuries, these thoughts were merged with sadness at having to do the will of God, and became one of the seven deadly sins to which all people, not only monastics, are subject. St. Thomas Aquinas teaches that sloth can be sinful in two situations: when we are sad about having to do what is spiritually good or so sad over our sins that we are prevented from doing good. Unlike sins such as lust or gluttony which can be avoided by fleeing temptation, according to Aquinas the remedy for spiritual apathy is to resist it by thought—"the more we think about spiritual goods the more delightful they become to us, and spiritual apathy goes away."[16] This foreshadows a relatively new technique of therapy, the systematic use of mental imagery and meditation to evoke scenes that will help achieve therapeutic goals. Nowadays the technique is used primarily in relaxation training and in the treatment of phobias. Aquinas is suggesting such a technique in the service of spiritual goals. Reflecting upon the benefits of virtue will generate emotions to dispel sadness and apathy and energize us to pursue virtue.

Using Aquinas's principle, St. Ignatius of Loyola and others developed spiritual exercises which include silent devotions, meditations, and focused contemplation on episodes from the life of Jesus or his teachings.[17] These exercises generate desirable religious feelings and behaviors in the devotee. In contemplating scenes from the life of Jesus one should imagine seeing Jesus and the various saints and apostles, with the aim of drawing some spiritual fruit from the imagined experience (p. 72). Ignatius suggests, for example, mental representations that alms-dispensers should use to ensure that they will distribute charity to the needy objectively, untainted by their own self-interest. One should imagine how a saintly man would distribute the monies entrusted to him, if his sole motivation were the greater glory of God and the further perfection of his own soul. Having imagined the rules of action in giving alms that such a disinterested person would follow, the alms-dispenser should do likewise. He should also imagine himself at the point of death and again, at the Day of Judgment, reflecting on how he would have ideally fulfilled his alms distribution responsibilities during his lifetime (p. 135). Such contemplations of future situations will enable him to overcome sinful inclinations he may now have, to neglect or abuse his status and power. Such techniques, designed to encourage altruism, can be adapted to modern use by therapists, teachers, or other who want to inculcate virtuous behavior. Perhaps political leaders deciding whether or not to go to war should be required to imagine in vivid detail the consequences of their decisions.

We invest more resources in trying to satisfy our self-centered goals than in enhancing our humaneness. Although many compassionate people contribute to human betterment, our society's preoccupation with self-gratification drowns out their efforts. To a superficial observer we may appear energetic, creative, and resourceful—the very opposites of sloth. However, as we noted earlier, this zeal in pursuit of wealth, status, and pleasure often conceals a widespread indifference to ultimate meaning, self-transcendence, and social responsibility.

Cotton Mather, the seventeenth-century Puritan preacher, applied New England ingenuity to the spheres of piety, morality, and ethics. In his *Bonifacious: An Essay upon the Good*, he encourages us to be as creative and ingenious in our religious and ethical lives as we are in our business endeavors. We should apply our wits to the pursuit of good deeds with the same methodical planning that the devil employs to ensnare us in evil. Slothful indifference to charity and good works must be countered by specific "devices" or stratagems for living righteously and helping others. Although Mather's ideas are formulated within a Calvinist theological framework, many of his "devices" can be adapted to modern use by all people, Christian or otherwise.

Doing good is self-rewarding. We should be grateful for opportunities to engage in benevolent acts, since it is through them that we become most God-like. Indeed, the devout Christian delights in such opportunities because they enable him to respond to the purpose for which he was created. Those who truly feel this way will even go so far as to pay others to apprise them of opportunities to do good.

Today we pay consultants for financial, psychological, or educational advice. We should be no less willing to pay consultants for advice on how to lead virtuous lives. We do so to a limited extent when we support clergy or scholars trained in analyzing the moral and ethical aspects of major medical, commercial, or military decisions we have to make. When it comes, though, to the moral challenges of everyday life, there are few people to whom we can turn. Some psychiatrists and psychologists feel that in our secular society it is the psychotherapist who is becoming, perhaps by default, an arbiter of our values. Unfortunately, there is little evidence that therapists are more attuned to virtue than are their clients.

Mather tells us to be continually aware of our failure to alleviate the misery in the world. Paradoxically, it is usually those who do the most good who are acutely aware of how much remains undone and who feel responsible for doing more. We spend much time and thought devising ways to enjoy food, clothing, and travel, to succeeding in business and other secular matters. Shouldn't we invest at least as much in activities that will elevate our souls? Today's newspapers carry special sections on sports, business, science and technology, health, food, home care, hobbies, fashion, arts and entertainment. But there are no regular sections devoted to spiritual and ethical improvement, although occasional feature articles will appear. Our social priorities are thus quite clear: we are bored by moral questions.

Mather reminds us that when Jesus wanted to encourage zeal in service to God he chose as his example the unjust steward, who is a symbol of wickedness. This is because it is much more common for people to be vivacious of spirit in performing illegal actions than lawful ones and the parable of the unjust steward would be easily understood. But why, says Mather, shouldn't we approach doing good with the same vigor and intelligence that the wicked employ in their evil arts? After all, the rewards of doing good far outweigh the fruits of evil.

We all have abilities we can use to help others but do not. At times we are not aware of our talents because we have not examined ourselves sufficiently. Although we may have great riches we behave as if were poor. Psychology has developed tests that reveal our interests and abilities, which we use for vocational guidance. However, they should also be used for moral guidance—to apprise us of how we can best use our aptitudes to serve those in material or emotional need. In Chaim Potok's novel *My Name Is Asher Lev*, a devout and artistically talented Jewish teenager is more interested in drawing and painting than in studying Torah, which deeply upsets his father. The hasidic rabbi whom he consults realizes, however, that there is more than one way to serve God, and that Asher will better serve God and man by following his artistic inclinations than by attending the yeshiva. To deny our talents or fail to use them for doing good is to squander moral opportunity.

Mather proposes that we set aside a specific time, to ask ourselves the question "What is there that I may do, for the service of the Glorious Lord, and for the welfare of those, for whom I ought to be concerned?" (p. 32). After considering this question, we should resolve to undertake specific actions and immediately record our resolutions in writing. We should periodically review our notes to see if we have implemented what we resolved to do. Regular moral accounting will energize us to do those things which we know in our hearts and minds we should do, but which in our sloth we avoid or neglect. Moreover, we will find that the more we think about and perform good deeds, the more we discover new opportunities to do good. For example, as a friend of mine who manages a charitable family foundation has become deeply involved in her work, she has found herself considering philanthropic projects worthy of support which she had never thought about before.

Devotional writers tried to harness the power of the group to influence the individual towards spiritual ends. Mather proposes the establishment of societies of a dozen or so associated families to meet every few weeks in each other's homes to provide mutual encouragement in serving God and doing good. One of the primary purposes of such family societies is to assist each other and the community at large in times of affliction and temptation. The society will consider who in the community is experiencing any special adversity and what can be done to alleviate their plight; what disputes have arisen in it and how the society can help reconcile the antagonists; and what inappropriate (sinful) behaviors are being engaged in by individuals and how may they be properly admonished so that they will desist from sin.

The past decade in particular has witnessed an explosive growth in support groups to help individuals cope with a multitude of problems encountered in life, from AIDS to zoophobia. Most people who join these groups are looking for ways to help themselves, although in the process they may also help others in the group. However, few groups are organized with the primary purpose of helping others, whether materially or morally. Even the modern forerunner of support groups, Alcoholics Anonymous, is essentially a self-help group run by alcoholics (or "former" alcoholics) to help themselves and other alcoholics. There are relatively few individuals not afflicted by adversity who group together to assist those who are so afflicted, which is the kind of small group that Mather is proposing. There are of course many philanthropic organizations in the voluntary sector, and government too plays a major role in "doing good." However, only a small percentage of our population is directly involved in such groups. Doing good is left to those professionals or volunteers who specialize in it, and we relinquish our individual responsibility to engage in acts of loving-kindness. This depersonalization of caring, benevolence, and charity desensitizes us to the needs of others and we become less humane as a consequence.

Although all people share the obligation and opportunities to do good, those with financial resources are particularly well placed to have a broad societal impact. Therefore, Mather devotes a special chapter to "Rich Men." If the values he advocates were internalized by all those of means in contemporary society, we would witness a remarkable alleviation of suffering.

The fundamental premise we should adopt is that whatever riches we have are to be used in the service of God and man—we are God's stewards. The only good aspect of wealth is doing good with wealth. According to a recent study, Americans donate about 1 percent of their income to charity, considerably less than the 10-percent tithe advocated by Judaism and Christianity.[18] Mather considers a tenth to be the minimum rather than the maximum amount that one should give to worthy causes. He tells of merchants he knew who decided upon a preset value as adequate to meet their needs and resolved that any additional income they earned would be devoted to pious uses. These merchants continued to engage energetically in business and trade long after they had amassed the sum they had preset for their personal use. The purpose of their continued commercial activity was to use their talents to earn more money in order to be able to do good with it. Our society would be much more compassionate if we were to adopt Mather's motive for generating income rather than the motives of accumulating power and achieving status.

In our discussion of sloth we have seen how Jew and Christian alike preached the virtue of zeal for the good and remonstrated those afflicted by spiritual apathy and despair. By becoming sensitized to the sin of sloth, we may be moved to lead lives of *hesed* (acts of loving-kindness) and *caritas* (love and charity). In so doing we shall find our lives invested with heightened meaning and purpose.

Sin and Responsibility

I held it truth with him who sings
To one clear harp in divers tones,
That men may rise on stepping-stones
Of their dead selves to higher things.
—ALFRED, LORD TENNYSON,
"In Memoriam"

The differences of opinion expressed by a judge, district attorney, and defense attorney in the trial and sentencing of a convicted criminal in New York illustrate the conflicting assumptions that characterize discussions of sin, responsibility, and punishment. They exemplify the difficulties we face when we try to ascribe responsibility for sins and crimes and determine appropriate remedies or penalties for them:

The Brooklyn District Attorney said yesterday that she may appeal a judge's decision to give five years' probation to a Chinese immigrant convicted of bludgeoning his wife to death with a hammer.

The judge said he did not treat the man more harshly, in part, because of testimony that Chinese attitudes toward adultery helped explain the crime.

The case . . . raised questions about a legal argument that cultural factors can relieve people of responsibility for violent behavior.

"There should be one standard of justice, not one that depends on one's culture," said the District Attorney. "I am deeply concerned by the statement that a man's cultural background should excuse him from serving a jail sentence."

The judge . . . said yesterday that he considered several factors—including cultural background—in giving [the defendant], 51 years old, the minimum sentence on a manslaughter conviction. Other considerations were his lack of a record, his remorse, his meek behavior during the year and a half he spent in jail awaiting trial and the unlikelihood that he would commit another crime.

But [the District Attorney] said sentencing should reflect "the seriousness of the crime, and the deterrent impact of the sentence."

In a nonjury trial last December, [the judge] found [the defendant] guilty of second-degree manslaughter, after reducing a charge of second-degree murder. [The defendant] had confessed to killing his wife . . . after she had admitted to him that she was having an affair with another man.

On September 7, 1987, after confronting her in their Brooklyn bedroom about their own sexual relations, he went to the next room, collected a hammer and then beat her eight times in the head, causing five skull fractures.

Legally, the lesser manslaughter charge means that [the defendant] did not intentionally kill his wife. His court-appointed lawyer . . . argued that the overwhelming sense of shame and humiliation brought on by his wife's adultery had put [the defendant] who had emigrated from Canton, China, in 1986, in a frame of mind where he was no longer in control of his actions.

To buttress his point, [the attorney] used an expert witness . . . an anthropology professor at Hunter College, who testified that in China, adultery is an "enormous stain," which reflects not only on the aggrieved husband, but "is a reflection on his ancestors and his progeny."

The defense argued that given the close-knit Chinese community, such private matters would have inevitably become public, making [the defendant] a pariah.

[The judge] said . . . that he had been "very impressed" by the testimony on [the defendant's] background. "I was convinced that what happened at that time was because he had become temporarily, totally deranged," said [the judge]. "I didn't feel that he had formed an intent to murder."

"He was the product of his culture. . . . The culture was never an

Sin and Responsibility

excuse, but it is something that made him crack more easily. That was
the factor, the cracking factor." (*New York Times*, April 5, 1989)

The emotions and behavior of the defendant in this case could be
analyzed from the perspective of anger, pride, and lust. How is one to
restrain one's anger when one's pride has been injured or one's lust
been frustrated?

What is of interest, however, from the perspective of freedom, determinism, responsibility, and punishment, are the different assumptions made by the three legal experts about these issues and the
inconsistency in the judge's analysis of the defendant's actions. If he
was totally deranged at the time he committed the act, and it was his
cultural background that caused his derangement, then why isn't his
culture an excuse? And if he was totally deranged, even if only temporarily, then why hold him guilty of a crime at all, even the lesser
charge of manslaughter? Would the judge have decided differently if
the defendant had been living in the United States for ten years, and
so been exposed to the different values of American culture with respect to adultery? On the other hand, what would the district attorney say if the defendant had been raised in a culture (of which there
are some) in which it is a moral duty for a husband to kill an adul-
teress? Would cultural considerations still be irrelevant in considering guilt and punishment? Part of the reason for the different views
is because a good part of the debate seems to be about whether or
not the defendant's behavior was inevitable under the circumstances.
If it was not inevitable, then we should punish him more severely
(the district attorney); if it was inevitable then we should not punish
him at all (his defense attorney); if it was partially inevitable (whatever that may mean), then we should be lenient in our punishment
(the judge).[1] Perhaps a more useful question to ask is: How should
we treat the defendant so as to deter him or others like him whose
wives commit adultery from assaulting and killing them? Of course,
the present legal system and legal theory do ask these questions too,
but the focus of their concern is more often on the "degree of in-
evitability" question. We will return to the question of free will, determinism, blame, and guilt after we compare and contrast Jewish
and Christian views of the nature, purpose, and responsibilities of
man with secular views.

We have studied the seven deadly sins in order to learn from the moralists what is useful for all who would like to lead better lives, morally and emotionally. We have also called upon psychologists and psychiatrists to be more open to moral thought in their professional practice. Although we have centered our interest on the seven sins, the moral literature discusses with equal discernment many other sins and vices, such as hatred, cruelty, callousness, deceit, slander, self-righteousness, and obstinacy. Uncompromising rigidity, for example, is a sure source of friction between a husband and wife, while slander and gossip permeate society and the press.

In addition to the specific causes, nature, and effects of each vice, the moralists were concerned with the purpose of man's existence and his proper relationship to the world. In order to fully appreciate the teachings of religious and classical moralists, we should understand their general views of man, his meaning and his obligations.

According to Judaism and Christianity, God has endowed man with unique, divine-like qualities which differentiate him from all other created beings and confer on him special privileges and obligations. Man should be aware of his unique status, but his consciousness of being superior to other creatures must be tempered by the realization that he owes his superiority to God's grace, not his own powers. Moreover, when he reflects on God's omnipotence he will have no cause for arrogance, since compared to God he is as naught.

The world which God has created and over which he has made man the master is essentially good and it is man's responsibility to maintain its goodness. Therefore, man must not be apathetic to evil, whether in himself or in others. Moreover, we must constantly strive to improve ourselves and help our fellow man do the same.

Modern secularism has a radically different view of man. The differences between man and other animals are products of evolution. Man's unique achievements such as language, reason, art, culture, technology, and morality can be explained naturalistically, without reference to God.

What are the implications of the secular view for man's sense of responsibility towards himself and others? If man is only a sophisticated animal without any divine-like qualities, why should we have any special interest in his welfare or reverence for his life? The religious view that man is created in the divine image restrains his aggression, whereas the secular one has weakened traditional moral and ethical restraints on aggression. Nevertheless, this does not prove it wrong. Secularists, however, need to develop theories that confer dignity, meaning, and morality on life as do religious beliefs. If they fail to do so, human society can degenerate into exploitation of the weak, violence against those with whom we differ, and even indiscriminate mass murder as did nazism, Stalinism, and Maoism, all secular ideologies.

Unlike Judaism and Christianity, secular psychologists and other social scientists adopt a relativist ethic. Good and evil are those things that any society approves of or condemns, and vary from society to society. They eschew notions of absolute values, be they based upon divine revelation, natural law, or rational analysis. Such an ethic has made it difficult to establish agreed-upon norms for interpersonal behavior, especially in our pluralist society. This makes the therapeutic endeavor difficult for a therapist who accepts the basic thesis of this book that psychotherapy is a moral enterprise. Hopefully our discussions of the vices have eased the psychotherapist's ambivalence by showing that many values can be shared by religious and nonreligious alike on rational and psychological grounds.

Classical and medieval moralists thought of man as having a body and a soul. The most popular view of the soul was a neo-Platonic dualist one in which the soul survived the body and could continue to experience pleasure and pain in an afterlife.

The soul concept endowed life with a meaning that transcended man's mortality. Belief in an immortal soul endowed even a life of travail and misery with significance and purpose. This belief is a powerful consolation when one has lost a beloved child, parent, or spouse. The grief-stricken mourner believes that his soul will be reunited with the deceased and this eases the pain of separation and loss. It also compensates for the apparent lack of justice in this world, as the wicked who prosper now will suffer later and the just who suffer now will prosper in the hereafter.

The belief in an immortal soul continues to be strong in many traditional Jews and Christians. Therapists who see religious patients must be aware of the functions that this belief serves in their lives and be prepared to anticipate emotional problems that may arise if it is called into question. Since secular psychotherapy has little to offer as an alternative to the consolation of religious belief in times of grief, or its hopefulness in periods of despair, it should not cavalierly destroy what it cannot replace.

Religious teachers used belief in an immortal soul to control the behavior of adherents, by promising rewards in the afterlife to those who lived virtuously and threatening punishment for succumbing to vice. Vivid, terrifying images of suffering in Gehenna or hell enhanced the effectiveness of the threats. Dante's Hell and Purgatory sections of his *Divine Comedy* describe punishments tailored to specific sins that souls undergo. Hieronymus Bosch painted grotesquely powerful pictures of the terrors of hell experienced by sinners. Although we may not be as worried as the medievals were about what will happen after death, the theological matchings of punishments to vices, which are the basis of these works of art, are psychologically astute. Punishments aren't arbitrary. They reveal the essence of sin and vice, and purge the soul of its defects by acting as remedies for flaws of character.

૨૦

Religions invest human existence with meaning by establishing goals and value systems that apply to all aspects of a person's life. These integrate disparate experiences and transform mundane and even painful experiences into satisfying ones. In rabbinic and medieval Judaism everything one does should be "for the sake of heaven." In Christianity one is to "bear witness with one's life" or act for the "glory of God." Religions provide standards which the individual can use to assess the worth of his life.

Joseph Karo, the sixteenth-century Jewish mystic and jurist, formulates the unifying end towards which all Jews should direct their activity:

Our sages have said "All your deeds should be for the sake of Heaven." Even permitted activities such as eating, drinking, walking, sitting, standing, sexual intercourse, conversation, and all of the needs of your body should be performed in the service of your Creator or towards something that will enable you to serve Him. (*Shulman Arukh, Orah Hayim*, section 231)

Since the ideals religion establishes are usually difficult to live up to, devout individuals experience life as a struggle and as a journey towards a distant and desirable end. Such a system also produces guilt when one perceives himself as failing to live up to the expectations of the religion or as incapable of ever succeeding by his own efforts. This sense of failure can be followed by intense spiritual joy if the sinner repents or experiences the grace of God.

Most religious Jews and Christians do not live up to the ideal of directing all their energies to the love of God. However, the aspiration to do so provides them with a unifying purpose in life which so many secularists lack. Religion is "catholic" in its embrace of all of life, and provides man with a clear focus on goals and ends. In contrast, secular man is fragmented and blinded by his freedom from God and authority. But his freedom from one master, God, makes him all the more vulnerable to enslavement by many gods, particularly his own passions and vices. The religious anxiety about failure to do God's will is replaced by a host of lesser anxieties, centered on failure to satisfy one's many desires. The secular person lacks a coherent framework by which to organize and evaluate all facets of his existence. This lack of an all-encompassing life goal and of an unambiguous standard of conduct is a major source of contemporary unhappiness. This does not mean that religion is "right" or feasible for someone who does not believe in God, or in the dogmas of Judaism or Christianity. But the fact that secularism is unwilling or unable to address these needs is one of its main shortcomings from a psychological point of view.

We will now turn to the subject of free will, essential to any discussion of sin and responsibility, as we saw in the legal case analyzed at the beginning of this chapter. The moralists' appeal that we restrain our impulses and control our behavior assumes that we are able to do so. In their final analysis we choose whether or not to sin or indulge our vices. This belief in the freedom of our will is central to traditional

THE SEVEN DEADLY SINS

Jewish and Catholic (but not all Protestant) concepts of sin. The idea that man is free to choose between alternative courses of action, and is responsible for his behavior has, however, an influence far beyond religion and theology. It is an assumption widely shared in our culture and permeates our legal system. It influences how we evaluate ourselves and others, and how we socialize our children.

We are most conscious of choosing when we are faced with conflicting goals or moral dilemmas. We weigh the different sides of a situation and anticipate the consequences of choosing one alternative over another. It is difficult for us to imagine ourselves as anything but freely choosing agents of our actions. When an individual violates a social, religious, or legal norm, we ascribe moral or legal guilt on the assumption that he could and should have done otherwise.

One traditional formulation of this belief in human freedom is that of Maimonides, which is very similar to the way in which Aquinas understands free will:

> Free Will is bestowed on every human being. If one desires to turn towards the good way and be righteous, he has the power to do so. If one wishes to turn towards the evil way and be wicked, he is at liberty to do so. And thus is it written in the Torah, "Behold, the man is become as one of us, to know good and evil" (Genesis 3:22)—which means that the human species had become unique in the world—there being no other species like it in the following respect, namely, that man, of himself and by the exercise of his own intelligence and reason, knows what is good and what is evil, and there is none who can prevent him from doing that which is good or that which is evil. . . . Accordingly it follows that it is the sinner who has inflicted injury on himself; and he should weep for, and bewail what he has done to his soul—how he has mistreated it.
>
> If God had decreed that a person should be either righteous or wicked, . . . or if there were some force inherent in his nature which irresistibly drew him to a particular course, . . . how could the Almighty have charged us through the prophets: "Do this and do not do that, improve your ways, do not follow you wicked impulses," when, from the beginning of his existence his destiny had already been decreed, or his innate constitution irresistibly drew him to that from which he could not set himself free? . . . By what right or justice could God

Sin and Responsibility

punish the wicked or reward the righteous? (*Mishneh Torah, Laws of Repentance*, Chapter 5)

This view of human freedom and responsibility has been challenged on theological, philosophical, and psychological grounds. For the determinist the causes of human behavior are not reason or acts of a "will," but biological, emotional, or social factors over which the individual often has little or no conscious control. Our legal system realizes that the premise of free will goes counter to much of human experience and our sense of what is just. Most of us too, in our individual lives, though affirming our freedom and that of others, frequently become aware of the inadequacies of the free-will doctrine to account for all behavior. Even Maimonides and Aquinas qualified their use of it. In effect, religious teachings about choice and accountability, legal theories about crime and responsibility, and our beliefs about the psychology of everyday behavior assume both free will and a measure of determinism.

What are some of the objections to the free-will model? One is that it is incompatible with a belief in God's omniscience. If God knows today what I will do tomorrow, as most medieval theologians asserted, then I cannot contradict His foreknowledge. Therefore, although I feel that I am free when I act, in reality there is only one course of action open to me, the one which God has foreseen.

Another objection to free will is based upon belief in causality. If all natural events are preceded by a cause or causes, and man is part of the natural order, his behavior too is caused. Where then is his free will? If you assert that his behavior is caused by his willing it, what caused the willing? If you respond that his willing was caused by (was a consequence of) his prior reasoning, as Maimonides and Aquinas seem to suggest, then the determinist will assert that there must be causes that made the individual decide the way he did. Whatever causes explain each earlier step in the sequence of events must have been preceded by other ones, ad infinitum. We may not be able to specify the actual causes in the sequence that culminated in an action, but if we accept the principle of causality, then we have to reject the possibility of free will on logical grounds.

A third argument is based upon the fact that much behavior, including moral choices and criminal acts, can be predicted with a high degree of certainty. There are significant correlations between what we think, feel, and do and our biological endowments and environmental histories. We are what we are by virtue of our genes and psychology, childhood experiences, cultural milieus, economic forces, and religious or political beliefs. The ability of social scientists to predict and control much of human behavior, thought, and feeling is a strong argument against the notion that man acts freely.

It is not the free-will model but determinism which dominates scientific conceptions of man. Thoughtful psychologists and social scientists know that there will always remain significant domains of human behavior that are unpredictable and beyond external control. The number of factors that influence us are large and their interactions complex; there are also practical and ethical limitations on studying them scientifically. However, the scientific advances of the twentieth century, based upon determinism as a working model of human nature, have vastly increased our ability to predict individual and group behavior. So it is reasonable, psychologists say, to assume that the determinist model is more accurate than the free-will one. The adoption of a determinist model has profound implications for our notions of sin, vice, crime, responsibility, guilt, blame, and punishment.

Maimonides and Aquinas would say to the determinist that the debate between them is in part semantic rather than real. We do not mean by freedom of the will that man's acts are uncaused. On the contrary, we who speak of the temptations of the flesh, the devil, or the evil inclination, of how differences in individual temperament, knowledge of Scripture, or the company we keep affect us, are acutely aware of how man's behavior can be influenced by biological and social factors. However, we believe that man has been endowed with reason and will. He is capable of using his rationality to apprehend what is good and do what is right. Surely you social scientific determinists do not deny man's ability to reason, weigh options, and anticipate the consequences of actions. Most of you do that all the time and recommend that others do so as well. You consider objectivity and rationality to be the very cornerstones of your scientific enterprise.

S i n   a n d   R e s p o n s i b i l i t y

To which the determinist, particularly Freud, would respond that belief in man as capable of rational decision making is wrong. On the contrary, man's reason is subject to great distortion by irrational biological and social forces of which he is usually unaware. He cannot control them with reason because they control his thought processes. What may appear to the untrained eye to be objectively rational is nothing more than a pseudo-rationality serving man's selfish interests and impulses. Even if man's reason were not distorted by these forces, their influence on him is far greater than whatever counterforce reason might exert.

In attempting to explain the violent opposition to psychoanalysis in his day, an opposition that included not only religious thinkers but many secular intellectuals and academicians, Freud proudly and defiantly declared:

> Humanity has in the course of time had to endure from the hands of science two great outrages upon its naive self-love. The first was when it realized that our earth was not the center of the universe. . . . The second was when biological research robbed man of his peculiar privilege of having been specially created, and relegated him to a descent from the animal world. . . . But man's craving for grandiosity is now suffering the third and most bitter blow from present-day psychological research which is endeavoring to prove to the "ego" of each one of us that he is not even master in his own house, but that he must remain content with the veriest scraps of information about what is going on unconsciously in his own mind. . . . This is the kernel of the universal revolt against our science. (*A General Introduction to Psychoanalysis,* Eighteenth Lecture)

Aquinas and Maimonides might respond as follows: To the extent that your theories about the irrational influences on human behavior are correct, you contribute to a better understanding of man's proclivity to sin. However, this is all the more reason to encourage rational behavior. In fact, that is precisely what you yourself are advocating in your own psychoanalytic therapy, which focuses on the patient's acquisition of insight (i.e., rational understanding) into why he thinks, feels, and behaves as he does. Presumably, this insight will enable him to change his behavior. We and our followers, some of whom have also noted the power of unconscious impulses, attempt to guide men to more effective use of their reason in fighting the irrational, sinful forces with which all of us must contend.

Notwithstanding their free-will position, Maimonides and Aquinas realize that sometimes there are exonerating factors when man does evil or fails to do good. Conversely, modern psychologists, while affirming determinism, use concepts similar to the traditional free-will model, particularly self-control. The debate between the theologian and the therapist about freedom is softened by the many points of convergence between a qualified affirmation of free will and a determinism which tries to cultivate self-control. Since much of what the moralists teach about the seven deadly sins is about practical ways to develop self-control—over our desires, thoughts, feelings, and behaviors—what they say can be useful even to an avowed determinist.

፨

Some qualifications of the free-will/moral responsibility model are found already in medieval religious literature.[2] Maimonides, for example, accepts that permanent and episodic insanity exonerates the insane from legal and moral culpability for his actions. Presumably, certain mentally unbalanced individuals do not have free will. This is consistent with the idea that free will is a function of the ability to reason.

He also recognizes the weighty influence of constitutional factors in some personality dispositions, though upholding free will in the face of this observation. Maimonides says that though we may be constitutionally predisposed to commit certain sins, we are endowed with the freedom to rise above our predispositions, presumably with our reason and will. When frustrated a mercurial individual will have to generate a greater degree of volition in order to control his anger than would a phlegmatic one, but he can do it. This implies though, that we differ in how much free will we need to exercise. Furthermore, since free will is contingent upon intellectual ability—our powers of reason and discernment—it varies as they do.

Maimonides acknowledges the compelling influence of one's social environment. Such influences, though not eliminating freedom, act as mitigating factors in ascribing blame for transgressions.

Maimonides formulates the social and physical rewards and punishments that should be used in raising and educating children. The expectation is that the desire for reward and the fear of punishment will influence the child's behavior in the desired direction. This reliance on external forces rather than appeals to reason and volition preempts freedom. One could argue that punishment and reward inform the child about what is right and wrong and induce him to think and to use his free will to choose rightly. Most probably, however, the carrot and the stick have their effects even when they don't stimulate thoughtful deliberation followed by rational choice. In children especially, they can have almost automatic effects, bypassing reason and conscious willing.

Thus, although Maimonides emphatically affirms free will, he doesn't apply it to all people and situations equally.

Similarly, Aquinas, when analyzing the relative gravity of sins, takes into account mitigating circumstances that lessen or totally remove the sinner's responsibility for his acts. Among them are ignorance, illness, strong emotions, and sensual enticements. These can hamper (or sometimes even prevent) the use of reason and the voluntary exercise of one's free will, thus lessening the degree of one's guilt.

There can be no doubt that the concept of free will serves the very useful function of making us feel that we are responsible for our actions and can play a role in modifying them. *The theological concept of free will is, in effect, often translated into the psychological one of self-control.* What can I do to effect change in myself? How can I modify or radically change my environment so that it will affect me less or more? How can I think or feel about my experiences in ways that will determine how they influence me in the future? How can I reflect on my past and interpret it in ways that will influence my present and future behavior? These are all forms of self-control. The fact that thoughts, feelings, and behaviors that I deliberately generate today (which themselves result from my prior experiences, education, or training) will function as causes in determining my future thoughts, feelings, and behaviors, is perfectly compatible with a strict determinism. The causes of behavior can be internal as well as external. The devotional writers excelled in cultivating these self-control skills.

Modern psychology denies free will but talks instead about self-control, ego-strength, internal locus of control, or phenomenological freedom. It teaches people techniques to help them delay gratification of immediate desires. Rational-emotive, cognitive, behavior, and reality therapy share a common goal of helping the patient assume greater control over what he does, thinks, and feels. *All of these reintroduce into secular, determinist psychology and psychiatry traditional religious concerns with self-control* and acceptance of responsibility for one's behavior. Interestingly, one of the most insightful analyses of self-control is by B. F. Skinner, the strict determinist and radical behaviorist.[3]

My own view is that the determinist model is more scientifically useful than the free-will one in the search for a better understanding of why we behave as we do. However, our use of the language of freedom remains valuable and even necessary. It enhances our self-esteem, encourages us to develop self-control, and reminds us how limited are our understanding of behavior and our ability to predict and control it. These useful functions of the free-will model should not, however, deter us from research to discover biological or social determinants of our behavior that are not subject to our direct, personal control. We must also be willing to face the logical implications of the determinist model. We have to reconsider our attitudes about guilt and responsibility, and the ways in which we ascribe moral or legal blame and administer punishment.

When considering the responsibility for certain sins or crimes, the free-will model will often be unjustifiably harsh, and the determinist model unjustifiably lenient. Uncritical free-will moralists will be less prone to acknowledge factors over which the sinner or criminal has little or no control. Thus, for example, they will lay exclusive blame on the individual for drunkenness, drug abuse, aggression, theft, rape, or murder. Free-will moralists will argue that he could and should have controlled himself and not committed the evil or criminal act. Therefore, because he could have freely chosen to refrain from such an act and did not, he deserves to be punished. Nor is it important to seek out biological, cultural, or social factors that might account for his behavior. As long as the person was not insane, he knew how to distinguish between right and wrong, legal and illegal. He should have just said no.

This rigid, moralistic stance is unjustified from a determinist perspective. At the time of his misdeed, the individual could not have acted otherwise. True, had he thought of the consequences before taking action he might not have proceeded. But the fact that he didn't think was itself determined. Therefore, the purpose of blame or punishment should not be to inflict pain as a "just deserts" retribution for a past deed. The deed is done and cannot be changed; when the action was taken the sinner or criminal had no other real option available to him. Although it might appear to both him and us that he had an option, this is an illusion.

Does this mean, then, that from a determinist perspective there is no justification at all for blame or punishment, moral or legal? Not at all. There can be several legitimate purposes for them. By punishment or blame, we are giving the sinner or criminal an experience that we expect will influence his future behavior. The next time he is faced with a situation in which he could kill, lie, cheat, steal, rape, murder, drink alcohol, or take drugs, he might refrain from doing so because of the effects of punishment and blame on subsequent behavior. These may be fear and anxiety, reflection or insight. Another justification might be to deter not the criminal himself, but others. When others see that society punishes certain acts, this might influence their future behavior. Punishment of the criminal might also serve as a useful catharsis for the rage or indignation of the victim, his family, or society that the crime generated. Punishment and blame could also educate the criminal and society about the importance of certain values.

I am not trying to argue here on behalf of any specific theory of punishment. I only want to point out that from a determinist perspective punishment should not be administered for what someone should have done, but for its future effects. If it can be shown in a particular instance that no justifiable future effect can be served by blame or punishment, then they should not be administered. Such an approach to punishment would probably eliminate a considerable amount of judicial deliberation about whether or not the accused could and should have done otherwise when he committed his crime.

On the other hand, a simplistic determinist model will often argue for the elimination of all individual blame, guilt, and punishment.

This happened in some of the more extreme applications of Freudian theory. The locus of all causality, and hence responsibility, for immoral or criminal behavior was shifted from the individual to the environment. Parents were blamed for the sins of their children, patients were told that guilt is always an irrational and harmful emotion, criminals were informed that childhood traumas or poverty are responsible for their crimes, and jurors were instructed by psychiatrists and lawyers that it is unfair and unjust to punish individuals because "society" is to be blamed for its own ills (and crimes became illnesses or diseases rather than moral violations). What this simplistic application of Freudian determinism fails to realize is that there are many instances where a sense of guilt, an acceptance of blame, and the experience of punishment can change the future behavior of a criminal or sinner in the direction that both he and society would consider desirable. By inducing him to think before he acts, he might act differently than were he not to think. It is necessary to avoid the two simplistic extremes. Granted, it is often very difficult, or even impossible, to determine in a given instance what the effect of blame and punishment will be on inducing change and enhancing self-control in an individual. There will continue to be differences of opinion on how best to punish violations of social, moral, or legal norms. However, a clearer understanding of the real and the specious issues involved in the free-will versus determinism debate and of the rationales for censure and punishment, will result in more just and effective responses to vice, sin, and crime.

❧

One way we avoid responsibility for our vices is to call them diseases or addictions. This suggests that they are caused by forces we cannot control. In a widely read psychology magazine one author, analyzing the motives for financial crimes committed by multimillionaires, quotes from a book on values in an age of greed: "I really do think that people get hooked on money . . . and one of the sad ironies is that the people who get hooked . . . tend to consider themselves very smart, cool-headed, and rational. . . . These are people who are very well-educated in the ways of money, but beyond a certain point, they're no longer behaving rationally at all."[4] She then comments, "Greed as addiction puts the problem into a clinical rather than a moral framework" and cites an article by a Wall Street psychiatrist which she considers to be "a plea for regarding such people as true addicts" who can benefit from treatment.[5]

Similarly, an article in a popular women's magazine, labels a pattern of female behavior that in a moral system might be called sexual promiscuity or unrestrained lust as "sex addiction." The article provides addresses and phone numbers of support groups and treatment centers for those afflicted with this disease.

On a television talk show featuring a psychiatrist and a compulsive gambler, the psychiatrist described compulsive gambling as an addictive disease much like alcohol, heroin, or cocaine addiction. The compulsive gambler, describing himself as a diseased organism now in remission, told how he almost destroyed his family by his compulsive gambling, but fortunately succeeded in getting out of the woods before final disaster struck. The psychiatrist pointed out that the best treatment for this unfortunate addiction was psychotherapy and Gamblers Anonymous, modeled after Alcoholics Anonymous.

It is very difficult to overcome the temptations of power, money, or sex, and the pleasures associated with them. However, it is deceptive and sometimes dangerous to use the language and metaphors of medicine, disease, and addiction to explain behaviors which we can learn to control. Such language encourages people to believe that they are not responsible for their vices and their disastrous consequences. To call a failure to exercise restraint an "addiction" or "disease" discourages the development of self-control.

The comparison of sin and vice to illness was very common in the Middle Ages. Sins were diseases of the soul, in the sense that the soul was not functioning as it was ideally meant to function, just as a diseased physical organ is not functioning as it normally should. The purpose, however, of comparing our diseased soul to a diseased body was not to excuse us from responsibility for our vices. On the contrary, it was to tell us that we are morally and spiritually deficient and that we should change our ways before it is too late. The sicker we allow our soul to become—the more we continue to sin—the harder it will be to recuperate. The person whose body is sick goes to a physician to advise him on what medication to take or which exercises to perform so that he can then apply this advice to himself. So, too, the person whose soul is sick should consult with the physicians of the soul who can advise him on what he should do to heal himself. The medieval use of a medical analogy to explain flaws in our character has the opposite effect to the contemporary vice-as-addiction model. Many professionals use the disease/addiction model to lessen their patients' feelings of guilt rather than to discourage self-control. But the patient, pleased to be "sick" rather than "guilty," will often deny that he is responsible for changing his behavior and that he is at fault for failing to do so.

We saw that one implication of the belief in man as a free moral agent in Judaism and Christianity is that he is called upon to renounce his sins and turn to God. If he does so he will be forgiven and no longer alienated from God. What are the psychological implications of this doctrine, especially as it relates to sins against our fellow man? How do differences between the Jewish, Catholic, and Protestant variants of it affect believers?

Let us first consider repentance (*teshuva*) in Jewish thought.[6] A sin committed by one person against another usually has several deleterious effects. By doing evil I have degenerated morally and am a less worthy individual. I have caused pain, insult, or injury to another. My victim and those close to him are angry at me so my sin has created bitterness and hatred.

Repentance requires that each effect of my sin be rectified. I must raise my moral level to what it was before I sinned. This means that I must acknowledge my sin, show remorse, resolve not to repeat it, and not sin again if faced with similar circumstances.

I must also repair the pain or damage—physical or psychological— that I caused, whenever this is possible. Often it is not. My victim may have died or be no longer accessible, or I may not have the means to rectify the damage I caused. What can be done to alleviate the feelings of guilt of a repentant sinner in such circumstances? Usually the moralists recommend that he do good deeds to others. If in my greed I stole but can't identify my victims, I should distribute money to the poor. Sometimes penitential acts are recommended as substitutes. If in my anger I insulted another I should subject myself to shame. If in my lust I committed adultery I should refrain from sexual intercourse for a period of time. If in my gluttony I ate a forbidden food or more than I should, I should fast for a while.

I must also do what I can to heal the breaches I caused in personal relationships. I must try to bring about a reconciliation with my victim and others who have been affected by my sin.

If I do all these things I am assured that God forgives me. If I am sincere in acknowledging my sin, in my remorse, and in my resolution not to repeat it, but for reasons beyond my control I cannot perform the acts that repentance requires, I am also forgiven.

The doctrine of repentance is a radical one. To appreciate why this is so, imagine your reaction to the following situation. A person has committed many brutal crimes against you and your family, causing inordinate pain, injury, and loss. Through a turn of events he has now come under your total control. You are understandably seething with hatred and obsessed with a desire for revenge. The suffering he has wrought is still before your eyes, and will be felt for years. You are about to inflict punishment on the vicious criminal. Suddenly you discover that he shows absolute and sincere remorse for all the crimes he has committed and that he will never repeat them even if given the opportunity to do so. Would you find it easy to forgive him and release him unharmed? I doubt that most of us would. Would a judge declare that, notwithstanding his earlier criminal behavior, he is now a changed man and therefore should not be punished? I doubt that many would, as such a judgment would go against our need not only for revenge, but for justice. Yet the doctrine of repentance and divine forgiveness teaches that this is how God will behave towards human sinners who repent. One can understand why the prophet Jonah was unwilling to call the wicked city of Nineveh to repentance. Jonah was uncomfortable with the doctrine of repentance and tried to sabotage its implementation.

The idea that God forgives the repentant sinner is based upon the awareness that, difficult as it may be to do, sometimes compassion and mercy should override justice and vengeance. However, it also follows logically from the concept of repentance. The authentically penitent sinner has transformed himself (or that aspect of himself in which he sinned) into a new self. He has undergone a spiritual and personality metamorphosis. Therefore the sinner, in effect, no longer exists. The body of the pre- and postrepentant sinner may be the same, but not his soul or essential character. Therefore it would be unjust to penalize the penitent for the crimes or sins of his old self.

This doctrine has profound psychological effects on believers. On the one hand, it is a doctrine of hope. One must never despair of the possibility of transforming oneself. On the other hand, though, it can cause great anxiety and guilt to the sinner. As long as he is still a believer, he knows that the failure to repent is itself a sin.

According to the Jewish doctrine of repentance, man can return to God and be forgiven without any intermediary or sacrament. Every person is responsible for and capable of repenting his sins and returning to God as an act of his own free will at all times.

In Catholicism, the sacrament of penance includes five components: remorse for the sin; resolve not to repeat the sin (these two being components of contrition); confession to a priest; sacramental absolution by a priest; and satisfaction (the imposition by the priest of a sacramental satisfaction or penance, such as prayer, fasting, cultivation of a virtue, or good works). As Anthony Koch and Arthur Preuss explain, "Besides conscientiously performing the penance imposed in confession, penitents are bound to atone for their sins by voluntary good works. . . . The duty of giving satisfaction in this wider sense implies a strenuous effort to neutralize the evil consequences of sin by making restitution of ill-gotten goods, repairing scandal etc."[7]

The similarities between *teshuva* and the sacrament of penance are evident. The devout Catholic and Jew who conscientiously perform the sacrament of penance and *teshuva*, respectively, probably have similar emotional experiences. These include a journey from self-deprecation, sorrow, and guilt, through firm resolve, to a feeling of cleansing and purification, culminating with repose and joy in God's grace and love. When they repent sins against fellow men they experience the removal of bitterness and the pleasure of reconciliation. Most Jews and Catholics, even the devout, rarely fulfill all the requirements of their respective faiths, since *teshuva* and penance are emotionally, psychologically, and behaviorally demanding. It isn't easy to say I was wrong, I am sorry, forgive me, to man or to God. To change our habits, to resist temptation, to uproot our vices and implant virtues in their stead are among the most difficult challenges we can face in life. However, penance and *teshuva* provide ideals for self-transformation towards which religious people must strive.

Secular culture does not provide an equivalent impetus to self-improvement in the moral sphere. It needs to develop one. At a minimum we should begin by educating our children and youth in moral philosophy and ethics. They should be exposed to the works of Aristotle, the Stoics, Spinoza, and other thinkers who grapple with the problem of what makes a good life, morally and emotionally, and what we must do to achieve it. They should learn to be self-critical of their character and how to change it for the better.

The differences between *teshuva* and the sacrament of penance give the devout Jew and Christian their own unique experience. The Catholic who depends on the priest for confession and absolution feels less autonomous than the Jew in his ability to change his ways. Protestant denominations that deemphasize or deny the salvational efficacy of good works, eliminate the sacrament of penance or its equivalent, and focus on man's inherent depravity rather than his potential for good, produce different feelings from Judaism and Catholicism. Howard Levine compares *teshuva* with the conversion experiences of Methodists and Revivalists.[8] In *teshuva* the individual repents of his own volition. He turns away from sin and towards God by changing his attitudes and behaviors. In the Protestant groups conversion does not result from good works, penance, or rectification of the harm produced by past sins, but by self-surrender to God. In response, God, in His grace, miraculously and usually suddenly, transforms the sinner.[9]

O. Hobart Mowrer, to explain why many Protestant clergy were attracted to psychoanalysis, pointed to similarities between the psychological and moral implications of Lutheran and Calvinist theology and psychoanalysis:

> Both Protestantism, insofar as it is Calvinistic, and the secular psychotherapeutic enterprise, insofar as it is Freudian, equally stress the helplessness of man. Calvin saddled us with the doctrine of predestination and divine election; and Freud spoke of psychic determinism and the tyranny of the unconscious. Both would have us believe that we are totally incapable of helping ourselves; and they differ principally in the extent to which they hold us accountable for the distressing predicaments in which we commonly find ourselves.

Protestantism has been curiously one-sided in its argument on this score. While holding that when we behave badly it is by our own volition and choice, it then insists, paradoxically, that when we behave well this is by the grace of God, for which we deserve no credit. In other words, the doctrine is that when we are confronted by an apparent option of good and evil, we can choose only the evil, and are fully accountable for having done so. . . . Salvation comes, if it comes at all, only by the grace and unpredictable favor of God. . . . Psychoanalysis takes the further step of making man irresponsible and unaccountable, not only for his salvation, but also for his sins as well. . . . Calvinist Protestantism took the first major step toward that brand of personal irresponsibility which is sociopathy, by making us supposedly powerless to do anything constructive about our guilt and sin; and then psycho-analysis came along and took us the rest of the way by insisting that not only can we not help ourselves move towards recovery; we are wrong to blame or punish ourselves in the first place. (*The Crisis in Psychiatry and Religion*, pp. 159–160, 162–163)

Mowrer argued that most neurosis and mental illness are caused by unethical behavior, which produces guilt and anxiety, as it should in socialized individuals. The guilt and anxiety disrupt mental health when we refuse to acknowledge to ourselves and to others that what we did was wrong. Only through secular equivalents of the religious con-cepts of sin (acts that violate sociality), guilt (acceptance of responsibility for such violations and feeling bad about the behavior), confession (self-disclosure, usually in group settings), expiation (making amends or res-titution for the material or psychological injury caused by the behavior) can salvation (restored mental health) be achieved.[10] Although Mow-rer's formulation may be extreme, every psychotherapist should be con-cerned about the relationship between morality, psychological well-being, and psychotherapy which he has raised.

Plutarch relates a story about Alexander the Great that bears upon the influence and responsibilities of psychological mentors, whether we call them philosophers, physicians of the soul, or mental health professionals. Once, Alexander, in a drunken rage, seized a spear and killed Cleitus, an old friend and faithful soldier, who had criticized him:

No sooner had Cleitus fallen with a roar and a groan than the king's anger departed from him. And when he was come to himself and beheld his friends standing speechless, he drew the spear from the dead body and would have dashed it into his own throat, had not his bodyguards prevented this by seizing his hands and carrying him by force to his chamber.

Here he spent the night and the following day in bitter lamentations, and at last lay speechless, worn out with his cries and wailing, heaving deep groans. Then his friends, alarmed at his silence, forced their way in. . . . Therefore they brought into him Callisthenes the philosopher . . . and Anaxarchus. . . . Callisthenes tried by considerate and gentle methods to alleviate the king's suffering, employing insinuation and circumlocution so as to avoid giving pain; but Anaxarchus, who had always taken a path of his own in philosophy . . . shouted as soon as he came in:

"Here is Alexander, to whom the whole world is now looking; but he lies on the floor weeping like a slave, in fear of the law and the censure of men, unto whom he himself should be a law and a measure of justice, since he has conquered the right to rule and mastery, instead of submitting like a slave to the mastery of vain opinion. Knowest thou not . . . that Zeus has Justice and Law seated beside him, in order that everything that is done by the master of the world may be lawful and just?" By using some such arguments as these Anaxarchus succeeded in lightening the suffering of the king, it is true, but rendered his disposition in many ways more vainglorious and lawless; he also made himself wonderfully liked by the king. (*Plutarch's Lives*, vol. 7, pp. 373–377)

Rather than encouraging Alexander to accept his guilt and mend his ways, Anaxarchus absolved him of guilt and fed his vanity and ambition. Alexander may have remained the Great as a conqueror but he was now less admirable as a human being. His vice of anger and its child, murder, compounded by his failure to complete the process of "repentance" which he had begun but which was stifled by his psychological adviser, induced him to commit additional crimes. And Anaxarchus bears part of the blame for Alexander's subsequent sins because he chose to foster his vices rather than nurture his virtues.

There is more that modern psychology can learn from the classical and medieval writers. Many of their descriptions and analyses of psychological processes are plausible once we understand their language and conceptual models, which revolve around the concept of a soul. And their use of literary and dramatic skill in the service of therapy of the soul are worthy of emulation by contemporary psychotherapists.

The moral literature on the seven deadly sins frequently refers to the soul. One component of the soul may be responsible for sin and sin will corrupt other parts of it. As we saw earlier, for the medieval moralists our soul contains the divine or the rational element in us and it is immortal, providing ultimate meaning to existence and consolation for suffering. Belief in a soul that survives the body makes it easier to believe in divine justice, since the rewards and punishments that are not apparent during life will be experienced by the soul in the hereafter.

Ancient and medieval ideas about the soul and its functions were also attempts to account for psychological and physiological phenomena that modern theories explain.

In the Hebrew Scriptures, the word usually translated as soul is *nefesh*. However, the Old Testament does not conceive of the *nefesh* as existing independently of the body. *Nefesh* is the vital principle which characterizes living beings. In some verses, the blood is the *nefesh*, because it was observed that death is correlated with the draining of the blood from the body. *Nefesh* also refers to emotions and thoughts. Dead people have no *nefesh*—they exhibit no consciousness. Although a few biblical passages suggest existence after the death of the body, the afterlife plays a negligible role in the thought of ancient Israel, and it has no significant religious or moral function. The *nefesh* is not a disembodied, spiritual entity that exists after death. Man is a psychophysical unity. In Genesis, we read that "the Lord God formed a man from the dust of the ground and breathed into his nostrils the breath of life. Thus the man became a living creature" (2: 7, NEB). What the verse is saying is that man originated in dust or clay and returns to the state from which he originated, as we see when the body disintegrates after death. During the period between the two stages of dust, man is an animate being who thinks, feels, and wills. This stage of life happens because God endows the dust from which he shaped man with the vital life principle. But once man dies, he reverts back to his origin. The same idea is expressed by Ecclesiastes the skeptic:

> For man is a creature of chance and the beasts are creatures of chance, and one mischance awaits them all: death comes to both alike. They all draw the same breath. Men have no advantage over beasts; for everything is emptiness. All go to the same place: all came from the dust, and to the dust all will return. Who knows whether the breath of the man goes upward or whether the breath of the beast goes downward to the earth? (3: 19–21, NEB)

Similarly, the Psalmist says that it is not the dead who praise God but only the living, and God's rewards to the righteous are physical and earthly. For him, man's religious activity and salvation take place on earth.

This biblical conception of the relationship between the body, life, and consciousness is closer to the views of contemporary psychology and biology than the body-soul dualism of Plato.

For Plato and those influenced by him, man is a composite of two different entities—the material body and the spiritual soul. The soul has various powers, such as sensation, movement, reasoning, willing, feeling, and desiring. Its reasoning and willing capacities control bodily movement and the emotions. It lives on after death when it is rewarded or punished according to how it behaved while in the body.

For Aristotle, the soul is the "form" of the matter of which man is constituted. It is that which makes man what he uniquely is, and which directs him towards actualizing his potential. Man's rational soul, or his rationality, differentiates him from all other creatures. For Aristotle, the rational soul does not exist apart from the matter of man—the matter is invested with being and purpose by its form. Although Aristotle himself might not have believed in the immortality of the individual soul, Aristotelian theologians such as Maimonides and Aquinas did. However, their conception of the afterlife of the soul was different from that of the neo-Platonists. Maimonides, for example, maintained that immortality of the soul is determined by how much truth we apprehend during our lifetimes as a result of intellec-

THE SEVEN DEADLY SINS

tual contemplation (i.e. how much we actualize our rational potential). It followed from this that the wicked, who for Maimonides were those whose evil traits and deeds prevented them from engaging in the contemplation of God and the apprehension of truths, could not be immortal. In other words, their souls perish with their bodies. Their "eternal damnation"—if one may use the term—is their nonexistence after death. This idea that the souls of the wicked do not experience any active, conscious suffering after death as punishment for sins committed during life was challenged by other theologians. One objection was that such a view would not deter the wicked from doing evil.

Soul concepts explained the puzzling difference between living and dead organisms, which to the naked eye often look the same. They accounted for the strange phenomenon that unlike inanimate objects, live people move in the absence of any external mover. They explained human experiences which are not linked in any obvious way to bodily organs. Our memories, ideas, and thoughts, the images we visualize, the dreams in which we see, hear, and feel in the absence of external sensations, the passions we experience, our consciousness of mental conflict—none of these can be linked to any specific part of our body. They seem independent of direct sensory experiences. What then causes them, and what accounts for their dynamic qualities? Soul concepts are to a large extent rational and often highly sophisticated answers of premodern man to these questions about his own nature and consciousness.

Contemporary psychologists and philosophers are still unsure of how to explain many of these same experiences. Their theories, while formulated in the language of scientific materialism, are incomplete and logically problematic. We know much more today about the relationship between the body and states of consciousness than was known in the ancient and medieval worlds. However, how and why we feel and think as we do—our love, anger, envy, guilt, moral anguish, self-control, deductive and inductive skills—are still far from fully understood. Some ancient and medieval analyses of the soul are more insightful than some popular and influential twentieth-century theories about human nature couched in the language of modern secular materialism. Circular formulations of orthodox psychoanalytic theory which can never be disproven, or radical behaviorist paradigms that try to explain human functioning solely in terms of relationships between overt behaviors and external stimuli, are sometimes less plausible as descriptions of our psychology than Aristotle's or Aquinas's analyses of the soul.

This is not to say that traditional soul concepts are the most useful ones in which to formulate psychological theories today. Operational definitions, measurement, quantification, empirical observation, and controlled experimentation are very important in developing psychological theories and in establishing psychological facts. However, although we can improve upon the analyses of our predecessors we should not ignore their contributions to our self-understanding, as academic psychology too often does.

え

We have seen that many discussions of sin and vice in classical and religious literature are aesthetic gems which make fascinating reading. Many great thinkers such as Seneca, Jeremy Taylor, Francis de Sales, and Moshe Haim Luzzato were also brilliant stylists. They merged content and form to create powerful works that can be read repeatedly with profit and delight. Besides relying on their own literary skills, they draw from biography and history, myth and legend, anecdote and life experience, poetry and drama to illustrate their themes, prod us to examine our consciences, correct our moral defects, and inspire us to strive higher. If contemporary therapists made greater use in treatment of the powerful appeal of art and imagination, they would probably have greater and more lasting impact. Perhaps the tantrums of the angry, the stinginess of the miser, the maliciousness of the envious, and the voraciousness of the glutton would decrease, if they periodically read literature or watched films in which the ludicrousness and self-destructive nature of their sins were portrayed. Therapists should at least test the hypothesis that the aesthetic-dramatic power of treatment programs can improve their chances of success.

え

The moralists often prefaced their works with the comment that most of what they wrote was already known to the reader. They insisted that they were merely reminding us of what in the depths of our souls we accept as true but because of moral and spiritual inertia we prefer to ignore. They expressed a hope that their books would not be read once and then put aside, but would be consulted regularly as guides on a lifelong journey towards greater virtue and true happiness. I close this book in the same spirit and with similar hopes. I would be deeply gratified if I have succeeded in making the rich legacies of the moral thought of the past useful to people today in their quest for good and meaningful lives.

NOTES

CHAPTER ONE: THE PERSISTENCE OF SIN

1. Susan Trausch, "Down to the Raw Nerve."
2. See Lyman's *The Seven Deadly Sins: Society and Evil* and Fairlie's *The Seven Deadly Sins Today* for thoughtful analyses of how the sins are reflected in and shape social attitudes, values, and institutions.
3. There are isolated voices in the dark. In the 1960s a leading learning theorist, O. Hobart Mowrer, argued against the prevailing Freudian view of guilt as essentially neurotic and maladaptive. He maintained that neurosis is often a consequence of immoral or unethical behavior. Only by facing up to their moral guilt and experiencing honest remorse could certain patients begin the road to recovery. In 1975, in a presidential address to the American Psychological Association, Donald Campbell stated, no doubt to a somewhat shocked audience, that

   > . . . present day psychology and psychiatry in all their major forms are more hostile to the inhibitory messages of traditional religious moralizing than is scientifically justified . . . in the areas of disagreement (as to how people should live their lives, child rearing, sex, duty, guilt, sin, self-indulgence, etc.), we are unable to experiment or in other ways to put well-developed theories to rigorous test. On these issues, psychology and psychiatry cannot yet claim to be truly scientific and thus have special reasons for modesty and caution in undermining traditional belief systems . . . the religions of all ancient urban civilizations . . . taught that many aspects of human nature need to be curbed if optimal social coordination is to be achieved, for example, selfishness, pride, greed, dishonesty, covetousness, cowardice, lust, wrath. Psychology and psychiatry, on the other hand, not only describe man as selfishly motivated, but implicitly or explicitly teach that he ought to be so. . . . They further recommend that

we accept our biological impulses as good and seek pleasure rather than enchain ourselves with duty. (*American Psychologist*, 1975, pp. 1103–4)

Campbell goes on to defend the view that much of traditional religious teaching relating to morality, sin, virtue, and altruism has had positive consequences for the survival of the human species and that on purely scientific grounds "recipes for living that have been evolved, tested and winnowed through hundreds of generations of human social history . . . might be regarded as better tested than the best of psychology's and psychiatry's speculations on how lives should be lived" (ibid., p. 1103).

4. Reality therapy, developed by William Glasser, shares the traditional moralists' emphasis on personal responsibility. Glasser teaches his patients that they have the capacity to control themselves and their lives, and should not perceive themselves primarily as victims of circumstance, addiction, or external forces. Unfortunately, reality therapy is not widely practiced, and most of its practitioners, along with other psychologists, are not familiar with and therefore do not avail themselves of the insights of the moral traditions.

5. One New Age center in New England sponsored a retreat devoted to swimming with dolphins. This experience was to have broken through barriers to meaningful interpersonal (human) relationships. See Interface (in Bibliography) for descriptions of how magic, witchcraft, shamanism, and dolphin interaction can bring happiness and p. 197.

6. Goodenough, *The Psychology of Religious Experiences*, pp. 32–35.

7. Aristotle, *Ethics*, Book II.

8. Although he employs the concepts of practice and habit to account for the development and modification of dispositions, Aristotle does not discuss at length how our vices and virtues are shaped by our experiences from birth through childhood. Why is one person courageous, another a coward? Modern theories of personality, on the other hand, study many environmental factors that produce our traits, such as our relationships with our parents, siblings, and peers or traumatic childhood experiences. They consider different ways of modifying traits such as altering the consequences of behavior or providing new models to imitate. Moreover, they would question Aristotle's faith in the power of mere practice to effect significant, long-term changes in personality. Although practicing the right behavior often works, many times it will not.

9. Gregory's distinction is not absolute and other writers parsed the seven sins differently. Carnal sins often include some mental pleasure (sexual seduction can include the psychological pleasure of having "won" the

seducted) and "spiritual" sins often include physical pleasure (vanity, a form of pride, includes a pampering of the body with fine clothing, jewelry, and cosmetics; sloth includes physical laziness).

Aquinas says that carnal sins incur less moral guilt than spiritual sins because they result from a very strong bodily urge—the concupiscence of the flesh. Guilt is inversely related to the strength of the drive to sin. This does not mean that spiritual sins are always worse than carnal ones, since guilt is determined by many factors, but only that all else being equal, spiritual sins are graver.

It would be interesting to test Aquinas's assumption empirically by devising some psychological instrument for comparing, for example, the drive for sex with the drive for fame—in the same person, between people, between men and women, or across cultures. Is it indeed the case that the sex drive is generally more powerful than the drive for honor or recognition?

Aquinas says we should be more ashamed of committing carnal sins since we are then more like the brute animals than when we commit spiritual sins.

10. See Bloomfield's *The Seven Deadly Sins*, which is an invaluable resource for understanding the seven deadly sins tradition.
11. Prudentius, "Psychomachia," p. 311.
12. Ibid., pp. 285–287.
13. Bloomfield compiled an extensive list of medieval associations of animals with sins (*The Seven Deadly Sins*, pp. 245–249).
14. *The Faerie Queene*, Book I, Canto IV, Stanzas 16–36.
15. Perry London, who discusses the moral dimensions of psychotherapy with insight and sensitivity, has made this point very effectively. "But if [psychotherapists] claim the ability to influence people, as they rightly can and do, then they must shoulder some responsibility for that influence. They must see themselves as moral agents as they are faced with moral problems. . . . Morals are the ultimate values by which we judge our acts. Psychotherapy is one arena in which such judgments now are made. . . . Psychotherapists may be ill-suited to assume this role, but they cannot escape it" (*The Modes and Morals of Psychotherapy*, pp. 12–13).
16. Modern New Testament scholarship acknowledges the great influence of Pharisaic Judaism on Jesus, the Apostles, and Paul. Although Christianity eventually divorced itself from and became hostile to Judaism, it retained many rabbinic moral and ethical values. This is especially the case with Catholicism and Puritanism.
17. Neaman, *Suggestion of the Devil: The Origins of Madness*, pp. 178–179.

18. Catholic theologians discuss with great psychological subtlety various states of mind that precede or accompany sins in order to determine whether they should be considered mortal or venial. Since mortal sins must be confessed, whereas venial sins need not be (though it is advisable to do so), people needed criteria for assessing which of their sins were mortal so that they could confess them. Studying such moral theology can cultivate skill at psychological self-analysis. Similar skills are acquired in Jewish seminaries in which the "musar" movement took root. Its literature is intensely introspective, seeking to ferret out the motives for an individual's behavior.

19. One New Testament list of sin not based on seven is Paul's enumeration of the depravity of the pagan gentiles of his day:

> Their women have exchanged natural intercourse for unnatural, and their men in turn, giving up natural relations with women, burst with lust for one another; males behave indecently with males . . .
>
> They are filled with every kind of injustice, mischief, rapacity, and malice; they are one mass of envy, murder, rivalry, treachery and malevolence; whisperers and scandal-mongers, hateful to God, insolent, arrogant, and boastful; they invent new kinds of mischief, they show no loyalty to parents, no conscience, no fidelity to their plighted word; they are without natural affection and without pity. (Romans 1:26–31, NEB)

First- and second-century rabbis single out certain sins that deserve particularly harsh punishment, often in groups of three. Sometimes they contrast vices with their opposing virtues, a pattern which was often used in Jewish and Christian medieval devotional or penitential literature. For example, Rabbi Elazar ha-Kappar said "Envy, lust and vainglory remove a person from the world" (*Ethics of the Fathers* 4:28) while Judah ben Tema observed, "The impudent is destined for Gehinnom [akin to Hell], but the shamefaced is destined for the Garden of Eden [Paradise]" (Ibid., 5:23).

20. It is possible that the anonymous rabbinic author of this midrash considers these seven sins to be the chief sins committed by Christianity, since they correspond remarkably with how Jews perceived that new faith.

21. See Bloomfield, *The Seven Deadly Sins*, pp. 74–75.

22. Aquinas analyzed the seven capital sins in his work *On Evil* and in the *Summa Theologiae*. However, he did not consider the notion of seven

capital sins, or the specific sins themselves, to be sufficiently central to his overall conceptualization of sin as to structure most of his extensive discussions of sin around the seven. Christian ideas about sin and vice, in terms of their definition, variety, psychology, causality, and implications for human life and society, were too broad and rich to be encompassed within the limiting constraints of the seven cardinal sins tradition. The tradition was more important and influential in medieval popular religious literature than in theology.

23. Aquinas also considered vainglory, gluttony, lust, and greed to be capital sins because they are distortions of the three primary "goods" which motivate all behavior: a good of the soul—such as beauty, knowledge, or recognition of our excellence in some endeavor or ability; a good of the body, which is necessary for self-preservation, such as food, or for preservation of the species, such as sexual intercourse; and an external good such as material possessions, which we have a natural inclination to acquire. The pursuit of these goods in proper measure and motivated by the ultimate good—the love of God—is virtuous. The inordinate pursuit of them or the pursuit of them as ends in themselves divorced from our ultimate good is sin or vice. Vainglory, for example, is the inordinate or misdirected pursuit of excellence, while gluttony and lust are excessive or misdirected pursuits of food and sexual intercourse. Avarice is excessive or misdirected pursuit of riches.

CHAPTER TWO: PRIDE

1. *The Individual and His Religion*, pp. 94–95.
2. See Donald E. Growan, *When Man Becomes God: Humanism and Hybris in the Old Testament*, Pittsburgh Theological Monograph Series, No. 6 (Pittsburgh: Pickwick Press, 1975).
3. As one studies the medieval Jewish and Christian devotional literature on pride and humility one is struck by the similarities between the two religious traditions. There is a tendency in the Christian treatments to focus more on man's inherent evil, sinfulness, and corruption than in the Jewish ones. This is related to the Christian doctrine of original sin and to the more pronounced anticarnal tendencies in Christianity. However, Judaism, like Christianity, considers pride to be a root sin and humility to be a primary virtue. Comparisons to worms and other symbols of insignificance as inducements to humility are not uncommon in Jewish writing. Both traditions share the view that man must humble himself before God and acknowledge his sinful pride in its various manifestations. Only then will he be able to redress the pain and sorrow that through his vices he inflicts upon himself and others.

4. *Summa Theologiae* 2a2ae, Question 162 (V. 44).
5. The relationship between pride, envy, anger, and homicide was tragically manifested when a graduate student in the physics department of the University of Iowa murdered in cold blood a fellow graduate student, three professors, and a vice-president, before killing himself. He had been envious and angry over the fact that his student victim had been awarded a prestigious prize for his doctoral dissertation while he was not. His other victims were involved in the award decision. A former roommate of the murderer said, "he had a very bad temper and saw himself as No. 1. He had a psychological problem with being challenged" (Marriott, "Iowa Gunman . . . ," 1991). Did he not also have a moral problem?
6. See for example David K. Clark, "Philosophical Reflections on Self-worth and Self-Love"; Dale S. Ryan, "Self-Esteem: An Operational Definition and Ethical Analysis"; Sol Roth, "Towards a Definition of Humility."
7. *The Rule and Exercise of Holy Living*, pp. 105–123.
8. Although this is something of an overstatement, it is true that neither Plato, nor Aristotle, nor the Stoics preached the kind of self-abnegation before God which constitutes the essence of Christian humility. The Christian virtue of humility, does, however, have its antecendents in the Hebrew Bible and in Pharisaic Judaism, as I already indicated. For a medieval Jewish treatment of humility see Bahya Ibn Pakuda, *Duties of the Heart, Treatise on Humility.*
9. *The Rule and Exercises of Holy Living*, p. 106.
10. Ibid., p. 107.
11. Ibid., p. 119.
12. Ibid., p. 120.
13. *Summa Theologiae* 2a2ae, Question 161 (V. 44).
14. St. Francis de Sales, *Introduction to the Devout Life*, pp. 110–119.
15. Ibid., p. 112.
16. See Daniel Goleman, "Narcissism Looming Larger as Root of Personality Woes."
17. Coopersmith, *The Antecedents of Self-Esteem*, pp. 38–42.

CHAPTER THREE: ENVY

1. Salovey and Rodin, "Coping with Envy and Jealousy"; Goleman, "Envy Seen as Sensitive Barometer"; and Queijo, "Jealousy and Envy."
2. Anonymous early Greek proverb.
3. *The Ways of the Righteous*, pp. 269–271.
4. I Kings 3:16–28.

5. *The Philosophy of Spinoza*, pp. 281–282.
6. *Rhetoric*, Book II, Chapter 10.
7. "Concerning Envy," Homily 11.
8. See Jerome Neu, "Jealous Thoughts," for a perceptive philosophical and psychological analysis of envy and jealousy.
9. Lyman, *The Seven Deadly Sins*, pp. 185–186, 190, and 194.
10. Richard Smith, as cited by Queijo, "Jealousy and Envy", p. 36.
11. *Envy—A Theory of Social Behavior*.

Chapter Four: Anger

1. Martin Luther King, Jr., in his sermon "Loving Your Enemies," offers several practical reasons for loving enemies that go beyond Skinner's. Hate begets more hate whereas love drives out hate and can transform our enemy into our friend. Hate destroys our objectivity and sense of values and corrodes our personality:

   > To our most bitter opponents we say: "We shall match your capacity to inflict suffering by our capacity to endure suffering. . . . We cannot in all good conscience obey your unjust laws, because non co-operation with evil is . . . a moral obligation. . . . Send your hooded perpetrators of violence into our community at the midnight hour and beat us and leave us half dead, and we shall still love you. But be assured that we will wear you down by our capacity to suffer. One day we shall win freedom, but not only for ourselves. We shall so appeal to your heart and conscience that we shall win you in the process, and our victory will be a double victory." (*Strength to Love*, p. 40)

2. The New Testament, while preaching meekness and forbearance, also expresses the anger of early Christians at the refusal of the Jews to accept Jesus as the Messiah and at their hostility to the Church.
3. Some Jewish and Christian theologians, uncomfortable with the idea that God can be angry, and even be pacified by a human, maintain that biblical descriptions of God's anger are to be understood metaphorically or in other nonliteral ways. See, for example Maimonides, *Guide of the Perplexed*, p. 126.
4. Aristotle, *Nichomachean Ethics* and *Rhetoric*, Seneca, "On Anger," and Plutarch, "On the Control of Anger." See also Schimmel, "Anger and its Control in Graeco-Roman and Modern Psychology."
5. Goleman, "When Rage Explodes. . . ."
6. Yudofsky's characterization of ordinary anger is too narrow, and many non-brain-injured individuals manifest explosive rage while many brain-

injured individuals do not. Moreover, many psychiatrists and legal experts do not agree that neurological rage is so uncontrollable that it exonerates the individual from responsibility for his violent crimes. See Tavris, *Anger: The Misunderstood Emotion*, pp. 74–77.

7. Seneca, "On Anger," 291–293. Harpagus's motivation in suppressing his anger was to escape an invitation to eat what still remained of his children's flesh rather than any philosophical acceptance of the value of self-control. In most of Seneca's other examples the motivating factor for suppression was fear of greater injury than had already been suffered. However, Seneca only wants to demonstrate that we have the capacity to conceal even intense anger. Actually he felt that a more honorable response for Harpagus and Praexaspes would have been to commit suicide rather than flatter monstrous kings.

8. There may be a hint of an early Christian controversy regarding justifiable anger in variant manuscript readings of a passage in the Sermon on the Mount as reported by Matthew. In one version Jesus teaches that "Anyone who nurses anger against his brother must be brought to judgment" whereas another version reads "anyone who nurses anger against his brother *without good cause* must be brought to judgment" (Matthew 5:22; emphasis added).

9. *The Rule and Exercises of Holy Living*, pp. 326–333.

10. *Beginning of Wisdom. Gate of Humility.* See Schimmel, "Education of the Emotions in Jewish Devotional Literature."

11. St. Francis de Sales, *Introduction to the Devout Life*, pp. 119–122.

12. See *Summa Theologiae* 2a2ae, Question 158, Article 2 (V. 44), and see also 1a2ae, Questions 46–48 (V. 21).

13. *The Seven Deadly Sins Today*, p. 98.

14. We have also pointed out in Chapter 3 that terrorism is often a manifestation of envy.

15. Unfortunately, too many people accept the angry terrorist's justification for his actions with the claim that he has been wronged and is only seeking to rectify an injustice, as in some way morally exonerating him from his vicious behavior. It is as if his anger at some (real or alleged) injustice endows moral merit on his behavior, despite the fact that he is denying justice to others and violating their rights. See note 13.

16. See Bandura, *Aggression*, pp. 107–113, for cross-cultural comparisons of the relationship between attitudes towards anger, aggression, and violence and their incidence.

17. "On Anger," pp. 209–213. Indeed, this is one of the most important methods for eliminating anger from a culture that Skinner advocates in

his utopian community, in which as much or more attention is paid to systematic training of the emotions from early childhood, as to training of the mind.

18. "On the Control of Anger," p. 99.
19. "On Anger," p. 283.
20. "On Anger," p. 281.
21. "On the Control of Anger," p. 149.
22. "On Anger," p. 305.
23. "On the Control of Anger," p. 125.
24. "On Anger," p. 313.
25. *Life of Christ:* "Of the Decalogue—The Sixth Commandment," and *The Rule and Exercises of Holy Living*, pp. 326–333.
26. "On Anger," p. 329.
27. "On the Control of Anger," p. 137.
28. *Rule and Exercises*, pp. 329–330.
29. "Upon Resentment and Upon Forgiveness of Injuries."
30. In this vein Martin Luther King, Jr., writes:

> We must recognize that the evil deed of the enemy-neighbor, the thing that hurts, never quite expresses all that he is. An element of goodness may be found even in our worst enemy . . . there is some good in the worst of us and some evil in the best of us. When we discover this we are less prone to hate our enemies. When we look beneath the surface, beneath the impulsive evil deed, we see within our enemy-neighbor a measure of goodness and know that the viciousness and evilness of his acts are not quite representative of all that he is. We see him in a new light. We recognize that his hate grows out of fear, pride, ignorance, prejudice, and misunderstanding, but in spite of this, we know God's image is ineffably etched in his being. (*Strength to Love*, p. 36)

31. "The Cognitive and Emotive Uses of Forgiveness," p. 630.
32. "On Anger," p. 341.
33. *Anger Control*.
34. "On the Control of Anger," p. 159. Plutarch employs the technique of gradual approximation in his commitment through a vow—first only for a few days, then a month, until finally he conquers anger entirely. An analogous procedure of gradualness in learning to inhibit undesirable emotional behavior, from brief to extended periods of time, is used by Skinner in *Walden Two*, although with a different technique than the vow (pp. 104–115).

Notes

35. Students of self-control have developed an effective behavioral contract analogous to vows, in which the patient commits himself in a binding fashion to perform or omit a specified behavior. In some cases the patient agrees to prespecified rewards and penalties in the event of fulfillment or violation of the commitment. A theoretical assumption underlying the technique is that in certain instances it is easier to commit oneself to a certain course of action or inaction at time A than to actually behave that way at time B. However the very act of commitment at time A, because of its psychological consequences, increases the probability that the behavior in question will now be performed or omitted at time B, which might not have been the case in the absence of a prior commitment. Furthermore, where the commitment includes actual penalties and rewards, the anticipation or application of them can encourage or deter behavior.
36. "On Anger," p. 319.
37. "On the Control of Anger," p. 107.
38. *Anger: The Misunderstood Emotion*, pp. 120–150.
39. "On the Control of Anger," p. 105.
40. *Aggression*, p. 257.

CHAPTER FIVE: LUST

1. Paretsky, "Soft Spot for Serial Murder."
2. Orthodox Judaism, Catholicism, and many Protestant denominations consider masturbation and sexual fantasizing to be sins. Jewish law severely restricts social contact between the sexes and forbids men from listening to a woman sing (other than one's wife) lest they become aroused; the use of contraceptives is forbidden in Catholicism, and in many situations, in Orthodox Judaism as well. Religious teachings about sex, particularly in Christianity, often produce unreasonable shame, guilt, and sexual dysfunction.
3. Aristotle, *Ethics*, Book III ("Nichomachean Ethics"), xii, pp. 140–141.
4. Cicero, *Tusculan Disputations*, IV, p. 415.
5. The following is a summary of the main Hebrew biblical laws which involve sexual behavior. Adultery, defined as sexual intercourse with a married woman, is a capital offense, in which instance both perpetrators are equally guilty and punishable by death. A married man who has sexual intercourse with an unmarried woman has not committed adultery since the Hebrew Bible recognizes the right of a man to marry more than one woman, but not the right of a woman to marry more than one man. A wife does not have exclusive sexual rights to her husband, whereas a husband has exclusive sexual rights to his wife. Other grievous sexual

offenses are male homosexuality, incest, and bestiality. Raping a woman in which no adultery or incest occurs is a lesser crime, of personal injury and/or property. Prostitution is not explicitly prohibited except in the case of a priest's daughter or when it is associated with pagan cultic practices. Though tolerated, the harlot is socially frowned upon. Concubinage is legal. There is no biblical reference to masturbation. Sexual intercourse with a menstruating woman who has not purified herself with ritual ablution is forbidden.

6. Jewish and Christian commentators of the Hellenistic and Roman periods, more wary of sexuality, sensuality, and romantic love than the biblical authors, interpreted the Song of Solomon as an allegory of the love between God and Israel (Jewish), God and the Church (Christian), or God and the individual soul (Jewish and Christian).

7. II Samuel 11 and 12 (NEB).

8. *Complete Woman*, p. 67.

9. Either Tamar needed time to recover her composure so that those who saw her would not suspect she had been raped; or having lost her virginity to Amnon, she wants him to marry her legally, lest she be condemned to a shameful spinsterhood. It is possible that marriage with a paternal half-sister was still permissible then in Israel in the royal family, although outlawed later.

10. See article on acquaintance rape by Lewin. Rape laws differ from state to state and have changed significantly in the past twenty years:

> Until the 1970s, rape laws in most states covered only those situations in which a man forced a woman to have sexual intercourse under the threat of bodily injury, she resisted strenuously, and there was outside corroboration . . . in most states you still have to show some kind of force or threat, and the woman's non-consent. What's changed is how force is defined, which can now include verbal threats or physically overpowering the woman . . . some states go further, eliminating any requirement of force. . . . In the most liberal states, it is a crime to have intercourse without consent, and consent is interpreted as a knowing and affirmative expression of willingness. . . . That means that if a woman is silent, or crying, or too drunk to give knowing consent it is a "no."

11. See Bardwick, *Psychology of Women*, Chapter 3. She summarizes women's answers to the question "Why do you make love?" as follows: "Perhaps the most frequent response was the perception of sex as an important technique for communicating love in a relationship which they hoped was mutual—or the observation that if they did not partici-

pate sexually the relationship would be ended. For most, the sex act is important because the male makes it important; for these women it tended not to be important in its own right" (p. 55).

12. Pieper, *The Four Cardinal Virtues*, pp. 161–162. See pp. 153–175 for a full discussion of Thomas's view of chastity and unchastity.

13. Sexual arousal is a function of a natural biological urge and of the learned association between environmental stimuli and sexual pleasure. Modesty in dress and restrictions on the public display of sexually arousing stimuli make it easier to follow the sexual norms of traditional religion. A major problem facing traditional communities today is how to deal with the high levels of sexual arousal and frustration which result from exposure to a sexually saturated environment, while insisting on adherence to norms that restrict sexual behavior. The level of sexual frustration increases the further the age of marriage is from the age of biological maturity. Some traditional communities encourage early marriage and will not allow televisions or popular magazines into their homes.

14. See Freud, *Civilization and Its Discontents*, particularly Chapters 3 and 4.

15. See, for example, Knapp, "Love, Lust and Romance: How Hollywood Shapes Our Reality." "In Hollywood romance plus lust equals love. . . . In the real world, romance often flickers and dies before it leads to long-term happiness. Lust can get people into trouble. And love? More often than not, it's just not the stuff movies are made of. . . . It's hard to maintain . . . and also a good deal harder to find than Hollywood would suggest." See also Silverman-Watkins, "Sex in the Contemporary Media," who observes that "in current depictions of sex in the media, there is much talk about sexual functioning, dysfunctioning, and deviation and little discussion of the emotional and relational contexts in which all of these arise."

16. *Women in Jewish Law.*

17. However, one lawyer defended his client, a prostitute, by arguing that she was a nymphomaniac and that her treatment was to have sex with different men (*New York Times*, August 1, 1991). If that were the case, she should have paid the men for their services, rather than the opposite.

18. Levine, "A Modern Perspective on Nymphomania."

19. Borowitz, *Choosing a Sex Ethic.*

20. Gittelson, *Love, Sex and Marriage.*

21. Foster, *Money, Sex and Power.*

22. Even among religious liberals there is debate about the practical meaning of "love and justice" as criteria for a sexual ethic. For example, most of

the regional presbyteries of the Presbyterian Church, which is considered by sociologists to be relatively liberal on sexual issues, rejected a 1991 report on human sexuality prepared by a commission of the Church, "Keeping Body and Soul Together: Sexuality, Spirituality and Social Justice." They felt it went too far in repudiating traditional Christian values. The moral evaluation and acceptance of male homosexuality and lesbianism remain a controversial issue even within the liberal camp. See Woodward, "Roll Over John Calvin: The Presbyterians Rethink the Sexual Revolution," and Steinfels's harsh critique of the Presbyterian Report, "Presbyterians are eager to read a new report on sexuality, but the excitement may end there."

CHAPTER SIX: GLUTTONY

1. Petronius, *Satyricon*.
2. One commercial, for example, uses a highly suggestive script and visual images to evocatively associate its product, a brand of coffee, with the possibility (hope?) of a sexual liaison between casual neighbors, one of whom comes to the apartment of the other in order to borrow some coffee. The creators of this commercial would probably argue that it is meant to be humorous (which, because of its absurdity, it is), but aside from the humor there is a sophisticated attempt to manipulate the viewer by conditioning his liking for coffee to sexual adventure. Thus is lust harnessed to gluttony, validating the strong connection between these two in the seven deadly sins tradition. The gluttonous and the lustful occupy adjacent places in Dante's Purgatory.
3. Henry Jaglom's film *Eating* explores women's obsessions with food, including their ambivalences, cravings, fear, and battles concerning it. America's historical preoccupation with dieting is surveyed by Schwartz in *Never Satisfied*.
4. Another weight-control program advertises that "graduates report experiencing a new guilt-free response to food. They learn that they are not helpless victims of their eating problems or their circumstances, but individuals who can take responsibility for what they eat and how much they weigh." Although a moral approach to gluttony would accept the last half of this statement, it would not exonerate the overeater who can control himself, but doesn't, from all remorse or guilt. Neurotic guilt about food is inappropriate but not all guilt is neurotic.
5. Much of the traditional moral literature includes drunkenness in the sin of gluttony. However, because of the unique physiological, psychological, and behavioral effects of wine, beer, ale, hard liquor, and other intoxicants, drunkenness and alcoholism raise special issues of control

that make it worthwhile to treat them separately from gluttony with respect to food (and nonintoxicating beverages). We limit our discussion to the vice of gluttony and the virtue of abstinence as they refer to food and do not analyze the vice of drunkenness and the virtue of sobriety which refer to the inebriating beverages. It is possible that gluttony and drunkenness were so closely linked in ancient and medieval thought because for many centuries wine rather than water was the most common liquid served with meals.

6. *Summa Theologiae* 2a2ae, Questions 146–148.

7. Five attitudes towards food are the ascetic, the puritanical, the thankfully accepting, the sanctifying, and the hedonistic. The ascetic avoids the pleasures of food as much as possible; the puritan partakes of food in moderation but considers doing so legitimate only to the extent that it can help him serve God better; the thankfully accepting enjoys food as a gift from God whom he thanks for the pleasure and benefit that His bounty provides; the sanctifier transforms eating into a spiritual, sacred act, in which one should experience spiritual rather than physical pleasure; the hedonist enjoys food for the physical and psychological pleasure it provides, which he tries to maximize. In Judaism and Christianity we find all except hedonism. See Jacobs, "Eating and Drinking as an Act of Worship in Hasidic Thought."

8. The glutton is not necessarily obese nor are obese people necessarily gluttons. A painfully thin, anorexic-bulemic adolescent girl, who alternates between self-starvation and eating binges and who is almost totally preoccupied with food, would be considered a glutton if she were thought to be responsible for her behavior and capable of controlling it. However, since there is a substantial and evident link between overeating and obesity, both medieval and modern descriptions of the glutton frequently depict him as grossly overweight.

9. Not very different in approach is Bahya Ibn Pakuda, the tenth-century Spanish Jewish author of the influential *Duties of the Heart*. He writes:

> Then strive to discipline the sense of taste. Only take of food and drink as much as you need for your sustenance and abstain from anything beyond it. The plan to adopt in this regard is to diminish varied courses and limit yourself to one course, if you are able to do so, and only partake of it as little as you can; and have it in mind that you do so in order that the bread shall be digested and not for mere enjoyment . . . and if you can train your soul to be insensitive to what you eat or drink, for the sake of disciplining it, do so.

Regard what you eat as a medicine [to keep you in good health], rather than as a food. (Ninth Treatise, "Abstinence from Worldly Interests and its Benefits for Us," p. 17)

10. Taylor, *Sermons. The House of Feasting*, and idem, *The Rule and Exercises of Holy Living*, pp. 64–83.
11. Wollersheim, "Behavioral Techniques for Weight Control."
12. Some modern psychologists consider gluttony to be a sublimation of frustrated sexual desire or the yearning for love. Although this is sometimes the case, such an explanation can also serve as a convenient rationalization for avoiding self-control.
13. Some ethicists maintain that the excessive way our society consumes food, distributes it inequitably and even recklessly wastes it, and siphons off resources that can be used to increase food production in less developed countries, is partially responsible for the food shortages they experience. Although the causes of famine and malnutrition are complex, and blame must be shared by others, something is definitely morally amiss when we see pictures of starving children in Africa and elsewhere on the seven o'clock news while eating our sumptuous dinners.
14. This effect was more frequently associated with the drunkard and also the gambler.
15. The harshness of the biblical penalty for disobedience, gluttony and drunkenness disturbed the rabbis who ingeniously interpreted the law as a theoretical one that was never implemented. But its moral message was clear—gluttony leads to violation of the fifth commandment, honoring parents, which in turn will lead to dishonoring God, to murder, and other capital crimes.
16. Gossip, slander, cursing, blasphemy, and other sins of speech were often associated with gluttony because they too are sins of the mouth and tongue. Moreover, socialization at meals is an occasion for gossip and slander, and drunkards are known to curse and use vile language. The moralists exhort us to use our mouths and tongues to praise God and to sanctify our lives. Gluttony and an evil tongue, in their many guises, are all uses of these organs in ways that defile us spiritually.
17. The halakhah was not content with a generalized blessing that could be recited before all food and drink, but classified foodstuffs and liquids into several different categories, and specified a particular liturgical formula to be recited before each category. This led to a large body of legal literature on "blessings over food." Given the extent of this sacred legal literature related to food, which the Jew was expected to master, it would be

incongruous to discourage eating. Could enjoying food be all that bad if so much intellectual energy is invested in the blessings over food?

18. There were, however, Jewish mystics influenced by neo-Platonist dualism who, like Augustine, believed that the body is a barrier to communion with God. They developed an intricate theory about the relationships between the soul, the body, and God, which allowed for the transformation of eating (and sexual intercourse) into sacred, spiritual activities when performed with the proper mental attitudes and meditations. Louis Jacobs, in the article cited in note 7, explains the system as formulated in the Hasidic adaptation of Lurianic kabbalah. Elijah de Vidas, in his *Beginning of Wisdom, Gate of Holiness*, explains how eating can be sanctified using the concepts of Zoharic kabbalah. See Gershom Scholem, *Major Trends in Jewish Mysticism*, for summaries of Zoharic and Lurianic mysticism and the relationship between them. The doctrines, myths, and practical teachings of the Jewish mystics can have a significant influence on the eating behavior and attitudes towards food of believers who try to live in accordance with them. Even Christians with a mystical bent will find much that is spiritually elevating in the kabbalistic approach, although it has little practical value for secularists.

19. In practice, though, the adherents of one approach often disparage the other. Similar differences of opinion exist with respect to treatment programs for nicotine, alcohol and drug abuse, all species of gluttony. Psychiatrists are usually more oriented to an illness/drug medication model and psychologists towards a maladaptive acquired habit/learning of new skills model. This is not because psychologists believe in free will but because, in general, psychologists are more interested in the interaction between behavior and the environment whereas psychiatrists, being trained as medical doctors, are generally more oriented to seeking and treating physiological causes of behavior.

20. Isaiah 22:13, cited by Paul in I Corinthians 15:32.

21. Petronius, *Satyricon*.

22. The relationship between overeating, obesity, and many illnesses is well established by modern medical research.

23. Another example of how the glutton can become desensitized to the pain of others comes from a "confession" made to me by a client, which I paraphrase. In his telling there was a deep feeling of shame and guilt:

> I have stolen candy from my own baby. He was hungry, whereas I wanted to satisfy my craving for sweets. He was in his playpen waiting for his mother to return home to feed him. To temporarily assuage his hunger she had left a few chocolate chip cookies for

him in the pen. Eyeing these cookies and desiring them, I diverted his attention from the bag, hastily removed some and went to another room to gobble them down without his seeing me. When he finished his last cookie he began searching for more, and not finding any in the bag began to plead "Cookie! Cookie!" Imagine the guilt that I experienced. I had eaten the last chocolate chip cookie in the house, and he wanted it. . . . For maybe sixty seconds of digestive pleasure I had caused my son to cry for several minutes. Is this what fathering is all about? If I can't control myself for a cookie, how would I behave if, God forbid, I was in a situation of famine with my child and I had to give up half of my ration in order to provide for him? Would I be able to pass that test? I have serious doubts about how I would behave under such circumstances, and my weakness scares me.

24. One example will suffice:

I want you to imagine that you are at your dinner table and have just finished your first serving of steak. You reach across the table to get another piece and, just as your hand reaches the plate, you feel a queasy, churning feeling in your stomach. You transfer the steak to your plate and, just as you do, a bitter spit comes up into your throat and mouth. You swallow it and raise the piece of meat on your fork. Just as the fork reaches your lips you vomit all over your hand, all over the plate in front of you. The vomit goes all over the table, and splashes on the people eating with you. They look at you horrified. You feel miserable, slimy, and the sight of the vomit mixed with food particles spread all over the table makes you vomit more and more. You hurry from the table and rush out of the room, and you feel better." (Cautela, "The Treatment of Overeating by Covert Conditioning," p. 106)

Although the patient knows that the imagined events are improbable in real life, the effects of conditioning by association do not depend on the "rationality" or high probability of the association between two juxtaposed images. Advertisers sell us food and cars by conditioning us to make the irrational association between them and sexual prowess. Many phobias result from chance associations between a stimulus and a traumatic experience. The fear of the situation created by the random association may be quite irrational but is nonetheless intense. Similarly, the association made by moralists and psychologists between excessive eating and aversive images can be effective, and both practitioners take advantage of our susceptibility to conditioning in order to achieve their objective of restraining our eating.

25. It is of course possible to munch potato chips while reading a book and thus defeat the purpose of reading the book. This is why a cardinal rule in weight control is never to eat and at the same time engage in some other pleasurable activity. One must isolate the act of eating as much as possible so as not to increase the range of stimuli that become pleasurably associated with it. A patient, who in good faith wants to acquire self-control, will follow this rule.

26. Perhaps, also, the gluttonous who have deprived others of food in order to satisfy their voracious appetites have to be subjected to starvation in order to teach them how it feels to be hungry. Only then will they be able to empathize with their victims and never victimize them again.

CHAPTER SEVEN: GREED

1. Greed is a vice which particularly flourishes in a social environment abounding with wealth, such as our own. As we pointed out in Chapter 1, from the late Middle Ages religious writers considered greed, even more than pride, to be the root of all sin. This emphasis on the dangers of greed, was probably related to the economic prosperity that developed at the time, making available a greater abundance of money and goods to be acquired by those who were willing to exert themselves in their pursuit. However, greed has existed always and everywhere, and has been inveighed against by moralists from ancient times until today.

2. Rothstein, "Getting a Tale of '80's Avarice on Screen."

3. Jewish spiritual leaders of seventeenth-century Poland debated the legitimacy of pursuing wealth at the expense of spiritual pursuits. Some argued that Jews were justified in doing so as a buffer against the threat of poverty that could result from antisemitic persecution, which was common. Other rabbis saw in these claims a rationalization for greed and a dereliction of spiritual duties. Ultra-Orthodox Jews in America, who don't share the fear of their ancestors, still debate the propriety of engaging in the pursuit of economic security. The issue today is the broader one of spiritual versus secular values. Some Orthodox rabbis discourage or even forbid students in their seminaries from going to college or mastering a "secular" profession, so that they can devote themselves exclusively to the study of Torah. They are to place their trust in God that he will provide for their needs and for those of their families. Others maintain that learning a profession or entering a business is a religious

duty since the Torah commands a man to marry, have children, support and educate them. There must be a reasonable balance between time invested in the study of the sacred texts and that invested in earning a living. However, even those adopting the latter view do not advocate the pursuit of wealth, but only the acquisition of sufficient skills and education to enable the individual to earn a moderate income and so avoid becoming dependent on the support of others.

4. I Kings 21:19.
5. Chapter 1:23, JPS.
6. *Economics and Ethics*, pp. 6–8.
7. See Newhauser, "Love of Money as Deadly Sin and Deadly Disease," pp. 318–320.
8. Thomson translation, Book IV, pp. 142–148.
9. *Summa Theologiae* 2a2ae, Question 118, Article 1.
10. "On the Happy Life."
11. Most first-century Jews were either poor or of moderate income, including many of their spiritual leaders, the Pharisees, who are described in the Gospels as avaricious, and devoid of all spirituality and righteousness. Luke tells us that when Jesus taught that one cannot serve both God and Mammon, the Pharisees, who loved money, scoffed at him. This stereotype of the greedy Jew persisted throughout Christian Europe in life and in literature, contributing its share to Christian and then Nazi antisemitism. It continues to influence the attitudes of many Christians towards Jews in the United States today (Glock and Stark, *Christian Beliefs and Antisemitism*, pp. 109–113). Ironically, but not surprisingly, Christianity adopted for most of its adherents an attitude towards money and wealth not much different from that of the Pharisees whom it condemned, reserving vows of poverty only for the select few who chose to live a monastic life. With the Reformation and the rejection of monasticism, Protestantism further blurred distinctions between the attitudes of rabbinic and medieval Judaism on the one hand and Christianity on the other towards wealth and the legitimate role it can play in the life of the religious person.
12. *Piers the Plowman*, pp. 173–175.
13. RE, pp. 333–341.
14. Rimland, "The Altruism Paradox."
15. RE, p. 335.
16. Pollay, "The Distorted Mirror: Reflections on the Unintended Consequences of Advertising."
17. Newhauser, "The Love of Money as Deadly Sin and Deadly Disease."
18. RE, pp. 338–339.

CHAPTER EIGHT: SLOTH

1. Jung, *Modern Man in Search of a Soul*, p. 264.
2. Frankl, *Man's Search for Meaning: An Introduction to Logotherapy*.
3. See Wenzel, *The Sin of Sloth*, for an excellent history and analysis of sloth, *acedia* and *tristitia*.
4. *Summa Theologiae* 2a2ae, Question 35 (V. 35).
5. See Schimmel, "The Book of Job and the Psychology of Suffering and Doubt."
6. This fact was recognized in a general way by medieval writers, who often associated what they termed *melancholy* with an imbalance in the distribution of bodily humors.
7. For example, a Catholic patient of mine in his twenties, was suffering from depression. One cause was the unexpected suicide, several months earlier, of his older sister, with whom he had been very close. His grief was compounded by an obsessive anxiety that since suicide is a mortal sin, his sister was consigned to eternal damnation. Whenever he imagined her pain and suffering in hell, a depressive episode was triggered. I am not a Catholic, and do not believe in hell. However, as a therapist, I felt bound to respect his religious beliefs which had the potential to strengthen and console him, and to try to develop a treatment strategy that would not threaten them. I did some research so that I could substantiate my understanding of Catholic moral theology that in certain circumstances suicide is not considered a mortal sin. His sister had committed suicide six months after her eleven-year-old daughter had died of brain cancer. I told my client that his sister's emotional pain and depression at having witnessed her daughter's suffering and then losing this only child of hers, would be considered by the Church to be a mitigating circumstance. Her suicide would not be considered a mortal sin and his sister's soul could be purged and eventually ascend to heaven. The young man was considerably comforted by these assurances of mine. I encouraged him to consult with a priest, who indeed validated what I had told him. I also explained to him that rather than worrying about his sister's punishment, it would be more constructive to pray for her salvation. How would I have proceeded if the position of the Church had been that the sister's suicide was indeed a mortal sin and no salvation was possible for her? Since my primary responsibility is to my client's mental health, I might have deliberately misrepresented the Church's position without questioning its authority. However, if he himself were expressing doubts about the authority of Church teaching on suicide, I would have explored his doubts with him. Perhaps he could reject that belief without

N o t e s

denying Catholicism in general. If, however, I felt that his depression resulted from a set of (what to me were) false or irrational religious beliefs, and that the restoration of his mental health was contingent upon the rejection of these beliefs, I would have broadened our psychotherapeutic discussions to encompass the overall role of religion in his life and in his psychological well-being.

Viktor Frankl, in *Man's Search for Meaning*, tells of his therapeutic use of an Orthodox Jewish patient's religious beliefs to assuage his existential pain:

> When a patient stands on the firm ground of religious belief, there can be no objection to making use of the therapeutic effect of his religious convictions and thereby drawing upon his spiritual resources. In order to do so, the psychiatrist may put himself in the place of the patient. That is exactly what I did . . . when a rabbi from Eastern Europe turned to me and told me his story. He had lost his first wife and their six children in the concentration camp of Auschwitz where they were gassed, and now, it turned out that his second wife was sterile. . . . The Rabbi evaluated his plight as an Orthodox Jew in terms of a despair that there was no son of his own who would ever say Kaddish for him after his death. . . . I made a last attempt to help him by inquiring whether he did not hope to see his children again in Heaven. However, my question was followed by an outburst of tears, and now the true reason of his despair came to the fore: he explained that his children, since they died as innocent martyrs (i.e. for the sanctification of God's name), were thus found worthy of the highest place in Heaven, but as for himself he could not expect, as an old sinful man, to be assigned the same place. I did not give up but retorted, "Is it not conceivable, Rabbi, that precisely this was the meaning of your surviving your children; that you may be purified through these years of suffering, so that finally you, too, though not innocent like your children, may become worthy of joining them in Heaven? Is it not written in the Psalms that God preserves all your tears? ("Thou hast kept count of my tossings; put thou my tears in thy bottle! Are they not in thy book? Ps. 58:6). So, perhaps none of your sufferings were in vain." For the first time in many years he found relief from his suffering through the new point of view I was able to open up to him. (pp. 119–120)

8. Genesis 4:9.

9. *Jacob's Well*, I, Chapter XVII.
10. Chapters 6–9.
11. Cited by Luzzatto, *Path of the Just*, Chapter 9.
12. See Shneur Zalman of Liadi, *Likutei Amarim*, Chapters 26–31.
13. "Ethics of the Fathers" 2:20,21.
14. Not all people, however, can control depression through reflection and reappraisal. For them chemical antidepressants (and alcohol) can be temporarily effective in alleviating sadness and listlessness. However, drugs do not address the spiritual malaise of which these feelings are often the external manifestation. Those who rely exclusively on drugs (whether licit or illicit) or alcohol to feel better, defer honest confrontation with the roots of their dissatisfaction with themselves. Antidepressant drug therapy must be complemented with a value-oriented psychotherapy
15. Music has been used to influence emotion and behavior since ancient times, in religious, military, political, educational, commercial, and therapeutic settings. Horace Mann, who wanted to create a public school system which stressed morality, sought to adapt the religious and political uses of music to social and moral education in the classroom.
16. *Summa Theologiae* 2a2ae, Question 35, Article 1.
17. Loyola, *The Spiritual Exercises of St. Ignatius*.
18. Based upon Deuteronomy 14:22–28.

CHAPTER NINE: SIN AND RESPONSIBILITY

1. Compare to this the request by the special prosecutor that Oliver North of the Iran-contra affair be sentenced to a prison term. One reason given for this request was that he had shown no remorse for his crimes. Would incarceration make him more remorseful? Or had he been remorseful, was there a greater probability that other government officials would be deterred from committing like crimes, so that the deterrent effect of his imprisonment would no longer be necessary? Probably not, and so if deterrence of others is important, he should go to prison whether or not he was remorseful. Perhaps the implicit argument is that had he shown remorse, there would be less chance that he would commit such crimes again in the future, and so there is no need for imprisonment to deter Oliver North himself. This is a fairly plausible argument, although I am not sure that this was the rationale for the special prosecutor's request. More probably, it was based upon a legal view comparable to the traditional theological notion that as long as the sinner (criminal) remains unremorseful, the stain of the sin (crime) remains on him, and he deserves to suffer for having voluntarily sinned (committed a crime) and for continuing to sin (to maintain his willful denial of the validity of the

law he violated or of the right of the legal system to have passed such a law and to enforce it) by not showing remorse. There might also be the element of society's need to assuage its own anger and indignation at his crime, and seeing Oliver North in prison would have that cathartic effect.

2. See Schimmel, "Free-Will, Guilt and Self-control in Rabbinic Judaism and Contemporary Psychology."

3. See *Science and Human Behavior*, pp. 227–241.

4. Laurence Shames, *The Hunger for More*, cited in Landi, "When Having Everything Isn't Enough."

5. Ibid., pp. 28–29.

6. See Schimmel "Joseph and His Brothers: A Paradigm for Repentence."

7. Koch and Preuss, *A Handbook of Moral Theology*, vol. 2, pp. 188–189.

8. Levine, "The Experience of Repentance," pp. 40–63.

9. In Judaism repentance can sometimes be sudden, and Protestantism knows of gradual voluntary conversion which involves the development of new spiritual and moral habits. The primary distinguishing characteristic between the two is the agent of change. In Judaism, it is the sinner who transforms himself; in Protestantism it is God who transforms the sinner contingent upon the sinner's surrendering his will to God.

10. See Perry London's analysis and evaluation of Mowrer's theory about the relationship between evil, guilt, and mental illness in his *Modes and Morals of Psychotherapy*.

BIBLIOGRAPHY

Allport, Gordon W. (1950). *The Individual and His Religion*. Macmillan.

Aquinas, St. Thomas (1964–). *Summa Theologiae*. Blackfriars, McGraw-Hill.

Aristotle (1952). *Rhetoric*. Great Books of the Western World, Volume 9. Translated by W. Rhys Roberts. Encyclopaedia Britannica Inc.

Aristotle (1943). *Nichomachean Ethics*. In Aristotle, *On Man in the Universe*. Translated by J. E. C. Welldon. Walter J. Black, Inc.

Aristotle (1976). *The Ethics of Aristotle: The Nichomachean Ethics*. Translated by J. A.K. Thomson. Penguin Books.

Arnold, Matthew (1965). *The Poems of Matthew Arnold*. Edited by Kenneth Allott. Longman, Green and Co.

Augustine, St. *Confessions of Saint Augustine*.

Bandura, Albert (1973). *Aggression: A Social Learning Analysis*. Prentice-Hall.

Bardwick, Judith M. (1971). *Psychology of Women*. Harper & Row.

Basil, St. (1962). "Concerning Envy." In *The Fathers of the Church*. Volume 9, *St. Basil, Ascetical Works*. Translated by Sister M. Monica Wagner. Catholic University of America Press.

Berke, Richard L. (1991). "For Hatfield, a Shining Image Tarnished by Ethics Charges." *New York Times*, 6 June, p. A1.

Biale, Rachel (1984). *Women in Jewish Law*. Schocken.

Blakeslee, Sandra (1991). "How You See Yourself: Potential for Big Problems." *New York Times*, 7 February, p. B15.

Bloomfield, Morton W. (1952). *The Seven Deadly Sins: An Introduction to the History of a Religious Concept, with Special Reference to Medieval English Literature*. Michigan State College Press.

Bohlen, Celestine (1989). "Holtzman May Appeal Probation for Immigrant in Wife's Slaying." *New York Times*, 5 April, p. B3.

Borowitz, Eugene B. (1969). *Choosing a Sex Ethic*. Schocken.

269

Bibliography

"Boston Teen-Ager Gives Motive for a Rape and a Murder: Boredom" (1991). *New York Times*, 27 May, p. 6.

Butler, Bishop Joseph (1897). "Upon Resentment and Upon Forgiveness of Injuries," In *The Works of Joseph Butler, D.C.L.* Volume 2, *Sermons*. Edited by W. E. Gladstone, pp. 115–141. Oxford, Clarendon Press.

Campbell, Donald T. (1975). "On the Conflicts Between Biological and Social Evolution and Between Psychology and Moral Tradition." *American Psychologist*, 30, 1103–1126.

Cautela, Joseph R. (1977). "The Treatment of Overeating by Covert Conditioning." In *Behavioral Approaches to Weight Control*. Edited by Edward E. Abramson. Springer Publishing Co.

Chaucer, Geoffrey (1958). *The Canterbury Tales*. Translated into modern English by Nevill Coghill. Penguin Books.

Cicero (1950). *Tusculan Disputations*. Translated by J. E. King. Harvard University Press.

Clark, David K. (1985). "Philosophical Reflections on Self-Worth and Self-Love." *Journal of Psychology and Theology*, 13 (1), 3–11.

Complete Woman (June 1991).

Coopersmith, Stanley (1967). *The Antecedents of Self-Esteem*. W. H. Freeman.

Dante Alighieri (1955). *The Divine Comedy: Purgatory*. Translated by Dorothy L. Sayers. Penguin Books.

de Sales, Francis (1966). *Introduction to the Devout Life*. Translated by John K. Ryan. 2nd Ed. Rev. Harper Torchbooks.

de Vidas, Elijah. *Reshit Hokhmah* (Beginning of Wisdom). (In Hebrew.)

Dickey, Christopher (1991). "The Blunderer from Baghdad." *Newsweek*, 25 February, pp. 34–35.

"Ethics of the Fathers" (1949). In *Daily Prayer Book*. Translated and annotated with an Introduction by Philip Birnbaum, pp. 477–534. Hebrew Publishing Co.

Fairlie, Henry (1978). *The Seven Deadly Sins Today*. New Republic Books.

Fitzgibbons, Richard (1988). "The Cognitive and Emotive Uses of Forgiveness in the Treatment of Anger." *Psychotherapy*, 23 (4), 629–633.

Foster, Richard J. (1985). *Money, Sex and Power: The Challenge of the Disciplined Life*. Harper and Row.

Frankl, Viktor (1962). *Man's Search for Meaning: An Introduction to Logotherapy*. Simon & Schuster.

Freud, Sigmund (1953). *A General Introduction to Psychoanalysis*. Translated by Joan Riviere. Pocket Books.

———— (1930). *Civilization and Its Discontents*. Translated by Joan Riviere. Hogarth Press.

Gittelson, Roland (1980). *Love, Sex and Marriage: A Jewish View*. Revised Edition. Union of American Hebrew Congregations.

Glock, Charles Y., and Stark, Rodney (1966). *Christian Beliefs and Antisemitism*. Harper & Row.

Goleman, Daniel (1990). "Envy Seen as Sensitive Barometer." *New York Times*, 27 February, p. C1.

——— (1990). "When Rage Explodes, Brain Damage May Be the Cause." *New York Times*, 7 August, p. C1.

——— (1990). "The Group and the Self: New Focus on a Cultural Rift." *New York Times*, 25 December, p. I37.

——— (1988). "Narcissism Looming Larger as Root of Personality Woes." *New York Times*, 1 November, p. C1.

Goodenough, Erwin R. (1965). *The Psychology of Religious Experiences*. Basic Books.

Hardy, Thomas (1978). *Selected Poems*. Penguin Books.

Horace (1968). *Satires and Epistles*. With Introduction and notes by Edward P. Morris. University of Oklahoma Press.

Ibn Pakuda, Bahya (1925). *Duties of the Heart*. Translated by Moses Hyamson. Bloch Publishing Company.

Ignatius of Loyola, St. (1964). *The Spiritual Exercises of St. Ignatius*. Translated by Anthony Mottola. Doubleday and Co.

Interface: New England's Center for the Education of Body, Mind and Spirit (Winter 1991 Catalog).

Jacob's Well. An English treatise on the cleansing of man's conscience (1900). Edited by Arthur Brandeis. Early English Text Society, Paul, Trench, Trubner and Co. Ltd.

Jacobs, Louis (1979). "Eating and Drinking as an Act of Worship in Hasidic Thought." In *Studies in Jewish Religious and Intellectual History*. Edited by Siegfried Stein and Raphael Loewe. University of Alabama Press.

Judah the Pious. *Sefer Hasidim* (Book of the Pious). (In Hebrew.)

Jung, Carl (1933). "Psychotherapists or the Clergy." In *Modern Man in Search of a Soul*. Harcourt, Brace and Co.

Karo, Joseph. *Shulhan Arukh*. (In Hebrew)

King, Martin Luther, Jr. (1963). "Loving Your Enemies." In *Strength to Love*, pp. 34–41. Harper & Row.

Klein, H. Arthur (1963). *The Graphic Worlds of Peter Bruegel the Elder*. Dover Publications.

Knapp, Caroline (1991). "Love, Lust and Romance: How Hollywood Shapes Our Reality." *Boston Phoenix*, 8 February, p. II 4–5.

Koch, Anthony, and Preuss, Arthur (1928). *A Handbook of Moral Theology*. Five volumes. Third Revised Edition. B. Herder Book Co.

Landi, Ann (1989). "When Having Everything Isn't Enough." *Psychology Today*, April, pp. 27–30.

Langland, William. (1968). [Piers the Plowman] *The Vision of Piers Plowman, Newly Rendered into Modern English by Henry W. Wells*. Greenwood Press.

Levine, Howard I. (1958). "The Experience of Repentance: The Views of Maimonides and William James." *Tradition*, 1 (1), 40–63.

Levine, Stephen (1982). "A Modern Perspective on Nymphomania." *Journal of Sex and Marital Therapy*, 8 (4), 316–324.

Lewin, Tamar (1991). "Acquaintance Rape." *New York Times*, 27 May, p. 18.

London, Perry. (1986). *The Modes and Morals of Psychotherapy*. 2nd Revised Edition. Hemisphere Publishing Co.

Lukas, J. Anthony (1990). "Illusion Is Slain in Camelot." *New York Times*, 16 January, p. A27.

Luzzatto, Moshe Haim (1966). *The Path of the Just*. Translated by Shraga Silverstein. Feldheim.

Lyman, Stanford M. (1978). *The Seven Deadly Sins: Society and Evil*. St. Martin's Press.

Maimonides. Moses (1963). *Guide of the Perplexed*. Translated by Shlomo Pines. University of Chicago Press.

——— (1937). *The Mishneh Torah, The Book of Knowledge, Laws of Repentance*. Edited and translated by Moses Hyamson. Bloch Publishing Co.

Marriott, Michel (1991). "Iowa Gunman Was Torn By Academic Challenge." *New York Times*, 4 November, p. A12.

Mather, Cotton (1966). *Bonifacius: An Essay Upon the Good*. Edited with an Introduction by David Levin. Belknap Press—Harvard University Press.

Mckinley, James C., Jr. (1991). "Tenant Held in Killing: Pressure and Tragedy." *New York Times*, 16 May, p. B3.

Merton, Thomas (1961). *New Seeds of Contemplation*. New Directions.

Milton, John (1965). *The Complete Poetical Works of John Milton*. Edited by Douglas Bush. Houghton Mifflin Co.

Mowrer, O. Hobart (1961). *The Crisis in Psychiatry and Religion*. D. Van Nostrand Inc.

Neaman, Judith (1975). *Suggestion of the Devil: The Origins of Madness*. Anchor Books.

Neu, Jerome (1980). "Jealous Thoughts." In *Explaining Emotions*. Edited by Amelie O. Rorty. University of California Press.

New English Bible (1972). Oxford and Cambridge University Presses.

Nordheimer, Jon (1990). "Young, Successful But Between Jobs." *New York Times*, 7 November, p. C1.

Bibliography

New Oxford Annotated Bible (1973). Revised Standard Version. Oxford University Press.

Newhauser, Richard (1968). "The Love of Money as Deadly Sin and Deadly Disease." *Zusammenhange, Einflusse, Wirkungen*, pp. 315–326. Walter De Gruyter.

Novaco, Raymond (1975). *Anger Control.* Lexington Books.

Paretsky, Sara (1991). "Soft Spot for Serial Murder." *New York Times*, 28 April, p. IV17.

Petronius (1951). *Satyricon.* Translated by Michael Heseltine. Harvard University Press.

Pieper, Joseph (1967). *The Four Cardinal Virtues.* University of Notre Dame Press.

Plutarch (1959). "On Envy and Hate." In *Moralia*, volume 7. Translated by P. De Lacey and B. Einarson. Harvard University Press.

——. (1939). "On the Control of Anger." In *Moralia*, volume 6, Translated by W. C. Helmbold. Harvard University Press.

Plutarch's Lives. Volume 7, *Alexander the Great* (1919). Translated by Bernadotte Perrin. Harvard University Press.

Pollay, Richard W. (1986). "The Distorted Mirror: Reflections on the Unintended Consequences of Advertising." *Journal of Marketing*, 50 (2), 18–36.

Potok, Chaim (1972). *My Name Is Asher Lev.* Knopf.

Prudentius (1949). *The Fight for Mansoul (Psychomachia).* In volume 1 of the collected works of Prudentius. Translated by H. J. Thomson, pp. 274–343. Harvard University Press.

Queijo, Jon (1988). "Jealousy and Envy: The Demons Within Us." *Bostonia Magazine*, May–June, pp. 31–36.

Ribadeneira, Diego (1989). "Wilding" Victims: From Addicts to Innocents." *Boston Globe*, 3 May, p. 24.

Rimland, Bernard (1984). "The Altruism Paradox." *Southern Psychologist*, (1), 8–9.

Roth, Sol (1973). "Towards a Definition of Humility." *Tradition: A Journal of Orthodox Jewish Thought*, 13 (4), 5–22.

Rothstein, Mervyn (1990). "Getting a Tale of 80's Avarice on Screen." *New York Times*, 31 October, p. C15.

Ryan, Dale S. (1983). "Self-Esteem: An Operational Definition and Ethical Analysis." *Journal of Psychology and Theology*, 11 (4), 295–302.

Salovey, Peter, and Rodin, Judith (1988). "Coping with Envy and Jealousy." *Journal of Social and Clinical Psychology*, 7 (1), 15–33.

Schimmel, Solomon (1988). "Joseph and His Brothers: A Paradigm for Repentance." *Judaism*, 37 (1), 60–65.

Bibliography

———— (1987). "The Book of Job and the Psychology of Suffering and Doubt." *Journal of Psychology and Judaism*, 11 (4), 239–249.

———— (1980). "Education of the Emotions in Jewish Devotional Literature." *Journal of Religious Ethics*, 8 (2), 259–276.

———— (1979). "Anger and Its Control in Graeco-Roman and Modern Psychology." *Psychiatry: Journal for the Study of Interpersonal Processes*, 42 (4), 320–337.

———— (1977). "Free-Will, Guilt and Self-Control in Rabbinic Judaism and Contemporary Psychology." *Judaism: A Quarterly Journal of Jewish Life and Thought*, 26 (4), 418–429.

Schoeck, Helmut (1970). *Envy—A Theory of Social Behavior*. Harcourt, Brace and World.

Scholem, Gershom (1961). *Major Trends in Jewish Mysticism*. Schocken.

Schwartz, Hillel (1986). *Never Satisfied: A Cultural History of Diets, Fantasies and Fat*. Free Press.

Seneca (1935). "On the Happy Life." In *Moral Essays*, volume 2. Translated by John W. Basore. Harvard University Press.

———— (1928). "On Anger." In *Moral Essays*, volume 1. Translated by John W. Basore. Harvard University Press.

Shakespeare, William (1969). *Complete Works*. Allen Lane.

Shames, Laurence (1989). *The Hunger for More: Searching for Values in an Age of Greed*. Times Books / Random House.

Shneur Zalman of Liadi, Rabbi (1973). *Likutei Amarim—Tanya*. Kehot Publication Society.

Silverman-Watkins, Theresa (1983). "Sex in the Contemporary Media." *Marriage and Family Review*, 6 (3–4), 125–140.

Skinner, B. F. (1953). *Science and Human Behavior*. Free Press.

———— (1948). *Walden Two*. Macmillan.

Spenser, Edmund (1909). *The Faerie Queene*. Edited by J. C. Smith. Oxford, Clarendon Press.

Spinoza, Benedict (1927). *The Philosophy of Spinoza*. Modern Library.

Steinfels, Peter (1991). "Beliefs: Presbyterians Are Eager to Read a New Report on Sexuality, but the Excitement May End There." *New York Times*, 25 May, p. 11.

The Talmud (1948). Soncino Press.

The Tanakh, A New Translation of the Holy Scriptures. (1985). Jewish Publication Society of America.

Tavris, Carol (1982). *Anger: The Misunderstood Emotion*. Simon & Schuster.

Taylor, Jeremy (1883). *The Whole Works of Jeremy Taylor*. Volume 2, *Life of Christ*. London.

Bibliography

———— (1857). *The Rule and Exercises of Holy Living*. Bell and Daldy Fleet Street.

———— (1840). "The House of Feasting, or the Epicure's Measures." In *The Sermons of the Right Reverend Jeremy Taylor* (XV–XVI, pp. 110–125). Robert Carter and Bros.

"Testament of Reuben" [Testament of the Twelve Patriarchs] (1985). In *The Old Testament Pseudepigrapha*, volume 1. Edited by James Charlesworth. Doubleday.

Trausch, Susan (1991). "Down to the Raw Nerve." *Boston Globe*, 30 January, p. 15.

"Vice Mayor Linked to Sex Scandal Quits in Fort Lauderdale." *New York Times*, August 1991.

The Ways of the Righteous (1969). Translated by Seymour J. Cohen. Feldheim.

Wenzel, Siegfried (1960). *The Sin of Sloth: Acedia in Medieval Thought and Literature*. University of North Carolina Press.

Will, George F. (1991). "After the Dust Settles." *Newsweek*, 25 February, p. 70.

Wogaman, J. Philip (1986). *Economics and Ethics: A Christian Inquiry*. Philadelphia: Fortress Press.

Wollersheim, Janet P. (1977). "Behavioral Techniques for Weight Control." In *Behavioral Approaches to Weight Control*. Edited by Edward E. Abramson. Springer Publishing Co.

Woodward, Kenneth, with Cohen, Alden. (1991). "Roll Over John Calvin: The Presbyterians Rethink the Sexual Revolution." *Newsweek*, 6 May, p. 59.

Yakovlev, Aleksandr N. (1990). Excerpts From Speeches at the Communist Party Congress. *New York Times*, 4 July, p. 16.

ACKNOWLEDGMENTS

I would like to express my gratitude to Hebrew College, which has provided an environment conducive to the interdisciplinary and comparative religious scholarship that is reflected in this book.

My wife, Judith, deserves special thanks for her encouragement and prodding. She had greater confidence than I did in my ability to write and in the value of what I had to say.

Adam Bellow, my editor at The Free Press, helped formulate the vision of the book, and his numerous suggestions influenced its style, structure, and substance.

My apologies go to my youngest child, Noam. The time and attention I had to devote to writing were often at his expense. I am particularly sorry for the occasions when I was impatient with him because I was immersed in the book. I hope he will eventually understand and forgive.

Name Index

Name Index

SUBJECT INDEX

Absolution, 236–37

Abstinence, 142, 146, 161, 162, 258

Acedia, 16, 25, 193; *see also* Sloth

Achievement(s), 31, 32, 40, 41, 47, 48, 49, 50, 52, 53, 56, 60, 65, 66, 71, 74, 76, 187

Addiction, 22, 140, 144, 162, 176, 177

 sin and crime as, 232–34

Adultery, 11, 15, 18, 111, 114–18, 131, 217–19, 235, 254; *see also* Sex outside of marriage

Advertising, 129, 132, 139, 145, 187, 188, 257

Aesthetics, 16, 48, 174, 243

Afterlife, 161, 163, 206, 221–22, 240–41; *see also* Hereafter; Soul, immortality of

Aggression and aggressiveness, 10, 11, 43, 86, 87, 109, 204, 221, 230, 252

Agnostic(s) (agnosticism, nonbelievers), 51, 52–54, 186, 195, 196

Alcoholics and alcoholism, 2, 199, 215, 257; *see also* Drunkards and drunkenness

Alienation, 141, 192

Altruism, 103, 122, 169, 183, 199, 201, 205, 212, 246

Ambition, 4, 32, 35, 66, 239

America, 27–28, 55, 198

Anger, 1, 2, 3, 4, 7, 8, 10, 11, 13, 14, 15, 16, 17, 22, 23, 25, 51, 58, 83–110, 115, 198, 200, 219, 228, 234, 235, 239, 242, 243, 250, 251–52, 267; *see also* Fury; Rage; Resentment; Temper; Wrath

Anguish, 17, 191, 194, 242

Anomie, 6, 9, 10, 192–93, 197, 200

Antidepressants, 197, 266

Antisemitism, 55, 262, 263

Anxiety, 5, 10, 28, 48, 49, 66, 85, 102, 116, 125, 126, 127, 128, 140, 148, 151, 152, 169, 175, 179, 182, 196–97, 204, 210, 223, 231, 236, 238, 264

Apathy, 10, 26, 155, 193, 194, 196, 197, 208, 210, 211

Appetite(s), 2, 13, 112, 142, 151, 154, 156, 163, 176, 188

Arrogance and the arrogant, 1, 4, 23, 27, 29, 32, 33, 36, 37, 38, 39, 41, 45, 46, 52, 54, 93, 97, 101, 184; *see also* Pride

Art and artists, 16, 17, 25, 34, 48, 131, 174, 213, 222, 243

Ascetics and asceticism, 14, 20, 24, 25, 143, 148, 175

Autonomy, 21, 237

Avarice, 17, 18, 25, 166, 168, 170, 172, 174, 175, 176, 179, 180, 181, 182, 184, 185, 186, 187, 188, 190, 249; *see also* Coveting; Greed

Avaritia, 25

Aversive consequences, 152

Aversive imagery, 157–58, 261–62

Beauty, 41, 43, 131, 132, 173; *see also* Physical attractiveness

Behavior, 6, 7, 10, 11, 12, 15, 17, 51, 85, 109

 determinants of, 223–34, 260

Behavioral contracts, 253

Subject Index

Subject Index

Subject Index

Subject Index

Subject Index